Alfred Lees
Ronald Nelson
Editors

Longtime Companions
Autobiographies of Gay Male Fidelity

Pre-publication
REVIEW

"*L*ongtime Companions is a wonderful testament to the fact that not only can gay men nourish long-term commitments, but they can do so with grace and dignity—and all this in the face of enormous prejudice and ignorance. Gay and lesbian people have long claimed that 'love makes a family.' But these stories clearly illustrate that the making of a family goes beyond love. Another key characteristic that is repeated in each very different love story is the courage to endure. Endurance and commitment encourage the ability to forgive. We find in these stories that partners are able to cherish each other, even as aging, illness, and even death take their toll.

A final striking common element in these stories is the affirmation that gay men, in spite of homophobia, are glad to be gay. And it is this very pride that attracts sometimes surprising support from straight people—friends, family, and acquaintances. Our joy in our unique culture contributes to the longevity and health of our relationships.

This book contributes significantly to the growing body of knowledge on resilience and longevity in relationships and should be read by anyone concerned with the health and well-being of couples and families."

Janet M. Wright, PhD
Chair and Associate Professor,
Department of Social Work,
University of Wisconsin,
Whitewater

Longtime Companions
Autobiographies of Gay Male Fidelity

HAWORTH Gay & Lesbian Studies
John P. De Cecco, PhD
Editor in Chief

The Bear Book: Readings in the History and Evolution of a Gay Male Subculture edited by Les Wright

Youths Living with HIV: Self-Evident Truths by G. Cajetan Luna

Growth and Intimacy for Gay Men: A Workbook by Christopher J. Alexander

Our Families, Our Values: Snapshots of Queer Kinship edited by Robert E. Goss and Amy Adams Squire Strongheart

Gay/Lesbian/Bisexual/Transgender Public Policy Issues: A Citizen's and Administrator's Guide to the New Cultural Struggle edited by Wallace Swan

Rough News, Daring Views: 1950s' Pioneer Gay Press Journalism by Jim Kepner

Family Secrets: Gay Sons—A Mother's Story by Jean M. Baker

Twenty Million New Customers: Understanding Gay Men's Consumer Behavior by Steven M. Kates

The Empress Is a Man: Stories from the Life of José Sarria by Michael R. Gorman

Acts of Disclosure: The Coming-Out Process of Contemporary Gay Men by Marc E. Vargo

Queer Kids: The Challenges and Promise for Lesbian, Gay, and Bisexual Youth by Robert E. Owens

Looking Queer: Body Image and Identity in Lesbian, Gay, Bisexual, and Transgender Communities edited by Dawn Atkins

Love and Anger: Essays on AIDS, Activism, and Politics by Peter F. Cohen

Dry Bones Breathe: Gay Men Creating Post-AIDS Identities and Cultures by Eric Rofes

Lila's House: Male Prostitution in Latin America by Jacobo Schifter

A Consumer's Guide to Male Hustlers by Joseph Itiel

Trailblazers: Profiles of America's Gay and Lesbian Elected Officials by Kenneth E. Yeager

Rarely Pure and Never Simple: Selected Essays by Scott O'Hara

Navigating Differences: Friendships Between Gay and Straight Men by Jammie Price

In the Pink: The Making of Successful Gay- and Lesbian-Owned Businesses by Sue Levin

Behold the Man: The Hype and Selling of Male Beauty in Media and Culture by Edisol Wayne Dotson

Untold Millions: Secret Truths About Marketing to Gay and Lesbian Consumers by Grant Lukenbill

It's a Queer World: Deviant Adventures in Pop Culture by Mark Simpson

In Your Face: Stories from the Lives of Queer Youth by Mary L. Gray

Military Trade by Steven Zeeland

Longtime Companions: Autobiographies of Gay Male Fidelity edited by Alfred Lees and Ronald Nelson

From Toads to Queens: Transvestism in a Latin American Setting by Jacobo Schifter

The Construction of Attitudes Toward Lesbians and Gay Men by Lynn Pardie and Tracy Luchetta

Lesbian Epiphanies: Women Coming Out in Later Life by Karol L. Jensen

Smearing the Queer: Medical Bias in the Health Care of Gay Men by Michael Scarce

Macho Love: Sex Behind Bars in Central America by Jacobo Schifter

When It Is Time to Leave Your Lover: A Guide for Gay Men by Neil Kaminsky

Strategic Sex: Why They Won't Keep It in the Bedroom by D. Travers Scott

Longtime Companions
Autobiographies
of Gay Male Fidelity

Alfred Lees
Ronald Nelson
Editors

Harrington Park Press
An Imprint of The Haworth Press, Inc.
New York • London • Oxford

Published by

Harrington Park Press, an imprint of The Haworth Press, Inc., 10 Alice Street, Binghamton, NY 13904-1580.

Cover design by Marylouise E. Doyle.

The Library of Congress has cataloged the hardcover edition of this book as:

Longtime companions : autobiographies of gay male fidelity / Alfred Lees, Ronald Nelson, editors.
      p.   cm.
    ISBN 0-7890-0641-3 (alk. paper)
    1. Gay male couples—United States—Biography. I. Lees, Alfred W. II. Nelson, Ronald, 1928- .
HQ75.7.L66 1999
306.76′62′092273—DC21   98-46138
                                                                     CIP

ISBN: 1-56023-957-3 (pbk.)

To Matthew Shepard
Robbed, at twenty-one, through unconscionable barbarism,
of his inborn right to discover who he was,
and whether a longtime companion awaited

ABOUT THE EDITORS

Alfred Lees and Ronald Nelson have maintained an exclusive relationships for forty-seven years. The two built, from scratch, a complex of buildings on their forested mountain in Pennsylvania's Upper Delaware Valley, and divide their time between this retreat and their loft in downtown Manhattan, where they are actively involved in the cultural life of the city. Their shared avocations include world travel and photography. *Longtime Companions* is their first collaboration.

Mr. Lees spent thirty-five years editing and writing for national magazines. He also published six previous books, mostly anthologies of his articles. Upon retiring from *Popular Science* at the end of 1998, he was elected president of the National Writers' Association and reinvigorated its newsletter while establishing a national competition for the best articles and books published nationally in the Do-It-Yourself (DIY) field.

Mr. Nelson retired in 1990 after thirty years in college textbook publishing as a development and acquisitions editor, spending twenty-one years with John Wiley and fourteen years with Prentice-Hall.

CONTENTS

WE'RE NOT LOST, WE'RE HERE

There is no map for where we go . . .
We're not lost . . . we're here.
There is so much that we don't know . . .
Oh, we're not lost . . . we're here.
Faint the trails and few the footprints.
Few and faint they disappear.
They have disappeared behind us . . .
We're not lost . . . we're here.

Philip Littell

This verse, and the one that appears after the Introduction, are lyrics from the song cycle for male chorus "Naked Man," by Philip Littell (to music by Robert Seeley), widely performed by the New York City Gay Men's Chorus under the direction of Gary Miller.

Foreword

We gays are, I sometimes think, a people without a past—or rather with a constantly shifting past depending as much on the teller as on the facts. Our legacy has not been passed down to us through the usual institutions of family, church, and school. Further, at certain times, in various countries, what continuity we might have once been a part of has been shattered, either by homophobic historians—who busily wrote us out of their slanted history books or made such obtuse references to us that we, the potential inheritors of that history, cannot recognize those who went before us as "our kind"—or our continuity has been shattered by genocide, as in Nazi Germany, by those who sought to wipe us out of existence, along with other peoples who stood in the way of the "master race."

We have also had a strange history of living in the shadows at times and, at others, attempting to stand in the light, attempting to bring the actors in that drama of history out into the open, so that those who came after would know that we trod the shores of the world, that we have always existed. But the simple crush of time has more often darkened the tenuous lights we shone than held back that darkness.

The bridges we attempted to build across the span of time have often been felled and each generation of us has had to restore those bridges to our past. It was popular before Stonewall for us to gather in small numbers and list the known homosexuals who came before us, in some sense celebrating our sketchy history; a few books were written to forever cast in print the names of the actors in the drama of our continuing. Yet time and time again the waters of obscurity have risen and washed away the evidence that we were ever there.

In most cases, each of us has led lives that shine for awhile and then, upon our deaths, have gone out, with no one coming after to remember us, to remember our individual struggles for self- and other-acceptance. Yet there have been those who have come together in lifelong relationships and lived together as mates through the tenebrous times. There are those among us now who began their lives together in the 1940s and 1950s and 1960s, who have seen history played out, through the genocide of the Nazis, and through the period in the United States, Great Britain, and elsewhere when our fate was in the hands of psychiatrists and medical men who, by amazing acts of barbarism, sought to eradicate our very souls through the use of such means as castration, lobotomy, and aversion therapy.

Those who were involved in relationships prior to Stonewall and are now living among us as elderly or middle-aged couples could tell us such stories, of how they met in times that are even less enlightened than today, who met and dated and fell in love and committed themselves to each other, so that they would have someone to share their lives with. They could tell us how they lost their families and clung, instead, to each other, for the support that most of us should be able to expect from our families. They could tell us of the shadow world before Stonewall, of the lack of books about us, or about the lack of allies anywhere in society. They could tell us so many things about our history and show us those bridges, and bring the past to light, and show us that each of us is a part of a rich and varied past.

That is what this collection of autobiographical essays by long-term gay couples is all about. Herein, they share slices of their own lives as they have lived them with each other or tell us of their mates who have passed on. And we have a thousand questions for each of them. In this treasury of essays, perhaps we can find the answers to some of those questions, maybe gain inspiration by reading these stories of real-life couples, some of whom have been with us since before Stonewall. And in so doing, we will not lose this rare opportunity to know our most precious past—one that is grounded in love, built on hope, and solidified in rare and beautiful partnerships that span the decades—like bridges that ultimately lead us to the future.

Ronald L. Donaghe
Las Cruces, New Mexico

Acknowledgments

Major help in assembling so diverse a collection of autobiographical accounts was given by newspapers who published our solicitation—notably *The Key West Citizen*, a Florida daily that well serves readers in the western Keys, and *Q-Notes*, "The Carolinas' Most Comprehensive Gay & Lesbian Newspaper," published every two weeks in Charlotte, North Carolina—as well as by one of the writers in this book, Martin Last, a U.S. expatriate in Montreal who proposed a number of potential contributors, resulting in three more of the strongest pieces in the book.

Our undying gratitude goes to New Mexico novelist Ronald L. Donaghe (*Common Sons, The Salvation Mongers, Letters in Search of Love*) who came up with the idea for such an anthology; we didn't always harbor such generous thoughts toward Donaghe—not after he felt compelled to dump the project on us (the first couple he had asked to supply an account). But since we agreed to take it on, he has been unstinting in his support, and volunteered his electronic processing skills to computerize the entire manuscript. He has also supplied our graceful foreword.

To Gary Miller, retired director of the NYC Gay Men's Chorus, who was good sport enough to authorize printing excerpts from our ultimately frustrating correspondence, and to wish us well with this book.

Finally, to Sheldon Soffer and Stanley Segal (a city/country couple like ourselves) who, while failing to collaborate on a promised account of their *own* late-blooming relationship—"We found we couldn't even agree on how we *met*," they confessed—put us in touch with a couple whose fifty years together makes such a fitting close to our collection. SS/SS also graciously hosted the boonies party to which we refer in the final section of our own account herein.

Introduction

The gestation of this project has been elephantine. My co-everything (including, now, co-editor) Ron Nelson and I first learned of it when we were asked to compose its initial essay, back in February 1994. The invitation came from New Mexico, from novelist Ronald L. Donaghe (that's DON-uh-gee—hard "g" as in geese, I learned) whose first book, *Common Sons*, I had admired, and wrote him so. A correspondence developed, and co-Ron (to distinguish one Ron from the other) and I even visited Donaghe and his then-new and still-younger lover, Cliff, in their Las Cruces home, on our way to a long-intended visit to Big Bend, Texas, in May 1993.

Six months later, when Donaghe was between novels, his agent proposed he edit an anthology, leaving it up to him to come up with a topic. Cliff suggested an anthology of reports written by long-term male couples, to counter the growing misconception that gay men were incapable (apparently *genetically* incapable!) of lasting, nurturing relationships. Cliff was enthusiastic.

"After all, *we're* well along toward one," he told Donaghe. "And look at Alfred and Ron in New York; they've been together for centuries! And don't you get travel postcards from another Manhattan couple like that?"

Thus was this book conceived, back in 1994; but birth was a long and painful way off. The minute Ronald Donaghe proposed participation to us, we both cried: "Way to go! Exactly the book that's needed, just now." Not only did we agree to contribute—we responded to Donaghe's entreaty to propose other participants.

We thought at once of previous New York friends—now scattered, couples with whom we'd played the "Who's been together longest?" game, years ago. Alas, we knew that death had reduced one of these couples (who had settled in Canada) to a solo act, but the surviving member quickly accepted our invitation. A now-ancient pair who had moved to the West Coast also immediately saw the need for such an anthology. Meanwhile, Donaghe had contacted "that other Manhattan couple"—strangers to us—and suggested the four of us get together to discuss the project.

The stories of these four *very* long-term couples formed the nucleus of the book you now hold in your hands. Unfortunately, Donaghe then got distracted by many personal editorial projects and discouraged by his agent's lack of success in lining up additional contributors. "He swears he put the word out over three national computer networks," Donaghe wrote us in May of 1994, "but this netted only one inquiry—a gay couple from Lubbock, Texas, who both got on the phone to assure me how 'anxious' they were for the book to appear, and that they'd 'definitely be contributing.'" (They never did—a declaration-of-enthusiasm/lack-of-follow-through pattern I was later to encounter myself.)

By August 1994 we had sent Donaghe the first two sections of what we had outlined as an eight-part account. What you'll find from us later on in this book may be said to be a labor of love, but it wasn't all that much fun. Even though I'm a well-published author (this is my seventh book) and Ron's entire career was in book editing, this writing didn't come easy—or fast. Collaborative autobiography is especially tough; it can open old wounds in the best of relationships.

Donaghe, who had been asked to contribute essays to two gay anthologies edited by the late John Preston (*Hometowns* and *Member of the Family*), after his novel *Common Sons* was first published in 1989, had expected the collecting of pieces for *his* anthology to be a snap. Everyone he told about it said, "Great idea! Much needed to counter the lies of the radical right!" But such enthusiasm did nothing to swell the number of his contributors.

Meanwhile, Ron and I kept plugging away, and finally mailed our last sections to Donaghe in May 1996. Since we had invested the better part of two years in the project—and felt responsibility to the friends we'd enlisted—we mentioned in our final cover note that if Donaghe had not managed to place the book with a publisher by year's end, we would have to ask for our contribution back, for marketing elsewhere.

Early in 1997, the "book thus far" plopped on our doorstep. Donaghe's cover note said, in essence: "Good luck!"

Overnight we had graduated from Principal Contributors to Editors in Charge. Though daunting, the project had by this time become a crusade for me—largely because of 1996's late-summer outrage: the Defense of Marriage Act. Had the author of Leviticus still been around, he would have labeled this congressional action—signed into law in the dead of night by a desperate-for-reelection Clinton—an *abomination*. (This is, of course, the Leviticus-writer's favorite word, and he hurls it at so many objects—from menstruating women and adulterers to whole categories of food!—that I've long been amused that Pentacostals fixate only on its use against men who lie with men. Obviously, these worthies are very selective in their choice of "biblical injunctions" to take seriously. In truth, the only value ancient writings such as Leviticus have is as historical record; they have nothing to teach us about contemporary behavior. But more on that in a moment.)

When the infamous legislation I speak of was first proposed, Clinton rightly saw it as a political ploy—an attempt by right extremists to embarrass him with a supposed national fear of the Hawaiian Threat. He admitted he saw no need for such an act, yet felt compelled to proclaim that marriage should be confined to unions between men and women—a startling confirmation that you can take our Bill out of the Arkansas hills, but part of him will always stay a hillbilly, stubbornly wedded to phony, outdated "country folk" attitudes.

Still, at that point, American gays had every right to suppose we were at last gaining civil-rights ground. After all, we had constituted a substantial political support for a vital young president, who flashily promised us emancipation from generations of second-class citizenship. Clinton had presented himself as a "some-of-my-best-friends-are-gay" kind of guy, promising major action against the long-standing (patently absurd) ban on gays in the military. But when push (by the military establishment) came to shove, the result was a waffle—a compromise policy that left the issue more muddled than before. To avoid a renewed Republican charge that he was weak on defending Moral Absolutes against a liberal gay onslaught, he capitulated on the marriage issue.

Clinton's double betrayal of one of his vital constituencies should have prompted a major defection—but where did we have to turn? Once Bob Dole desperately sought the support of the Christian Coalition (even stooping to being photographed on their convention podium in a grinning solidarity handclasp with the noxious Pat Robertson) we knew we had no choice. (What next, Bob? Ralph Reed for attorney general?) And Clinton cynically counted on that; he had nothing to lose with his double betrayal.

The Defense of Marriage Act remains, then, the most reprehensible governmental insult to a section of the citizenry since the Dred Scott decision; it brazenly denies basic rights to a vast category of citizens, branding them as "officially inferior." It will, of course, be eventually struck down as unconstitutional, but in the meantime it behooves every gay American who gives a damn about civil rights to expose it for the total fraud it is.

Truly, has there ever been a more fatuous or hypocritical spectacle in the halls of congress than that summer's circus, as somber senators and smug congressmen elbowed each other for a turn at the podium to proclaim their devotion to the sanctity of heterosexual marriage—that linchpin of Family Values? I'll not soon forget Senator Robert Byrd (D., West Virginia) reading into the record that letting the scourge of same-sex marriage take root on our sacred (mainland) soil would be to give "legal sanction to aberrant behavior." At least twenty of the senators he was addressing—some of whom joined Byrd in extolling the unassailable nature of hetero marriage—are themselves divorced.

When both Bob Dole and Newt Gingrich jumped on this bandwagon to uphold the sanctity of such unions, one could only recall that Dole walked out on his first wife (and their daughter) and Newt left *his* first (and two daughters)—both to marry younger women. Other members of the Family Values First Wives' Club would include the first Mrs. Dick Armey, the first Mrs. Phil Gramm—and even the first Mrs. Rush Limbaugh—the list goes on!

But I suppose my favorite exchange was when a gay-rights spokeswoman could take no more pontificating from thrice-married Bob Barr of Georgia—a *sponsor* of DoMA—and demanded, in an interview: "Congressman, just *which* of your marriages are you defending?"

The lunacy and self-contradiction hardly stop at Capitol Hill. The following summer's treat came from the Southern Baptist Convention in Dallas, where 12,000 delegates of America's biggest Protestant denomination voted to boycott all Disney enterprises because the company extended health benefits to employees' same-sex partners and then—horrors!—let Ellen come out on their ABC network.

I've posted by my desk *The New York Times* photo of these smug, mindless folk unanimously holding aloft their voting cards, eager to be counted in this ridiculous crusade. Whenever energy flags, a glance at these faces brings renewed vigor for *my* crusade—this book.

Reverend Tom Elliff, pastor of the First Southern Baptist Church of Del City, Oklahoma, spoke for this vast group when he announced: "We believe homosexuality is a choice and it's a bad choice." Since such "belief" flies in the face of all social enlightenment and scientific evidence, it's the modern equivalent of the church's unshakable belief (in Galileo's time) that the Earth was the center of the universe, around which all else revolved. It's yet another example of fundamentalism getting it all backward and stubbornly refusing to be enlightened.

If there's one thing every writer in this book knows as Infallible Truth, it's that homosexuality is not now, never has been, nor ever will be a *choice*. It's an inborn trait like being left-handed or freckled. Environmental influences can *shape* or pervert it. No one's *born* a pedophile, an S&M freak, or even a drag queen—these *might* be said to be "lifestyle choices," though even here the term "choice" is dubious: these twists occur through childhood trauma or aping bad role models. It's hard for most of us to accept that anyone—of either sexual orientation (and there are basically only two)—would *choose* to be a child molester. The psychological causes of such perversions are complex and often tragic, and of course society must be protected from the end result. But to claim society must isolate and control your normal garden-variety, born-that-way homosexual is as paranoid and delusional as a similar discrimination against women or racial minorities.

The photo by my desk also reminds me of an earlier sense of disgust I had had over "religious" bigotry. A friend was a deacon of Downtown United Presbyterian Church in Rochester, New York, and served on the search committee that extended a call to Californian Janie Spahr to come east as copastor. Although the congregation voted overwhelmingly for Spahr, who openly celebrated her relationship with another mature woman, all hell broke loose within the denomination.

Uptight Presbyterian churches in the Rochester synod went out for blood, demanding a ruling by the General Assembly (the denomination's national congress). Alas, the "official" Presbyterian denomination has often proven reactionary—or at least craven—when challenged by its militant-right members (a fact that led me to leave the faith I was raised in—my father was a Presbyterian minister). So, ultimately their Permanent Judicial Commission canceled Spahr's call—effectively booting another Christian leader out of the church. All in outraged response to same-sex marriages.

On January 5, 1993, the *Times-Union*, Rochester's daily, provided a major forum on their "Readers Say" page to Reverend G. Robert Geyer, pastor of the suburban Brighton Presbyterian Church (who had been a major agitator against Spahr), publishing his very long defense of the commission under a banner headline: Spahr ruling was just! (The fact that the *Times-Union* chose not to put quotes around the head suggests a bit of off-the-top editorializing.)

This long self-justification of Reverend Geyer's was so full of specious reasoning and distortion of biblical truth that I felt a response was necessary. On January 16, I mailed mine off to the *Times-Union*—which refused to publish it. Since the Spahr incident remains of national concern—and since I'd spent a fair amount of time researching my response—I offer my "lost" letter here. But first, let me quote the concluding paragraphs of the good pastor's published defense of the commission's ruling:

> We at Brighton Presbyterian Church certainly agree that narrow-mindedness and bigotry have no place in Christ's

church. We not only welcome homosexuals but we have had an active ministry for over five years with a group of homosexuals in reorientation. Currently, 16 to 20 meet each week, with over 60 having been involved over the years. We did not seek this ministry, but as some people who had been involved in the "gay" lifestyle began attending Brighton and expressed their struggle and desire to be free, their needs began to be met.

Many of these can attest to finding reorientation in repenting and receiving God's forgiveness in Christ. Some have come "into the open" in the congregation and have found love and acceptance by the Brighton church.[1]

Shades of Ronald Donaghe's new horror novel, *The Salvation Mongers*! Here was my response:

Since I must assume that the congregation of Brighton Presbyterian would not call a stupid or uneducated man its pastor, I must conclude that Reverend Geyer is being hypocritical. He sternly informs your readers that "We can't as Christians pick which Scriptures we will follow and which Scriptures we will not."

What patent nonsense! Reverend Geyer does precisely that every day of his life. The Book of Leviticus (which many bigots rush to quote as the scriptural condemnation of homosexuality) is a book of church law. It sternly directs Reverend Geyer that the following are unclean and to be avoided: Every beast not cloven-footed nor cud-chewing; every mouse, tortoise, lizard, or snail. There are no two ways about these scriptural demands: "Every thing that creepeth upon the earth shall be an abomination"—and if any of these critters chance to fall into any pot, the *pot* must be destroyed.

Even worse, Reverend Geyer, is a menstruating woman—or heaven forbid! one that's just given birth. The latter must be ostracized as unclean for seven days after bearing a male child (which, by the way, *must* be circumcised on the eighth day) and then the poor soul must continue rites of purification for thirty-three days, touching no hallowed thing or coming *near*

Reverend Geyer's sanctuary. It's even worse if she's unlucky enough to give birth to a mere female. Then she's unclean for *two weeks* and must continue her purification for three-score-and-six days; and *then* she must drag a yearling lamb and young pigeon to Brighton Presbyterian and kill them on the altar.

I also hope Reverend Geyer is scrupulous about instructing his parishioners that *no* family member may ever see another member naked. Scripture makes this very clear, Reverend Geyer, so don't let the parents watch while you perform that circumcision on the eighth day!

Quoting Old Testament sources back as a directive for *Christian* experience is unfair, you say? Well, as Reverend Geyer will be first to assert, *all* Scripture must be obeyed! But let's be Christian about this and examine the very Scripture Reverend Geyer presents—Matthew 19:1-12. Here, Christ himself answers Pharisees who ask: "Is it lawful for a man to put away his wife?" and Christ answers unequivocally that "the twain shall be one flesh . . . what therefore God hath joined together, let man not put asunder . . . whosoever shall put away his wife (except it be for fornication) and shall marry another, commiteth adultery: and whoso marrieth her which is put away doth commit adultery."

Now, nowhere in Scripture is it recorded that Jesus uttered one word either for or against homosexuality, but there are repeated references (in other gospels and in the teachings of Paul—which are even harsher toward divorce than Matthew) that specifically ban divorce. Until Reverend Geyer can assure me that Brighton Presbyterian has no divorced parishioners and certainly recognizes no remarriage by them, I suggest he pull in his horns and keep his own counsel.

Where has Brighton *been* this past decade? Homosexuality per se is not a lifestyle choice. For Reverend Geyer to announce that the only way a gay or lesbian can be a Christian is to repent the way God made them and live a celibate life is even more absurd than for him to decree that any divorced person must abstain from all further sexuality. We mustn't *pick* which Scriptures we'll follow, Reverend Geyer!

Seriously: the only valid requirement Brighton's congregation can make of its professing Christians is that (whatever the sexual circumstances) each strives for a faithful and loving relationship, treating the mate with the respect they demand for themselves. Anything further is clearly none of the congregation's business.

Even more clearly, the decisions of their neighboring parish are not! That Presbyterian hierarchy has nullified Downtown United's call to the obviously qualified Jane Spahr because of her same-sex marriage is hardly a cause for Reverend Geyer's celebration. From my objective distance, DUPC's congregation is obviously on the side of the angels and Reverend Geyer's is sadly misled.

If the fact that "openly gay and lesbian elders and deacons serve on DUPC boards" means that DUPC has, as Reverend Geyer claims, "entered into a form of open rebellion," their actions bring hope to my despairing Presbyterian breast. DUPC and equally enlightened congregations may yet drag Protestantism into the twentieth century before it draws to a close—leaving Reverend Geyer fulminating in nineteenth-century darkness.

It was found years ago that an upstate New York paper refused to let a voice of reason be heard—just one more example of why social justice and progress and change are moving so slowly in America. I would guess what most of us find so exasperating is the intellectual laziness most bigots display. Each time they're challenged by social progress they revert to the same old stances. Equality for *blacks*? Blacks in the military? Too disruptive! Couldn't be assimilated! Equality for *women*? Equal pay for equal work? Women in the military? Too disruptive! Couldn't be assimilated! Equality for *gays*? No discrimination in employment or housing? Gays in the military? Too disruptive! Couldn't be assimilated! (The hoot *this* time 'round was that this was claimed by the top *black* in the military, who had managed to surmount just such claims against him*self*.) We never learn.

Still, the hope that education is possible if truth and reason are disseminated is what motivates books such as this one—and such as the anthology *Beyond Queer: Challenging Gay Left Orthodoxy* edited by Bruce Bawer, and *The Case for Same-Sex Marriage: From Sexual Liberty to Civilized Commitment* by William N. Eskridge.[2]

So, after having accepted the unsought challenge of expanding the initial premise of *Longtime Companions* to book-length proportions—how to proceed? How to find such couples "out and proud" enough to agree to tell their stories, in their own words, under their own names? Obviously, accumulating enough joint accounts was no simple task. Getting *anyone* to compose an autobiographical essay is like pulling teeth; our natural lethargy makes all of us prefer to read than to write. Getting a *gay* to do it involves greater effort; not only is there what Eskridge terms "Fear of Flaunting" (examples in a moment), but for men past a certain age there's memory of the real risk of exposure to unsympathetic neighbors or employers. To get a *pair* of gays to write about themselves is still more problematic. *Both* partners must agree—and time after time I found one willing party unable to convince his longtime lover to participate.

My initial resource was a manila folder in which I had filed clippings from magazines, newspapers, or performance programs—intending to send them along to the original editor of this project once I'd learned of the difficulties he was having lining up contributors.

CASTING FOR COUPLES:
THE ONES THAT GOT AWAY

After a number of rejections from couples I had learned of from my clipping file, my confidence in the possibility of this book began to erode. There was the pair of painters in rural Pennsylvania who each summer play host to a group of underprivileged children from Manhattan's Hell's Kitchen—kids brought together with theater professionals to produce their own plays. And then there was the well-known composer of operas and art songs, living in upstate New York with his lover of many years. Both couples responded to my invitation with a resounding NO! That's when I truly came to appreciate Eskridge's aforementioned theory: Fear of Flaunting (expounded in the Epilogue of his book *The Case for Same-Sex Marriage*):

> I grew up in a small town in West Virginia. My aunt explained to me how small towns accommodate homosexual couples. Same-sex couples can live together all their lives in a small town, and everybody will understand that they are committed partners in the same way that husband and wife are partners . . . their families and neighbors will know to invite them both to social events. Gossips who speak maliciously against the couple will be disciplined by polite society. . . . The trade-off is that the couple is expected not to flaunt their sexuality. They should . . . not speak as open lesbians or gay men, and definitely should not marry one another . . .[4]

—or publish a joint account of their relationship in a book such as this! My months of subsequent search for participants confirmed again and again that couples least likely to say yes live in rural communities where Fear of Flaunting reigns supreme. They would rather die than rock the boat—or jeopardize the security of this unspoken truce.

Nearly every refusal letter received from such semicloseted pairs has concluded: "—but we fully support your project and wish it success!" With such well-wishers, who needs opposition?

ENTER: KEY WEST!

Over our years together, Ron and I have several times escaped New York's harsh winters on brief vacations to Key West, southernmost city in the United States. "Escape" is the operative word for the place—it's Land's End, literally as far as you can go (without continuing into the Gulf by boat; it's 150 miles from Miami but only 90 from Cuba). Our favorite means of getting there is by rental car, bouncing out the chain of Florida Keys on the 123-mile Overseas Highway, which is laid mostly on bridges from an old railroad, abandoned after hurricane damage early in this century.

Once in the city, the car's a drag, and we either hoof it or rent bikes from our B&B. It's always a joy to cycle past the charming conch (that's "konk") houses, all featuring porches, many of which fly rainbow flags. Key West is the personification of "laid back," so it's gay-friendly by nature. While we were there in March 1997, staying in a gay-owned guest house, I was reading the local daily at breakfast on their porch when it struck me that this paper—*The Citizen*—could provide a podium for announcing our project. I dashed off a letter to the editor:

> As a gay visitor to your gracious town, I was put off by a headline in your paper: "The Gay Lifestyle." Though there are certainly "gay lifestyles" (not all of them commendable) there's no such thing as "the" Gay Lifestyle (singular). Gays come in just as wide a range of types and attitudes as straights do—as I've become newly aware while collecting autobiographical accounts for an anthology to be titled: *Longtime Companions: Joint Accounts by Gay Couples Who've Weathered Over a Dozen Years Together*. It now strikes me that this book can't be complete without a contribution from at least one Key West couple, and I welcome queries from any that qualify.[5]

The paper ran my name and address.

The response was heartening. We had scarcely made it back to New York City before the letters began arriving, each more enthusiastic than the last. From these many would-be volunteers we were able to encourage three couples to work up contributions to this book, nearly doubling the joint accounts we had gathered to date.

So Key West will continue to hold an even warmer place in our hearts: it provided the first much-needed boost to this project we had inherited.

COME TO THE CABARET

This boost was soon followed by two additional acceptances to my solicitation letters. On our hundreds of drives up to our country place (see The Retirement Project in the chapter "Lives Long Entwined"), our shortest—and thus most frequent—route was through a lakeside village in the Catskills where we always noted a once-proud, now-dead hotel looming above the road that ran between its lofty perch and the dark waters of White Lake—dark waters rumored to be a favorite dumping ground for the cement-shoe victims of gang assassinations; the bodies were trucked up here from New York City, rowed out over the great depths and—kerplunk! We were heartened when we learned the derelict hotel had been purchased, and continued to be delighted as, on each subsequent trip past, we noted the progress of rejuvenation.

In a couple of years, the sad old relic had been joyfully revived. It now crowned its high lake bank with three-story pride. Three large dormers marched across its broad roof and a covered verandah ran the full length of its facade—from one of the posts of which fluttered a modified rainbow flag—always a symbol to perk up one's interest.

When ads for a weekend cabaret at the newly opened hotel began to appear in local country papers, we were further intrigued, and finally ventured over one Saturday night to sample the quality. The solo star of that night's cabaret was one of the two new owners responsible for the restoration, and the public manner in which these young men celebrated their partnership was most refreshing. In introductory and closing statements bracketing the show, they paid obviously sincere tribute to one another and to their relationship-for-life.

The show itself had been notable. The performer was tall, broad-shouldered, dark, and theatrically handsome, with flashing eyes and a stunner smile; he could also sing—in a flexible baritone, and in the best cabaret tradition, he *acted* each song.

Still, the most memorable thing we carried away from that cabaret was this hotel pair's casually open presentation of their life partnership—and this to an audience which (although obviously sympathetic and supportive) couldn't even be described as "mixed"—Ron and I were the only same-sex couple in the hall; *and* in a community that might well have triggered Fear of Flaunting. Not that this hotel pair flaunted *anything*: their tributes were exchanged "across a crowded room," and weren't backed up, after, with physical display. Still, the village in which the hotel sits might be dubbed Hasidic Heights: the blinker-light intersection a few blocks uphill of the hotel usually swarms with Orthodox Jews in uniform—the men in vests and long black coats even on hot summer days. The local county newspaper runs virulently homophobic letters from redneck subscribers, often signed with Jewish names.[6]

Yet, here, in this packed cabaret corner, two men were frankly announcing themselves as devoted life partners. I recall turning to *my* life partner to murmur, "These guys have to be in Donaghe's anthology!" When, a few months later, it—surprise!—became *our* project, the White Lake hotel duo was one of the first couples I solicited. When they phoned their agreement to participate, I turned to Ron in triumph: "I think we have a book!"

So we've given this pivotal contribution to our project "pride of place" as the lead-off account.

THEN, A SOUR NOTE (WITH CHORUS)

The second spring acceptance, which so buoyed my hopes for the project, proved (alas) less salubrious—perhaps the most crushing disappointment of my "casting for couples."

Ron and I have for years supported the New York City Gay Men's Chorus, a courageously "out there" group that offers several professional-quality concerts each year in Manhattan's best halls (they've also toured extensively, in the United States and abroad).

Their musical director for eighteen seasons has been Gary Miller, and I would guess I've watched Gary get kissed by more major celebrities in Carnegie Hall than anyone else I can think of—from the late greats Colleen Dewhurst and Larry Kert to Marilyn Horne and Frederica Von Stade, Eartha Kitt and Elaine Stritch, Faith Prince, Barbara Cook, Cyndi Lauper, and both Channings (Carol and Stockard)—all of whom have shared the stage with Gary as guests during chorus concerts.

Gary's bio in every concert program concludes: "His partner in life, Daniel Starr, is chief librarian at the Museum of Modern Art." So, one mid-March day, off went my solicitation. Gary replied within a month with a letter saying:

> Daniel and I would be interested in exploring our participation in your project. It would be an interesting process for our

relationship. . . . We've been together for thirteen years, are deeply (though silently!) committed to one another, and proud of our enduring relationship. . . . Neither one of us would have time to devote to this project until the summer months. . . . We leave this Friday (on vacation) and when we're back I'll give you a call (once) we settle back into our routines.

He provided his home phone number: "If I'm negligent about getting back to you in a timely manner, please feel free to call me."

Though I followed up with repeated notes over the next four months, I could never elicit a further response. When I finally had to write that they were holding up the whole project, Gary huffed back (in August!), "At this late point in the summer, Daniel and I simply don't have the time this project requires."

Several months later, in accepting a lifetime achievement award at SAGE's twentieth anniversary celebration in a Lincoln Center concert hall, Gary spoke (with the New York City Gay Men's Chorus arrayed behind him, filling the stage). Allowing as how his early fifties seemed premature for such a career-capper, Gary warned he might just come 'round for another one, a few years hence. He announced that he would be retiring as musical director after his current (eighteenth) season with the chorus, and acknowledged the sense of bewildering unfairness his long-term status as an HIV-positive man arouses in him as the chorus sings at a seemingly endless chain of memorial services for its own members and other AIDS victims. His speech was both moving and witty and only heightened my sense of loss that he and Daniel Starr couldn't get their act together to participate in this anthology.

I did not go in paparazzi pursuit of major celebrities for this project. One could compile such a book from the ranks of the famous, retelling the familiar stories and notable achievements of such long-term male relationships as those between composer Benjamin Britten and the tenor for whom he created such memorable roles (*Peter Grimes, Death in Venice*), Peter Pears; the esteemed filmmaking partnership of director James Ivory and producer Ismail Merchant; the nurturing relationship of architect Philip Johnson with David Whitney; the thirty-year collaboration of composer Lou Harrison and Bill Colvig; the controversial documentary filmmaker

Marlon Riggs and his steadfast lover, Jack Vincent, who nursed him through the agonies of his final illnesses; theatre director Marshall Mason and his lover Danny Irvine, both teachers at Arizona State and soon to celebrate their silver anniversary; French esthete, artist, playwright and filmmaker Jean Cocteau and his favorite actor, Jean Marais (the original Beast in *La Belle et la Bête*); choreographer Anthony Tudor and dancer High Laing (finest male interpreter of Tudor's work); artist Paul Cadmus and the live-in model of his later decades, Jon Andersson (of whom he's drawn and painted such exquisite nudes); modern-dance choreographers Murray Louis and the sixteen-years-older Alwin Nikolais—the mentor he pursued into one of the most creative collaborations in the history of dance (until Nikolais's death in 1993 at age eighty-three); composers and sometime-collaborators Samuel Barber and Gian-Carlo Menotti; writer Christopher Isherwood and artist Don Bachardy.[7]

It might be said that long-term celebrity marriages are more remarkable than most because of the greater odds against their success—especially when one or both of the partners is in the arts or entertainment. Inevitably, fame and acclaim create a "groupie" atmosphere, and wherever ardent admirers make themselves available (in a rather pathetic hope that some sheen of glamour will rub off on their drab lives) the temptation to stray from a core relationship increases. "Whoring around" seems to come with the territory of celebrity, where it's so easy; basically, though, gay promiscuity is no worse than—or different from—the heterosexual variety. It just (starting with the 1980s) became more foolhardy.

What my co-editor and I sought for this collection was *diversity*. We wanted as broad a spectrum of relationships as possible—in age, profession, geography, and attitude. Some of these romances began in high school or college, some were very late blooming, even coming after failed experiments with conventional marriage (at least one writer was sixty-one when his gay relationship *began*).

We've gathered professional men, teachers, bankers, blue-collar workers, innkeepers, arts managers, political organizers, gardeners, florists—even book and magazine editors and a pioneer porn filmmaker (sorry, not one hairdresser, though he would have been welcome if one had volunteered). We said to them all: "Tell us about yourselves—how and where you met, how and when you decided to commit for life, how you've juggled careers, how you've made it all work." Our arbitrary criterion was that each couple had to have made it through twelve years in tandem. The resulting collaborative autobiographies in this book transcend the solipsism of most gay memoirs—those my-first-time, lonely-eminence confessionals that are the morose legacy of the Edmund White school of self-revelation. We think you'll find these shared experiences refreshing and even inspirational.

So can the couples in this book be considered typical of contemporary male unions across the United States and Canada? Hardly—no more than such a varied and scattered sample could ever count as "typical" of any vast and diverse group. But they *are* representative—in their multiplicity and the dedication of their commitment.

Yet if you assembled these writers in one room, I would expect a cacophony of disagreement on many issues. Nor do the editors embrace all the opinions expressed in these essays. We would give expatriate Martin Last an argument re the livability of New York City, needless to say! And the "open marriage" several of these couples advocate would prove disastrously unworkable for other couples in this book.

THE MONOGAMY ISSUE

Since several couples in this anthology happily admit their union is not an exclusive one sexually (and even credit this aspect of their relationship as contributing to its longevity), it's important to discuss it here. We've included such views because they expand the diversity of this book, further demonstrating that male unions come in as many forms as heterosexual ones. I would venture to say there are, proportionately, as many "open," unbinding experimental two-sex marriages as there are male unions of this type.

Still, you only have to read the other joint accounts in this book to see how destructive such openness would be to some unions. Indeed, you may find it surprising to see how naturally monogamy comes to the majority of male marriages—since there's virtually no tradition of it in male homosexuality. I don't doubt for a moment that famous gays in the 1920s, 1930s, and 1940s (Valentino, Monty Woolley, Noel Coward, director George Cukor, Cesar Romero— even Cary Grant and Lenny Bernstein) might have pursued less frivolous sex lives had society been less judgmental. But since their homosexual desires were already banished to the shadows, there was no incentive to direct them upward, into the light. Social opprobrium (or, at the very least, even among sophisticates, a superior smirk) would have greeted any serious liaison with another man. So they had little choice but to "go cruising," and certainly little motivation toward more mature behavior.

Even in today's committed couples, the temptation to stray is understandable. Though sex is properly the most profound expression of loving commitment, it is, at the same time, one of life's supreme recreational pleasures. (And homosexual lovemaking is, by its biological nature, recreational rather than procreational.) The young have an almost irresistible urge to grab as much of this stimulating joy as possible, feeding their erotic hunger with as little discrimination as they gorge on junk food. But surely it didn't take the AIDS plague to teach most of us that since casual overindulgence is bad for your health (as well as for mature development of interpersonal relations) promiscuity might be said to be a symptom of arrested development.

Paul Newman once observed (explaining *his* marital fidelity): "Why settle for hamburger when you have steak waiting at home?"—a crude-but-apt analogy not much appreciated by his classy wife, Joanne Woodward. But this again is personal opinion, and what else could you expect from me, who once began notes toward a book to be titled *Monogamy Is for Grown-Ups*?

Still, as editors, both Ron and I appreciate the frankness with which several of our essayists chose to treat so personal a subject, and as one of them says (I paraphrase): "Hey, it's worked for *us* for seventeen years!"

And, once again, such a divergence of outlook only makes our point that gay unions come in as many types as heterosexual marriages do. One has only to examine contemporary culture to realize how little monogamy is regarded by many straight husbands. Who else makes grotesque Broadway shows glorifying 42nd Street whores, countless movies about adultery, and all those sleazy flesh books so profitable? Not to mention "day-rate" motels! As Bill Maher recently pointed out on *Politically Incorrect*, straight married couples are "poor advertisements for their product." And *their* marriages come with the stamp of social approval—and with Congress rushing to "protect" their sanctity. Yet half of them end in divorce.

JUST ONE THING MORE

Each account herein represents a couple—as listed in the Contents. In most cases, one member of the pair agreed to do the actual writing in close consultation with his partner. In these instances, the dual byline reads (for example):

> Scott Samuelson [the writer]
> with Eddie Dudek [the helpmeet]

In a case or two each partner elected to submit a separately bylined piece; these are always paired. In two accounts, the surviving mate tells of his long-term union with a partner who has died. When Ron and I faced up to our own autobiography, we decided to split it into sections, by subject, alternating on the main texts while the other kibbitzed with marginal comment. Thus, in the text and the Table of Contents, each section is separately bylined, for clarity. The end-tab of every account indicates where it was written. All accounts were completed from 1996 to 1998.

One thing these joint accounts make abundantly clear is: there's no such thing as a "homosexual lifestyle." I can only hope this book hastens that silly cliché (promoted by the radical right and fostered by a lazy press) to a well-earned grave. There are as many lifestyles among gays as there are among a comparable sampling of straights. Let's not forget that straights can sport perverse and grotesque lifestyles, too—though nobody pretends such fringe behavior is *typical* of heterosexuals. And while I can't indiscriminately applaud *all* lifestyles (I'm certainly wearied and annoyed by the endless image-loop of parading hairy leathermen with chain-strung nipples that the Right projects as their obsessively one-note version of the "gay lifestyle"), this book is meant to celebrate gay diversity.

That said, there's one thing every partner in this book would agree on: (perhaps mis-) appropriating the brothers Gershwin, each of us would sing out, "I've got my man! Who could ask for anything more?"

The only thing *more* all us Longtime Companions could ask for is formal recognition. We've all worked diligently to make our partnerships sound, nurturing, enduring. We've done this without any social motivation, largely without role models, and in the face of "official" disapproval or contempt. We've told our stories here to refute—by the simple facts of our experience—the grotesque misrepresentation (by politicians, fundamentalists, and the world's rednecks) of gays as being incapable of stable, committed relationships.

Loving commitment and life sharing are not exclusive to heterosexual unions, guys, however desperately you pretend they are.

The testimonies in this book are living proof. If, taken together, they present one message, it's that DoMA is discriminatory and unjust and must be pronounced unconstitutional. A legal challenge is inevitable—even if it must be pursued all the way to the Supreme Court. I only hope I live to read Clarence Thomas's sputtering dissent from the majority opinion.

Meanwhile, however, repeal isn't moving in our favor. Lest gays ever become complacent with advances we've made toward social equality, we need only recall the recent backlash vote in Maine—a "people's veto" plebiscite that made Maine the first state to repeal its protection of gays from discrimination. If one gives any credence to the political cliché "As Maine goes, so goes the nation," this chilling confirmation of the clout of the Christian Coalition should be as much a wake-up call-to-arms as the national passage of DoMA.

Organized "Christian" extremists poured into Maine's churches with the same false generalizations and scare tactics they've used elsewhere. Because of complacency on the part of Maine's knowledgeable citizens, turnout was low (only 30 percent of registered voters), thus handing the radical right its dubious victory. These extremists don't give a damn about democracy; they have no faith in rule by the majority. Their only concern is power where it counts, and winning by a handful of votes is heady because it permits them to force their restrictive agenda on everyone.

We gays still have an immense job of reeducation before us—a job unlikely to diminish in the foreseeable future, and a job to which this book is dedicated.

NOTES

1. G. Robert Geyer, 1993. Spahr ruling was just. *Times-Union* (Rochester), January 5, p. 7A.

2. Bruce Bawer, ed., 1996. *Beyond Queer: Challenging Gay Left Orthodoxy.* New York: Free Press; William N. Eskridge, 1996. *The Case for Same-Sex Marriage: From Sexual Liberty to Civilized Commitment.* New York: Free Press. Incidentally, you'll never find the term "queer" used seriously in this book in place of homosexual or gay. To embrace this enemy term of contemptuous derision in hopes of taking the sting out is one of the more absurd defiant gestures of young radicals. I found myself applauding black dancer Bill T. Jones on a recent television roundtable with Martin Duberman and other rather desperately liberal homosexual spokespersons who kept lauding "queer cultural values." When Jones had heard enough of this, he snapped: "I never answer to 'queer' any more than I'd answer to 'nigger.'" And when Duberman tried patiently to explain the new term's usefulness, I wished Jones had asked if he would answer to "kike." "Queer" belongs only in the title of Bawer's anthology, in which the essays all strive to reach *beyond* it—as do the autobiographical accounts in our book.

3. Luis Torres, 1996. Reader's Forum. *Time,* September 9.

4. Eskridge, *The Case for Same-Sex Marriage,* p. 184.

5. Alfred Lees, 1997. Letter to the editor. *The Key West Citizen,* April 23.

6. The pertinence of these comments is further sharpened by the fact I'm writing them on the day sixteen orthodox rabbis filed a federal suit to block the imminent opening of Manhattan's new museum, A Living Memorial to the Holocaust. Lead plaintiff, notorious homophobe Rabbi Yehuda Levin of Brooklyn, explained that he and his colleagues were outraged by the museum's inclusion of gay victims of the Nazi death camps, "elevating homosexuals to the martyred status of six million Jews." While it's difficult to conceive of such a public obscenity as this action (and statement), it's another reminder that few things are as offensive as "religious" bigotry—and it doesn't all flow from Protestant camp meetings.

7. One could, of course, also list many notable lesbian unions, such as that between novelist Mary Renault (who wrote so eloquently of love between men in ancient Greece) and Julie Mullard, with whom she lived for fifty years. But these relationships are beyond the scope of this anthology.

MARRY US

I who would serve you, who would serve
I your love, your love would earn.
I who would love you,
who would love,
I would be loved in return.
I who am created,
Lord by your touch and word,
Perfect image of my God,
I would be seen and heard.
What we promise is our prayer;
Let us love, love for aye,

Each others care for all our lives.
Marry us today.
In the sight of God and Man,
two are now as one.
We affirm this visibly,
Man is not alone.
To our Father's house we come
to rejoice and pray
we live and die like all your sons,
Marry us today.

Philip Littell

THE JOINT ACCOUNTS

The Ballad of Eddie and Scott

Scott Samuelson with Edward Dudek

Our story together actually begins in the early fall of 1980—thank God! This makes it mathematically convenient to remember which anniversary we are celebrating at all times. But before we go there we wanted to give a little individual background for some added color. To this day, and by my calculations this would be sixteen and a half years into this relationship we call ours, neither of us can quite figure out how we ended up here. Had you asked either one of us seventeen years ago what our idea for the ideal mate would have been, I don't think we would have described each other. Be that as it may, here we are and here we intend to stay.

I (Scott) was born on March 14, 1957 and raised on the East Coast in a formerly industrial city in Connecticut called Waterbury. My father, from whom I've been estranged for over ten years (a tale I might get back to—but probably won't, since it has nothing to do with my being gay or my relationship with Eddie), was a machinist in small shops around Waterbury throughout my whole time in his house. He was not a specialist of any kind, meaning he wasn't a tool-and-die man or such, just the guy who was fairly proficient on any number of machines and could move around the shop as he was needed. Although this sounds like it would make that person a valuable asset, my father was probably the lowest man on the totem pole as far as salary went. Somehow, and I'm still not sure how, we managed to survive—albeit not in the best of neighborhoods, yet always clothed and fed and every now and then treated to a little family recreation. I must say that being raised with a little less always makes you appreciate what you do get when you do get it.

My mother is a terrific lady whom I adore, not that she is in any way perfect, but she has always been my champion and our (Ed's and my) biggest supporter. My mom was diagnosed with a rare kidney disorder when she was nineteen years old. Consequently, she spent quite a lot of time in and out of the hospital while I was growing up. I guess if I really thought about it I could come up with a sad story about this situation, but when you are not aware of any other way of living your life, you just move on. Today, my mom lives, sans kidneys (dialysis three days a week), back in Connecticut. Although she is pain-free for the first time in her life, she is truly frustrated by her inability to pick up and move around as she would like to do. But valiantly she marches on. My parents divorced shortly after I left home and Mom married again—more happily.

To move on quickly, I will tell you that I have three sisters back in Connecticut. They all, as I, are doing the best that they can with what they have. Due to circumstances that you will have to wait to read about in a different book, their road is not always as smooth as I would like it to be for them. But we all continue to love and support one another the best that we can.

I moved out of Waterbury in 1977 at the age of nineteen, heading for New York City to pursue a career in the theater—what a cliché. I attended the American Academy of Dramatic Arts and went on to professional theater a couple of years later. That brings us up to the time that Eddie and I met, except to tell you that I did not come out completely until I was twenty-one years old, although I believe I knew I was gay from about the age of nine or ten.

Eddie, on the other hand, says he feels he knew he was gay when he was about six years old and acted on it at a very early age. He was born on May 14, 1951 in Detroit, Michigan. He is of Polish descent and his family is steeped in those wonderful ethnic traditions. To this day he tries to carry on those traditions in our household. That is not so easy, since I, coming from a mixed bag, was not used to those kinds of traditions and am not always as flexible as I wish I could be. I have gotten better over the years, I hope, and Ed is extremely tenacious.

When Eddie was six years old, his father passed away. It was terribly unexpected—a brain aneurysm—and it left his mother to make some extremely difficult decisions. There were family properties that had to be sold off and a move that took them away from the neighborhood that they loved. I suppose it was more difficult for his two older sisters than it was for a six-year-old. They helped his mom the best that they could, all of them. His mother was a fiercely independent woman with a will of iron and a heart of gold. She provided well for the family and kept everyone in line. She passed away in January 1997, not an easy passing, and she is sorely missed. She struggled long and hard her entire life and may she now truly rest in peace.

*   *   *

Eddie was a great student throughout his school days and loved it. He was also a vehement member of his church's choir and was devoutly religious from a very young age. He was very active with local community theater and studied ballet with the Detroit Savero Ballet. When he was twenty, Eddie auditioned for and got a part with a touring company of Disney on Parade—a part he performed for over three years before moving to New York to continue his professional dance career. He worked steadily and made his living as a dancer for over twelve years. This is about where our story *together* begins.

It was in 1980: I had just auditioned for and gotten my first union show and was very excited and very nervous. It was a production of *Good News* that was being performed in a theater restaurant in northern Connecticut called Coachlight Dinner Theatre. I got this job because I had just finished working in a summer theater with a musical director who was now the resident musical director for this place. He thought I would be right for the show and invited me to come to New York City for rehearsals. Eddie, on the other hand, had already been performing at this theater with the resident director and choreographer for a few years. He was tremendously comfortable and had established himself as chorine in residence. He was the life of the rehearsal process—and pretty obnoxious from my insecure point of view. He sat behind me with a friend of his, another regular dancer at this theater, in the chorus musical rehearsals. All throughout these rehearsals, in breaks between the actual learning of the music, he and this guy would chatter incessantly. I, of course, being the good little first-timer, thought they were being totally rude and disruptive. Although I never was sure what they were talking about, my paranoid little self was sure it was nothing good and it was about me. It was very disconcerting, but I thought I had just better ignore it, as I had enough to think about with the show itself.

Years later, Eddie would tell me that what they were talking about was how broad my shoulders were and wouldn't they just love to try me out. For that I will just have to take his word, but at the time no one could have convinced me that was the topic of conversation. As you will probably get to understand throughout this account, I—despite my many genuine positive attributes—am overly insecure and slightly paranoid. You would have a very hard time finding anyone to corroborate that statement, but nevertheless I'm being sincere. That is actually, probably, the one thing that Eddie and I have in common. To the world we probably appear to be very much in control of everything at all times, but we are constantly questioning ourselves and each other.

When the rehearsal process in New York was finished and it was time to relocate to the theater, we had various ways of getting up to Connecticut. Most just took the bus from Manhattan's Port Authority depot. This is where everything really began.

As it turned out, Eddie and I chose, totally coincidentally, to take the same bus. When I arrived at the bus platform, I saw Ed standing with a very attractive young man, and Ed introduced him as his lover, John. He was a very nice guy and actually was on his way to get Eddie something to drink on the bus and would I care for anything? He walked away and Ed started to talk, informing me that he and John had been together for six years, and was I involved? The answer to this was not really, but I had met someone recently and we had gone out a few times, but I wasn't sure where that would go because I would be away for a couple of months. John returned and it was time to depart. They said their good-byes and off Ed and I went.

There happened to be a female cast member on that bus and we all sat near each other and had a great trip up to the theater. There was lots of laughing and dish about the show and other cast members. One thing that I have to confess to (since it's still brought up to me to this day) is a stupid little thing I said to Eddie on that trip. I need to explain my behavior, sort of, in advance.

When I was in school, I had the opportunity to stage manage for a professional Shakespearean workshop group. One winter evening as we were beginning a new rehearsal process, and all the actors were arriving at the rehearsal space, an actor of some renown arrived with a substantial dangle from his nostril area. The director and founder and mentor to this group met this gentleman with a hearty hello and, "Richard, you have a big snot hanging out of your nose." It was not in the least bit discreet, nor did it matter really as everyone there had already noticed the problem. So Richard cleaned himself up, everyone had a good laugh, and the tension was broken. I had found this quite brilliant. The director, being the one that everyone looked up to and regarded as the one in charge, saw that he was the obvious choice to inform Richard of his unfortunate situation. Since everyone there had seen it, and there was no way to do this privately, he made a big deal of it and by doing so put everyone at ease. Back to our story.

So, as Eddie and I and Regina were talking, I noticed this accumulation of a white substance in the corner of Ed's eye. Having had the aforementioned experience, I said to Eddie, "If you don't get that gook out of the corner of your eye, I think I'm going to puke." To this day, I insist I handled the situation with wit and sensitivity. I'm sure you see the similarity between the two incidents.

I'm not positive, but I think this might be where we connected. For sure, *something* was different between us, now.

When we got to the hotel at which we would be staying, we found out that by coincidence our rooms were right next to each other. After settling in we made plans to have dinner together. We went across the street to a nice little place called Two Mattoon. We had a great dinner and even better conversation, and it was at this dinner it became apparent that we were in trouble. There was no mistaking our intention to go further than that.

As I stated earlier, I know that neither of us was what the other would have considered to be his "type," but things had absolutely transcended that. We were definitely in *something*, whether it was love or lust; it was happening. Without going into the gory details, we did sleep together that night and it was truly the beginning of the end on one hand and the beginning of the beginning on the other.

*   *   *

What you need to know at this point is that Eddie is a tremendously loyal and faithful man, and this was not a simple matter. He was, after all, in a six-year relationship and had a lot of baggage. I did not. After a few weeks of this "affair," I called in the chips. It was to be me or John. It was not that I wanted John out, it was that I was at the point where I didn't want to continue in this situation if there was nothing in it for me in the long haul. An ongoing adulterous affair was not what I was looking for. At that point, I told Eddie to take the time to figure this out. He eventually decided that things were not as good at home as he would have liked them to be. He decided to leave John. Again, none of this was frivolous or easy for either of us, and it took a lot of time and was very painful for a lot of people—not just Eddie, John, and me. There were family and friends that were involved and no one was particularly pleased with this situation.

When the show was finished we returned to New York and had to make arrangements for living. My apartment was still being sublet and Ed had to vacate his and John's. So we sublet for a while and then moved into my apartment. We lived together for almost a year and suddenly things got weird. Eddie informed me one night that he was having second thoughts and wanted to return to John. I thought I was going to die. It was one of the most devastating things that has ever happened to me. I didn't know what to think or do. I would go to work and come home and not even remember what I had done. And I am not a fragile person. Eddie eventually moved out and back to John.

For some reason we stayed in close contact. Soon after he moved out he got a show that was going to tour the East Coast for the summer. Over the course of this tour we stayed in touch, and at some point, Eddie asked me to meet him in the Poconos where the show was playing. I wanted to know why but he wouldn't say. Still, I went. It was then he informed me that it was not working out back with John and he wanted to return to me. There was one hitch. He and John had put a deposit down on the purchase of a house in the Catskills. He stood to lose $10,000 if he backed out at that point. I had some serious thinking to do. At the age of twenty-three, and a theatrical hopeful to boot, how was I going to be able to handle this financial burden? We talked long and hard, and I decided I would go for it. Much of the mortgage maneuvering was left to me because Ed was still on tour, but we actually were able to pull it off.

John, at this time, was a very confused and angry man. I certainly don't blame him. But after a few years we actually became very good friends. I even got him a job with me at a restaurant in Queens where we performed together for a couple of years. John was a very handsome, very talented, and very intelligent man. He and I had a ton of fun at the restaurant, and the three of us became extremely close. John even stayed in our house upstate (the one he was supposed to buy with Eddie) for a vacation one year. It was devastating to both of us when John informed us that he had AIDS. He suffered with the disease for a couple of years and passed away on December 3, 1988. The day we got the call, Eddie happened to be upstate and I had to call him to tell him. It was not only sad that John was gone, but that we were not able to be together at that moment to console each other. He was a big part of our lives, in the end a wonderful part, and we still miss him a lot.

In 1984, Eddie decided he did not want to continue as a dancer and I was not very happy in my pursuit of stardom, so we decided to leave the theater and open a business of our own together. What could we possibly do? After agonizing hours of conversation and debate, we decided we would both be happy owning and operating a bed-and-breakfast. So that became our quest. Because we owned the house in the Catskills and had met a lot of people, we chose to look there for a piece of property to be our B&B. In September of that year, we purchased a run-down, dilapidated old summer hotel on the shore of White Lake, in upstate New York. The place was truly a disaster. It needed to be gutted and rebuilt, but it was what we could afford.

So Eddie, Tom (a fabulous stray weimaraner we adopted the year we bought our first house), and I started tinkering and playing at the hotel. We spent the next few years trying to put enough equity into the place so a bank would lend us the real dollars for the major renovation. We did this by working on the cottages that surrounded the main building. We worked full time in New York City, Eddie in his apartment-cleaning business and I at the restaurant mentioned before. We would take the money we made, whatever was left over after expenses, and run upstate and buy supplies or give it to whoever did some job for us during that week. As you can imagine, it was a slow process.

It was in those years, 1985 to 1989, that I think some of our fondest memories lie. We always had friends up to visit. We had parties in this tumbledown mess. We made some great new friends;

people were always stopping by to see what was going on there. The building is on a main road in a small town—need I say more? My mother and her husband were always there—they had given us part of the down payment when we bought the hotel, and part of the deal was that they got the use of one of the cottages for ten years. They were a great source of encouragement (most of the time) during those years. Ed's family—his mother, and one of his sisters and her family—were out from Michigan a few times and actually stayed with us there. My boss at the restaurant and his family, truly our adopted second family, were always up to help and play and fight and cry and laugh and eat! We still howl when we reminisce about the silly things we did at that time.

As with everything in life, all was not perfect. There were certainly financial worries. Our Tom was hit by a car before our (and all our friends') eyes in front of the hotel—he wasn't killed but very shaken up. Unfortunately, and we don't know if one thing had to do with the other, Tom developed stomach inversion one night six months later and we couldn't save him; that was a rough one. The restaurant in Queens was having some problems and eventually closed. John passed away. All the usual life occurrences, I guess, but our experience seemed to be so intense at that time. It was as if everything was electrified.

One of the best things that happened, but almost didn't, was the acquisition of our Sophie—an incredible little Tibetan spaniel that my mother got for us. After Tom died, she told us she wanted to get us one of these dogs. She had one, my aunt had one, my sister had one—we would love it. We fought with her, telling her that we didn't want the responsibility of another animal. We loved Tom, but in the city, a dog was a burden all the time. Feeding, walking, vets, cleaning, whatever. Tom had just died and we were simply not ready to take that on again.

Finally, she wore us down. Or I guess she wore me down. Ed was in Detroit visiting and she caught me in a weak moment. I called him and talked him into it. Now with the decision made we had to wait. Then we got the call we were getting a little girl. What were we going to name her? That was another whole deal. Her pedigree name was Jo Jevon Sweetdreams. So, Jo-Jo? JJ? Chantilly? Tilly? It went on for a while. You would have thought we were having a real child.

At that time (actually forever), I had a habit of imitating Bette Midler doing her Sophie Tucker jokes: "I will never forget it, you know." And it came to me: Here we were up in the "Jewish Alps" having a girl. When I suggested the name to Eddie he loved it, and so Sophie it is. She is the best. What else would proud fathers say? She is gorgeous, friendly, talented (she sings with me), and quite the princess! She's ten years old now and she thinks she is still a puppy, in looks and in actions. People can't believe it when we tell them her age.

She has really been like our child and such a joy. Whenever we get cards or notes from friends, or even customers, often they want to know how Sophie is, or tell us, "Say hello to Sophie." And it is truly because of her personality. People just love her. We never have a problem with babysitters when we travel. In fact, we have friends who are offended if we don't ask them to watch her if we go away. I think we obsess!

Speaking of coming up with a proper name—our hotel project was now far enough along to suggest we needed a name for it. "White Lake Manor" had a bit too grand a ring to it—and we certainly weren't about to call it "The White Elephant"! But since we had merged our *lives*, it seemed appropriate to merge our *names*—or at least the middle names we never used. Thus was born the Bradstan Country Hotel.

By 1989, Eddie and I knew we had to make some other major decisions. There were things going on in our White Lake building that had to be addressed. The roof was leaking even more and causing serious damage; there was a two-story attachment on the back of the building that had detached itself and was about to collapse; the front porch had done the same; there was a large section of the foundation that was crumbling —the list went on. We knew if we didn't do something we would lose the entire building. We started looking for contractors. What a joke! How could we afford one? We had already sold our first house to work on the cottages; we were never there because of all the work we were doing on the hotel property.

We finally called a guy who had stopped by months before looking for another work site. He had left his name and number in case we ever needed a contractor. He came over and we told him what we wanted to do and that we had no money to do it. He said sure we did, no problem. He told us to go to the bank and get an equity loan. We told him we didn't think we would be able to get enough. He said, sure you will—go ahead! We did. We got it! It was unbelievable. It seemed impossible but there we were. This is really where there is another whole book, so we'll try to be succinct.

This gentleman's name was Carl and he took us on a journey over the next year that gave us an education that we couldn't have gotten in twenty years in a school. He brought the hotel not only up to the grade we needed to save the structure but well beyond. It was, after this one year, at a point where it was ridiculous to not try to go on to completion. But we needed more money, obviously. Well, the building now was worth a lot more. So we went back to the bank and asked. Surprise: this time it was no. Carl to the rescue again. He introduced us over the phone to this guy who was a mortgage broker. Actually, he was a legal loan shark. He set us up with a legitimate broker who actually cut him out of the deal in the end because he was such a dog. We got the money we needed, albeit at quite a price. This was May of 1990 and the Queens restaurant closed in June. Eddie and I decided that instead of looking for another job, I would just move up to the hotel and work for us. So much of the work that was left to do was work I could actually do. All finish stuff: painting, stain, refinishing, tiling, papering, trimming—that kind of work. So to the hotel I went. What a year! The stories I could tell. Up at seven, to bed at midnight. I still can't believe I actually was able to keep myself motivated. And Eddie would work all week in the city and then come up and work even harder here. I should tell you now that Eddie was the absolute brains on this project. Don't ever tell him I said so,* but it's true. He saw the project totally complete in his head from day one. He had to guide me through every inch of the way. His design work and organization was and still is astounding to me! I was, as I tell people all the time, the mule. If I knew what was to be done I could eventually figure out how to do it.

After the most intense year of both of our lives, we were nearing the completion of our dream. In April, there was about a week's

---

*Footnote by Eddie: Actually, I'm looking over Scott's broad shoulder as he keyboards this. I had done the outline for this account, so I am naturally concerned with how he's fleshing it out. I see he's giving it to you straight—so to speak.

worth of intense work to be done and then we could open by our projected date, May 3. Things were moving at a feverish pitch. Our friend Helene (pronounced LN) had taken a vacation from her nursing-care coordinator position at the Cabrini Medical Center in Manhattan to help with the final details. All of our friends, both in New York and upstate, were going to be on hand for the opening. I had called and hired the pianist that I last worked with in the city to come up and play for us. People were donating time and things to help out. Plants were arriving, plaques were made, and Helene, Eddie, and I were, it seemed, forever covered with paint, stain, and polyurethane and about ready to drop! May 2 arrived, and we had accomplished the impossible; people that were staying the weekend were arriving, and somewhere we found a new burst of energy. That was Friday and the grand opening was Saturday.

From the start, we had planned that our B&B had to include a cabaret—after all, we were both theater people. The front-corner cabaret room was where the party would take place. The liquor license had not come through yet, but that really didn't matter as we were just throwing a party. Saturday arrived and the party began! In our lives I don't think we could ever reach that high again. We all laughed and cried and jammed and drank and ate, and had the best time ever! I will never forget walking to that cabaret stage for the first time to sing and looking out at Eddie and all of our friends and family just beaming. I started to sing and everyone started to cry. I *hope* it was just from the relief everyone felt! Everyone had been so involved and supportive that I think it had become as important to most of them as it was to us. Not just old friends and family, but the new friends as well. This is something that Eddie and I have been blessed with— the most extraordinary group of friends and acquaintances that you could ever meet. The list is endless and they come and go and come and go, but the feelings never wane. We can pick up with any one of them at any time and we are all there. We miss the ones who have passed away and we think of them often and always feel special for having had them in our lives.

*   *   *

This is our seventh year in business. The liquor license came two weeks after our party, and the cabaret opened. It has been as suc-

cessful as our area can allow. We now have a cabaret series that is
rivaled by none. We are able to present the best-known performers
in the cabaret industry right here in White Lake. This is due in great
part to the generosity and support of the late Nancy LaMott, a
cabaret star who took a chance and agreed to perform here. She
went back to New York and told everyone she knew in the industry
to come and perform here. It paid off for them all: our audiences
treat the performers like gold and Bradstan doesn't treat them so
badly either; still, it was a risk for Nancy and she did us proud.
Consequently, upon her passing, Eddie and I dedicated our cabaret
corner to her memory. It is now called the Nancy LaMott Room.
Some of the performers we have had the pleasure to present are
Karen Mason, Ann Hampton Callaway, Tom Andersen, Baby Jane
Dexter, KT Sullivan, Debbie Gravitte, Lee Lessack, Michael McAssey,
Christine Andreas, Tim DiPasqua, Jeff Harnar, Alix Korey, Marga-
ret Whiting, Julie Wilson—the list goes on.

These artists solo in our Sunday night series, each summer. On
nonstar Fridays and Saturdays, I share the stage with up-and-coming
cabaret singers (who also double as accompanist or wait staff)—so I
keep my tubes from rusting, and our audiences remain indulgent.*

We love and are both very proud of our hotel and cabaret. We
take great pride in our accomplishments here. We both think it is
one of the reasons that we have been able to sustain our relationship
for so long. It has also caused us to come close to calling it quits on
occasion. But fortunately our love and common sense prevail. Our
business is well respected in the community.

Now, here is where we're least comfortable talking about ourselves, but we are out in the community and everyone knows and
accepts our relationship. We think it is because we just *are*, and
have been together for all the time that people in the community
have known us. There is no more to gossip about in our relationship
than anybody else's. Plus, we have been together longer than many
straight couples in the area. Another sign of acceptance in the

---

*Another over-the-shoulder from Eddie: Don't let him kid you. Our audiences
love him—and why wouldn't they? He's a seasoned performer with great versatil-
ity, who can be funny or moving as the song demands—and he's gorgeous up there
(if you'll pardon a prejudiced view).

business community here is that I was elected chairman of the county chamber of commerce in January 1997. As I said, there is really no one who doesn't know that I'm gay; I get a kick out of being in a meeting with legislators, county managers, and local officials and have someone ask how Eddie is or did he redo such-and-such, and no one blinks an eye. On social occasions where spouses are included, Eddie is always invited. I guess that is how it is supposed to be, but I know it ain't always that way everywhere.

In closing this chapter I need to say that this is just an idea of the life that we have had and continue to have. We've only shared some of our highlights here. We have, from the very beginning of our relationship, treated it as a marriage and take it very seriously and work very hard at it. It, like any relationship, has its good and bad moments. We are surrounded by extraordinary people, and we never hide our relationship. Nor do we flaunt it or hold it out there to be judged by anyone but ourselves. Our family and friends are very supportive and know their place in our lives. We have met and welcomed many people into our life, and home, and business. We will continue to do so for as long as we go on. They are our joy and our food. It has been a fantastic sixteen-and-a-half years, both positive and negative, and we look forward to the rest of our lives together. If it is only 50 percent of what we have already experienced, it is more than most will ever know in an entire lifetime.

White Lake, New York

Park Bench to Forever

Roy Strickland and William Wynkoop

SURVIVING THE CURE
by Roy

My mate, William Wynkoop, and I met on a park bench in Washington Square Park, Greenwich Village, on a mild winter night, December 19, 1949. I was getting over an unhappy relationship and went into the park, never realizing this action would mark the start of what is now a forty-seven-year relationship! William came along, saw me on the bench, sat down, and we started to talk. He sounded gentlemanly, was going to Columbia working on his master's in English. After about a half hour, I said, "Would you like to go have a beer at The Old Colony?" a gay bar on Eighth Street. William agreed, we had a beer, a cousin of mine came in, we talked with him a bit, and then I asked William to come back to my place on West Ninth Street. I had a small room in the apartment of a gay fellow there (we were not lovers) and that was the beginning. We hit it off beautifully, both physically and mentally.

Our families eventually knew about us. I'm a survivor of the "hormone imbalance" theory for "treatment of homosexuality" that was popular before the war. I was twenty back in 1938 and after graduating from high school I was working at a beach club in Huntington, Long Island. I had met this attractive boy, several years younger, and we spent a lot of time together, singing pop songs as we walked the beach at night. One rainy afternoon we went to the movies, and I held his hand in the balcony. We hadn't had sex yet, or anything; we just really enjoyed being together.

Well, my older sister spotted the hand-holding and called me on it that evening. I told her how much I liked this boy, and she sent me off to an Austrian doctor who told me I had to stop seeing my friend. To help make me "normal" he gave me shots of male sex hormones—six sessions, which cost my poor sister $150—a lot of money in 1938.

The result, of course, was that I got hornier and wanted to see my friend worse than ever. I told my sister she was wasting her money, and she reluctantly agreed. She finally accepted my nature. We stayed good friends and I handled all estate details a couple of years ago when she died; she had grown quite fond of William.

After working at Grumman Aircraft on Long Island from 1941 to 1945, and living at home, I had realized that, being gay, I would be happier in New York City. I got a job at R. H. Macy, in display, then at McCreery's, then at Lord & Taylor.

I am sure my father realized the situation, too, after I moved to New York and came home weekends bringing William; Dad took a great liking to him. We would go out with Dad in his boat, and several times went down Long Island Sound on overnight trips. I think my father was glad to see I had finally found a permanent mate! William had an older brother and a younger brother, both with families, and they, too, accepted our partnership.

I have not had a problem with church or religion. I was raised in the Presbyterian Church, in Huntington, but shortly after high school, I became an agnostic, and still am.

I am openly gay in my community—it being Greenwich Village. While I worked at Grumman during World War II I was careful to hide my gayness from all my co-workers, but when I went into display, I had no problem, because most all of my co-workers were gay!

I have no children, and never had a feeling I wanted any, even though family and friends were always asking, "When are you going to get married, and have children?" I think too many gays and lesbians do get married, just to please their families, and then regret it later. I think there are too many children in the world already!

It was hell to be gay when I was growing up. I knew I was "different" from a very early age, and had to hide my interest in the other nude bodies in the showers in school. When I was in high school, about 1935, I was playing tennis with a schoolmate, whom I always suspected, and he yelled at me, "I'm going to start a Phi-Beta Club; you can be the masturbator!" I nearly dropped my racquet!

Also, a chap lived three doors away from me during my years in high school, and once came by our house and said, holding a BB gun, "Want to go up to the woods and shoot some crows?" We did not shoot crows (fortunately) but had mad, lovely sex—the beginning of many such occasions. We went to the house of a friend of his, who was in late middle age, a doctor who had been married, who stood by the bed and directed us as to what to do next—holding a jar of Vaseline and never touching either one of us!

But I can honestly say there's only been one real love in my life. More than forty-seven years have passed since I first met William on that park bench. We've never broken up, but have had disagreements on various subjects, including abortion, the death penalty, religion—and pigeons. Early in the relationship, we were not monogamous, because we were separated by jobs—him in Detroit and me in New York City—but we've been faithful ever since we both found jobs in the New York area. I've always felt I couldn't imagine life without William and have been most fortunate to have had him as a mate for so many years. As to the "love life" these days— it is still great, just not as often! (No, I've never gone back to the hormone treatments.)

I would guess the thing people find most remarkable about our relationship is that after so long together, William and I still not only love each other, we *like* each other. We enjoy travel, plays, ballet, opera, dining out. Not every aspect of life is cheery, of course. The day after Thanksgiving, in 1993, I had my esophagus removed because of cancer, at Memorial-Sloan Kettering Hospital in New York. I don't think I could ever have made it through without William. And he's *still* helping me with my hospital and doctor bills!

People continue to find us remarkable: we've been on television thirteen times and many articles have been written about us in magazines and newspapers. This interest seemed to peak around our forty-seventh anniversary on December 19, 1996—but we're girding our loins for a new flurry in December 1999, when we observe our fiftieth—just before the world goes mad celebrating the new millennium!

Our *public* wedding dates from June 16, 1996, however. On that Sunday afternoon, we were a proud part of the "Great Wed-In" in Bryant Park, behind the New York Public Library at Sixth Avenue and Forty-Second Street, along with many other couples, on a great stage. Tom Duane, an openly gay city councilman, read the service from the Episcopal prayer book; the woman rabbi from Beth-Simchat Torah, Reverend Pat Baumgardner, pastor of the gay Metropolitan Church in New York, and Dr. Robert Williams, a pastor at the Marble Collegiate church on Fifth Avenue, were on the stage with us—and all of them spoke. We were given a certificate of marriage, which we later had framed. It now hangs in our kitchen!

The following evening, June 17, we were married again in a most impressive ceremony at Marble Collegiate, by Dr. Williams. Starting at the back of the large church, we joined other couples in a long line that moved slowly down the main aisle, as the wonderful organ played a wedding march. Reaching the pulpit, we couples moved alternately either right or left of Dr. Williams, who then performed the ceremony. The uniqueness of the occasion, the beautiful stained-glass windows, the music, and the surprising number of couples—it all gave us an unforgettable experience.

(Marble Collegiate sponsors a fine organization called "GIFTS"—an elaborate acronym for Gays and Lesbians in Fellowship, Tradition and Service—which meets once a month in the parish hall. They provide a good dinner at a reasonable price, followed by a two-hour program that can be both entertaining and thought-provoking. In various ways GIFTS makes a valuable contribution to the lives of gay men and lesbians in New York City.)

After all these ceremonies, I told William: "You have *finally* made an honest man of me!"

Since the rise of the Gay Rights Movement, William and I have been active in many gay organizations, especially SAGE (Senior Action in a Gay Environment).[1] For many years, we were Friendly Visitors to older, gay shut-in men and women. We would shop for them, visit, walk with them (if they could walk). We still are part of a group that goes to speak to young people at Hetrick-Martin Institute (which works with gay and lesbian youth who've left home), at Green Chimneys (a residence for homeless youth—mostly gay, many kicked out by their families), at Cornell University, and just recently at a symposium at New York University's school of social work. We regularly attend SAGE brunches and socials, held once a month (William and I have always loved dancing together). For many years, I answered the phone at the SAGE office.

Last June, I retired as a volunteer in the flower program at Memorial-Sloan Kettering Cancer Center, where I had worked for twelve years. Our group did 180 arrangements of flowers in champagne bottles that were placed throughout the hospital. I was the sole male volunteer, and the women there called me "the thorn among the roses!" But it was a natural outgrowth of my career as manager of a florist shop catering to celebrities and the well-to-do on Manhattan's Upper East Side. Another memorable outgrowth of that career was being invited to do the floral arrangements for a state dinner at the Ford White House. The gracious first lady was a joy to work with.

This June I retired as a volunteer at the Associated Blind on West Twenty-Third Street, where I read to people once a week for three hours, for seven years—even after the loss of my esophagus! I miss doing all this volunteer work, but there comes a time in life when one has to cut down. I am eighty to William's eighty-two.

We spend much time, mornings and evenings, reading aloud to each other, now—and this we thoroughly enjoy. Our current book is a hefty biography of Somerset Maugham; now there was quite a guy! (Remember photographer George Platt Lynes' portrait of him, all buttoned up, confronting a nude youth?) It's also good preparation for our trip back to England in a few weeks on the Queen Elizabeth. William and I have always been Anglophiles; not sure which we enjoy most—our six-day crossings aboard that elegant floating city or our days in London. I hope we'll be celebrating our fiftieth anniversary with such a trip.

CORROBORATIVE TESTIMONY
by William

Roy has shared with you his recollection of our first meeting—and of our double ceremonies in June 1996. Here's my version of the former—as well as my account of an even earlier commitment ceremony Roy neglects to mention.

Late that first night we spent together, Roy suddenly, silently slipped out of bed in the dark and lighted all six white candles in the black, fancifully designed wire candelabrum hanging on his wall above us. Then he flopped back down on me and the narrow bed in his small room. We both laughed, but those white candles burning in the dark seem to me now, looking back, somehow symbolic, even prophetic.

Roy had recently moved downtown into the Greenwich Village apartment of a gay male friend, not a lover, at 8 West Ninth Street. I lived nearby in 45 West Eleventh Street, a large men's rooming house called then the University Residence Club. We had met, for the first time, earlier that December evening. I had been taking a long way home after a sad meal in the diner at Sixth and Greenwich Avenues.

Still rather disturbed by a conversation I had there with a homosexual man, I felt I could have said more to help him. About my age, he was a musician of some kind whom I had met once before in the home of a mutual friend, also a gay musician, a pianist. When I entered the diner, he was finishing his supper. He beckoned for me to join him, which I did.

He was, I think, dangerously depressed, mainly about our outcast state as homosexual males—especially at Christmastime. Between Thanksgiving and New Year's Day, December was his cruelest month with holiday decorations, the music, alienation from old friends and family, the lack of a respected home life with wife and children, no support from the religions and the gods, just universal condemnation and loathing.

Shocked but fully sympathetic, I spoke about favorite writers who had written supportively—Plato, André Gide, Magnus Hirschfeld, and others. I quoted from Rene Guyon's book, *The Ethics of Sexual Acts.*

Almost evangelically, I tried to show him that, to survive and find peace, even happiness, as gays, we had to fight against any tendency in ourselves to accept as justified society's homophobia, which could destroy us. When we said good night on the corner of West Eighth and Sixth, I knew I had failed to reach him. Perhaps I should have told him about my lifelong religious experience, which had sustained and enriched my existence. He had taken the subway to his lonely room way uptown. I walked slowly through Washington Square.

Ten minutes later, I first saw Roy. He was seated near the end of a bench. Something about his form in the dim light of the dark park attracted me. I stopped, turned quickly, and sat down near the other end. We were soon talking about life in the Village. About half an hour later we were ordering beers in a popular gay bar on West Eighth at the foot of MacDougal Street. While there, Roy was surprised by a male first cousin of his own age who, passing on the sidewalk, saw us through the window. We had lively talk and another round of beers. After his cousin left, we hurried around the corner to Roy's place.

He was thirty-one, I nearly thirty-four. I had begun to feel that, despite the differences, he was more like me than anyone I knew.

We left early next morning, Roy to go uptown to his Lord & Taylor department store display job, I to my nearby room to resume my studies as a Columbia University candidate for a master's in English. We had made a date to meet about seven that Thursday evening, December 22, at his apartment for a drink before going out to dinner.

During the intervening time I realized that our meeting had been for me uniquely significant. I grew hungry to be with Roy again, to share his being.

Arriving at seven on Thursday, I got no answer to my ring. Ten minutes later, I rang again, thinking he might have been in the shower or asleep. No response. I decided to wait until seven thirty on the sidewalk outside the front door of the house where he lived. Soon the sudden racket of fire engines converged with shrieking sirens on the Hotel Fifth Avenue across the street. I waited, watching the excitement and gathering crowds, until about eight. Then, hating to leave, I left.

Making my way through all the people watching from the downtown side of Ninth Street, I began to think of where on West Eighth Street I could find nearby an inexpensive meal. Sad and mad, I tried not to let myself feel too deeply my disappointment. He had probably forgotten our date or just decided he didn't want to see me again. We had exchanged phone numbers, but he hadn't called. I had stayed home working most of the day. "Oh, forget it!" I tried to.

Eighth Street was filled with Christmas. Swags with colored lights swung above and across this main thoroughfare of the Village. Shop windows blazed and carols blared from open doorways. Sidewalks swarmed with people of all ages, the street itself crowded with cars.

When I approached the corner, I saw a familiar two rows of public telephones, one on the Fifth Avenue side, the other on the Eighth Street side, of the old drugstore. All phones but one were in use. Spontaneously I went in and tried one last time.

Roy answered immediately. He sounded greatly relieved and elated. He had attended an obligatory Display Department holiday cocktail party, then had trouble catching a cab. Nearing Ninth Street they were slowed down and finally stopped by the hotel fire. Roy had jumped out and run from there.

I'm sure we spent more than we could afford that evening— probably for dinner at an expensive gay restaurant, and a gay bar later. December 22 was, of course, the darkest night of the year, but this one was our brightest nearly fifty years ago.

*   *   *

Prior to my making "an honest man" of Roy with the public ceremonies he's described, we had availed ourselves promptly, back in 1993, of a new opportunity offered by the City of New York to register as domestic partners. (After all, we'd been exactly that for nearly forty-four years by that time.) On March 3, 1993, we presented ourselves at the city's municipal building (appropriately wedding-cake architecture, just north of City Hall in lower Manhattan) and when we reached the office to which we were directed, were assigned registry number 145. The woman clerk gave us a paper to take to another office down the hall, where we were given the certificate.

When Roy and I got there, we were the only ones, but gradually more duos appeared—male couples and female couples. We were the oldest pair there, and when we started talking to the others, they were so impressed with the time we had been together that one woman, who had brought a camera, proposed we step outside for a group photo. Once that was done, someone else suggested we all have lunch together to celebrate our nuptials, but Roy and I had to hurry to a meeting uptown. We only hope the other couples, frozen with us in that photo, have fared as well as we.

Speaking of photographs, one of our favorites is a dual portrait taken several years ago for a coffee-table book on gays in America. In it, Roy clutches and kisses my hand in so touching a way, the shot has become something of an icon for long-term gay marriages. *OUT Magazine* featured a blow-up of it in an early subscription brochure. Talk about playing role models!

The long-established male couple in Terrence McNally's fine play and film, *Love! Valour! Compassion!,* muses sardonically: "We're role models—it's very stressful." (This duo—Perry and Arthur—is celebrating fourteen years together, so qualifies for inclusion in this anthology!) In truth, Roy and I are pleased the privilege of playing role models has fallen to us—though, as Roy has indicated, it can prove rather stressful for people our age.

Greenwich Village, New York

NOTE

1. Senior Action in a Gay Environment, Inc. (SAGE), 305 Seventh Ave., 16th Floor, New York, NY 10001; Terry Kaelber, Executive Director.

Loss of Sharing:
The Bereavement Continues

Martin Last

YOUR PRESENCE IN ABSENTIA

You are away from me
in another place, a
remote locus, yet in
focus here where
you belong, your body,
your private self rests
best here near me,
and I feel you close,
yet know you away.

The space of you is
empty, but still
filled with some
eidolon of you,
which is part of me,
inseparable, stable,
able to fill the space
I need filled to be
complete, replete,

full of myself, my
space filled by you,
and alone I am not
incomplete, as you
inhabit where you are,
for now, not.

For forty-three years a very large part of my life was shared with Baird Searles. We met in 1950, fell in love immediately, and never separated. Although we had vaguely known each other just enough to say hello (he was studying ballet at a local studio and was the dancing partner of the younger sister of my close friend Dick), our apocalyptic meeting was on the Fourth of July at a roof garden party given by Dick at his family's spacious home. It was a singularly romantic situation: the national holiday, the Florida moon shimmering over Lake Worth and across Palm Beach to the ocean, the display of *feu d'artifice* celebrating more than it could know. I had brought a girl to the party and after the fireworks ended, on the pretext of being tired, I drove her home and sped back to Dick's where Bay was awaiting me. Somehow, almost wordlessly, as I drove him home after the party ended we both knew that we were destined to be lovers. He was still in high school and I was between college years. Above and beyond the casual "hi" on such occasions as we had previously met (before that wonderful night)—in the local record store, at Dick's house, at the library—we each knew that there was something special in the way we looked at each other; there was a recognition, a more than incidental interest, and I knew that I was becoming infatuated with this fascinating boy. Perhaps in the sense of "it takes one to know one," neither of us questioned whether the other was gay. Bay had had no actual sexual experience, but he clearly knew what he wanted. I, on the other hand, had been sexually active, off and on, since the age of thirteen—but then, I did have a few years on him.

An ecstatic but difficult year in Florida followed. Ecstatic because we were so very much entranced with each other and were making grand and optimistic plans for our future together, and difficult because although we had a number of sympathetic friends there were some who were not so, including my mother, whose worst fears were confirmed when she (uncharacteristically) read a letter from a college friend of mine to whom I had written candidly about my relationship with Bay. In 1950 in a relatively small city in a very benighted culture an overt love affair between two boys of sixteen and twenty was, in the eyes of most, hardly thought of as a thing of beauty and a joy forever. Bay and I had decided right from the beginning that we would not shield ourselves from the world, or, for that matter, the world from us, and with a combination of ingenuousness and forthright bravado we took our places on life's stage. My mother was shattered and tried various ploys: a psychiatrist who found me quite healthy psychically; the county sheriff, with whom she was acquainted, who advised me that my acts were illegal; a Christian Science practitioner whose response was nebulous and uneducated. My always tranquil father seemed to take the fact of my homosexuality and my relationship in some sort of stride; he was much more concerned about my mother's reaction than he was about my circumstance, and rightly so, for she was traumatized by the revelation. My mother appealed to Bay's mother who, in turn, found herself able to accept the situation and embrace me. "So, now I have a second son," she said.

It soon enough became apparent to us that we would have to leave our hometown and head north. As a young gay couple we simply faced too much antagonism and scorn in the Florida of that time. And, too, we knew that to pursue our interests—his in dance and mine in music—we would have to plant ourselves in a more fertile field than south Florida. With precious little money between us (but with considerable buoyancy) we headed north to continue our studies, and our life together. Boston was our destination. We had met a couple of Harvard gays who were vacationing in Florida, and they were the only friends we had in the north. After two years of working and studying in Boston—Bay danced with several local companies and I had a scholarship summer at the Tanglewood music center, thanks largely to Aaron Copland—we moved to New York, where we initially held various subsistence jobs. Although Bay continued to dance with various New York groups and in summer stock, and I to struggle with music, it had become increasingly clear to both of us that we were not prepared to make the sacrifices which our once-cherished careers demanded.

We gradually moved upward. Bay worked in the library, became drama and literature director at WBAI radio (where he produced America's first openly gay program—and that was before Stonewall), then did publicity for MGM. I managed several bookstores, wrote for various magazines and finally (mirabile dictu) became an A and R manager for RCA Records.

In 1973, we decided that we were fatigued, discouraged, and ill-suited to corporate life and, with minimal capital and great trepidation, opened a bookstore which we operated for some fourteen years. When, after we were confident of the success of our venture, and could squeeze the time free, we traveled: the British Isles, Holland, France, Egypt, Mexico, Canada, the American West. These voyages contained innumerable adventures which we shared with amusement, dismay, enlightenment, and always love and care for each other. In Egypt, for instance, the boat on which we were traveling up the Nile became stuck for twenty-four hours on a sandbar. (The following summer it sank in the great river, never again to sail.) Once freed by, finally, the Egyptian Navy, we landed at the small village of El Wasti where a waiting bus took us to explore the ancient pyramid site of Meydum. On our return to town the bus was stoned by local thugs who had no use for "rich" tourists, and we had a bit of a time in getting from the bus to the boat unscathed. Our first trip to England was most special. We had met the steward of Kensington Palace, and after dining "below-stairs" there on pheasant shot by Prince Philip, and dancing with the staff through a wine-filled night, we were invited by one of the guests, a footman to the queen, to witness, a few days later, the presentation of the colors to the Welsh Guard in the great quad of Buckingham Palace. Our host slipped us into his room at the palace, from which we were able to watch this once-per-reign ceremony. Of course it rained and the queen covered herself with a huge black umbrella while her equerry carried her voluminous purse (what on earth does she carry in it?). The peerage are the only guests invited to view this event; the ordinary Englishman is excluded from such rarefied pageantry. On a later visit to Ireland we traveled for a gloriously rustic, low-speed week around County Cork via horse-pulled gypsy van. All of our trips were oriented to our many mutual interests, particularly those of history (Bay was strong in Egyptian dynastic and Celtic history; I had acquired a good deal of fascination for pre-Columbian cultures), music, dance, and the plastic arts, and almost all things French. After our first trip to France in the mid-1980s we kept going back there and never got to other parts of the world again.

July 4, 1975 was our twenty-fifth anniversary, and we decided to have something of a bash, a reasonably sober, reasonably drug-free and civilized bash, but a bash nonetheless. A block away from our West Village apartment was a small, intimate restaurant that we frequented and whose owners, a gay couple, had become at least culinary friends. We decided to take this charming eatery over for the night and invited a number of friends for an evening of celebration and revelry. For the chef and his waiter/lover, preparing full dinners for some twenty-five people was daunting. Then waiter Josh had an inspiration: he acquired a Sabrett hotdog stand, complete with wheels and an umbrella, somehow got it into the tiny space of the restaurant and furnished it with steamed franks, cooked-to-order hamburgers, fries, and all of the trimmings one could want for scrumptious repletion *à l'américaine*. The help-yourself bar thrived. The food and drink were campy and fun, but the joy was found in the presence of our friends. Gay couples (male and female), a brace of straight couples, and gay and straight singletons joined Bay and me in rejoicing. We finally left the restaurant and in the quiet dimness of late-evening Perry Street we fired illegal stick-rockets into the night, nostalgically recalling the fireworks on the night of our fall into love in 1950.

Throughout our union, there were periods of very rough going as well as halcyon times of loving relationship. Outside intrigues were, for both of us, a periodic source of pain, anger, depression, and tension. That we each had such external affairs, a few of which on my part were dangerous in that they came perilously close to separating us, was undoubtedly inevitable. That we, somehow, survived them often seemed, in retrospect, miraculous. There was milk and honey, but there was also nettles and bile. As we matured, and sometimes it seemed that we never would, we grew ever closer and external liaisons became less and less desirable.

We both continued to write (pragmatism prevailed; he had given up dancing and I composing) and although I had poetry, magazine articles, and critical pieces published, it was Baird who achieved commercial and artistic success with several significant books on film. Meanwhile our bookstore business had grown into a strong one with an international trade. Yet after fourteen years of operating our enterprise we were tired and ready to sell it and leave once and for all what we felt to be an increasingly unlivable New York. We did that in 1990, opting for Montreal, a very special, friendly, civilized, and polyglot city we had often visited and had come to love.

I don't have a clue as to just when it came to me that inevitably one of us would die before the other, although a wide acquaintance-ship over many years surely provided plentiful examples. I was not, however, obsessed with this vision; it merely appeared in my con-sciousness from time to time and for no prompting reason I could ever discover. I don't know whether Bay had experienced this reve-lation or not; I don't remember that we ever spoke of it. Occasional-ly, but without specific occasion, the image crossed my mind. Could I survive without him? Could he without me? I worried considerably more about the second question; I could fuzzily ex-trapolate the answer to the first.

In the fall of 1992 Bay, for the first time in his life, became seriously ill. Major surgery was indicated and he underwent it with enormous courage and strength. He knew that he had cancer but he kept that knowledge from me, as did his doctors at his insistence; I was told that there was no malignancy. In early 1993 he required further surgery. By that time I could not but be suspicious, yet Bay, even under the mind-bending palliative drug doses he was receiv-ing, was determined to protect me from knowledge of his terminal condition, and it was he who reassured me. Only when one of his doctors inadvertently mentioned cancer to me in the course of a conversation about his condition did we confront the inevitable together. Bay died in his sleep in March 1993.

The recollection of the occasion of his last trip home from the hospital still remains vividly with me. He wanted to stop on the way to look at a jacket he had seen in a shop not far from our apartment. He was so feeble that I was loathe to let him, but hadn't the heart to refuse him. We left the taxi and he headed for the store. I needed a few grocery items and hurried across the street for them. I was quick and returned to meet him at the men's shop. He wasn't there. I waited uneasily for him on the sidewalk, and just as I was feeling the beginning of real anxiety I saw him coming along toward me. He said that he had gone around the corner to check out another store, but failed to find the jacket at either. The following day was that of St. Valentine. I laid out things for breakfast and took our dog, Miel, out for her morning promenade. When I returned it was to find a compact disc on my breakfast plate—a valentine from Bay. The jacket was a ruse. He had gone to the nearby record shop and, with the recommendation of a friend who shared musical interests with me and usually knew what I was questing for, purchased chamber music by the marvelous and nearly unknown Italian Giuseppe Martucci. He did this loving thing while dreadfully debilitated by his cancer, often so weak that I had to help him walk. It was the last thing he was able to do on his own, and that courage and persistence was a major part of the mental strength he maintained until his death.

Bereavement is a state of many parts: some are obvious and immediately evident and active, while others remain concealed, or only partly revealed. After all, *no one* knows us. It is those late-coming realizations of kinds of loss that have the potential to overwhelm; they have a sneaky way of insinuating themselves into the consciousness just when one is beginning to recover.

Sharing was a very large part of our union. In many areas Bay and I had different—if not differing—tastes. And we certainly had some divergent interests, and diverse ways of looking at things, and of seeing things, too. This does not, of course, preclude sharing, it enriches it, and as time passed our repertory of shared books, movies, music, travel, friendships, trivial and serious communication, inside (and outside) jokes, the solemn and the silly, grew. And often from many differences we learned from each other, and perhaps grew a bit as well.

There is, certainly, sharing with friends; friendship, too, is strongly based on sharing. But it isn't remotely the same as sharing with one's lover. Some immediacy is important in sharing, as is considerable proximity and continuity. Unless you live high on the electronic highway and spend your time on the phone, at the fax, or move in with your friends, immediacy, proximity, and continuity are all lacking. Lacking, too, is intimacy of the kind that can only be shared by lovers.

The ongoing problem in dealing with the loss of sharing is that each new day inevitably presents at least one (usually many another) thing that wants sharing. It is a subtle and slippery thing, neither anticipated nor avoidable. Very suddenly it is there, manifest in the half-formed sentence I am about to articulate to Bay, the thing I want to share with him. Again I am caught off guard, and yet I would rather not be on guard. For me now many things I experience are incomplete precisely because I am not *sharing them in their time and place*, nor am I now able to share them with Bay who was so large a part of my life. Not all experience is shared, of course; not all can be, and not all should be. Each of us is, finally, alone, eremitic, private, and at least partly impervious. Perhaps the recognition of that reality is what we use sharing as a defense against. It seems likely that the loss of sharing—or its absence in those who never were so fortunate as to share—may lead to an excessive overconfrontation with the lonely, private, and mostly impenetrable self. Perhaps what I miss most is that I have no way to relieve myself of myself, nowhere to share in that particular way which growing together over a long period can provide. There seems nothing to replace it with.

ARRIVING AT SOME END

The trouble is that now
time is wrapping around itself
like some mocking helix,
with only banal events to
mark its eccentric movement.

I sing internally, orchestrating
the ambiguous music in my head
with some solemn instinct.
Subtlety is not in question now, and
only irreversible, incalculable
reality demarcates day and night and
the buried pain I cannot
locate or bring illumination to.

There are some closed rooms within,
their doors locked, their keys lost:
it is perhaps best so, for they
are the deep resources that hold
my mortal architecture together.

Knowing where I am now does not
tell me where I may soon be
now that decades of love and
oneness are continually compressed
into each succeeding moment.

In my heart be it.

All of his books, journals, films,
mementos, this and that, surround
my animus, along with mine. So much
incunabula, the concordance of a
life fully lived, too soon over.
Yes, too soon over as the music
plays on, remote, indifferent and
disinterested in this commonplace
parade of life and not-life.

There is some amorphous question
which can never articulate itself
as it drifts throughout my space.
I try to catch it, for I believe that
I may have its answer, but grasp or
grab, sneak up on it as it lurks
around and it slips out of reach.

Where is it now? In some dim corner or
surrounding the brilliance of a bulb;
spreading across the floor or
running down the walls?
Perhaps it is time that is the question,
wrapping around itself like a
helix. Mocking. Mocking.

I recently watched the Joffrey Ballet's *Billboards* on PBS. It is a provocative, fascinating, engaging and innovative dance work. Although I much enjoyed seeing it, and felt a touch of that nearly forgotten frisson of excitement I used to feel when seeing something new and good, I was naggingly conscious of the fact that I was watching alone. When the telecast was over I felt very solitary, unable to share. The experience, like so many others, was incomplete, unsatisfying.

As I have—sometimes slowly, sometimes agonizingly, sometimes simply—overcome and come to terms with some of the aspects of my loss, I have come late to realize that there are surely other aspects now coming to the fore, and for which there is, perhaps, no amelioration. They must be lived with. Of these I find myself most vulnerable to the loss of sharing.

Sharing is a large part of the network called communication that must develop between two people if the relationship is to work. Communication has and takes many forms: body language; eye language; sensitivity; respect; cooperation; trust. Some areas of this communication network are nameless, and though they surely exist they do so in another dimension; they cannot be articulated and they remain enigmatic.

Much of the foregoing may seem to suggest that the loss of Bay has left me almost completely empty, vacuous, apathetic. Certainly I have lost much that I must accept as irreplaceable; many aspects of my future life can never again be as they once were. The passage of time solaces some of these wounds; a great deal of effort in self-examination, with some outside help and therapy, ameliorates as well. Coupled with this endeavor is that of fashioning a new life and recognizing that I must live for myself now, without allowing the past to overwhelm me. And I always know that my continued well-being is what he wanted. For the rest of my sentient life, I will miss him. He is gone from me in the three tangible dimensions, but for those beyond—the impalpable dimensions—he remains forever a part of me.

During Bay's illness and beyond his death I wrote fifteen poems intimately revealing my feelings and thoughts. There was some catharsis in this act, and those poems, collected into a small folio called *Arrival, Departure and Arrival*, unquestionably helped me through the crisis. The last two, which follow, I could not share with Bay. I could only share them with our friends and associates.

FINAL ACTS

Turning, spinning, searching
for respite and rationality,
seeking the rest that knits up
that eminent ravel'd sleeve
of care, bisected between those
practicalities which must be dealt
with and those irresistible emotions
which like unavoidable torments
will no doubt rip the soul,
I rage for the narcosis of sleep
as so many consummations become
inevitable. Is escape the only answer,
oblivion the only solution?

How very abhorrent is self-pity,
the gritty fear of one's delicate
friability, the trepidation of
one's interior decrepitude.
That we find ourselves so
infirm in times of trial
is frightening; that we seek
the mock death of slumber
suggests our vulnerability
and lends a kind of angst to
the already quaking being.

His life stopped in sleep at 3 AM
on March 22.

When Eliot wrote of the "Hollow Men"
his view was cosmic.
Now there is an even greater vacuity.
My feelings are null and there is
only an overreaching vacancy, a
protective emptiness of perception,
some sort of defensive refusal to

admit that unacceptable sensation.
That will come later.
The last things I said to him were "à bientôt"
and "à demain": there is no
demain now. Only the void.

AND SO TO ENDURE

After days of dim, dank sky,
drizzle and shifting miasma,
the cumbersome cloudcover has
wandered away, like a discontented
cat, and left a turquoise
day, ripe with omens of spring.

Here is regeneration, finally, and a
celebratory sentience: the gulls
are back from winter's unknown habitat,
stertorous, startling the hushed
clarity of a sweetened, soft morning.
The anxious call of a crow, seeking
its like, sounds from some nearby
rooftop, seeming rootless in expectancy.

My love's body is ash now, but
he inhabits me and my domain
at every ordinary and special
event of the often shapeless day.
That I live with that with some
accepted contentment maintains
my animation and my reveries.

Carpe diem seems a diurnal
resurrection, renewing and enriching,
as the nocturnal cats, the incubi and
succubi of the dark, perform their
customary plaintive sacre du printemps,

and in that eternal, sensual ritual
there is a curiously calming comfort.
The persistence of some
perpetual poignance will
always abide in me; a mellifluous
melancholy will live in my mercurial
mind, but I will cherish these
slumberous sensations, cling to them
as they endlessly clarify the ambiguous
urgencies to continuance and
duration, maintaining the will to
continuity as he lives on in me.

Montreal, Quebec, Canada

Married—with Children

Fred Knoerzer and John Strong

When we first met, in 1982, at a party in Manhattan, we were both in other relationships: Fred was dating the party's host, Elliot, and among Elliot's other guests were John and his then-lover, Ray, who were living in New Jersey. In the ensuing months, the two of us encountered each other at least twice more—once on a theater date with Elliot and Ray, and again at a birthday party John threw for Ray.

On these occasions Fred found himself considerably attracted to John, so it was rather thrilling—and flattering—for him to receive a postcard from John while he was on a vacation with Ray in the summer of 1983. At this time Fred was in the middle of an affair with a man named Randall, but he acknowledged John's card with a letter. In it he admitted his attraction to John, assumed that because of the postcard the feeling was mutual, and suggested that if they should ever be unattached at the same time, they should get together.

This was to happen sooner than either of us expected. By early October Fred's affair with Randall was virtually dead, and John had broken up with Ray and moved to Manhattan. By an almost novelistic coincidence, on the very day after Fred had made his final break with Randall, John called Fred to invite both him and Randall to a housewarming party in his new Manhattan digs. Fred asked if he could come alone, because he and Randall were no longer a pair, and John said okay. Fred came to the party alone and wound up staying overnight. This began a four-month courtship and engagement that culminated in John's moving in with Fred on February 1, 1984. John was sixty-one, and Fred was fifty-three. The rest is history, as they say.

A happy history? Yes. Why? First, there are those things that drew us together initially. Of these the most obvious and basic was sexual and physical attraction, but that alone would not have been enough over the long haul. From the start there were two other basics: we each appreciated the other's intelligence and sense of humor.

Another common bond we had soon discovered is that we had each been married for about twenty-seven years in spite of our always knowing we were gay (and subsequently bisexual, of course). Fred had been divorced in 1979, his gayness a factor. John had also been divorced in 1979, his gayness was not a factor. We were also fathers, John of two sons, then ages twenty-five and twenty-three, and Fred of two sons, then twenty-seven and thirteen, and three daughters, then twenty-six, twenty-three, and seventeen. In the first year of our relationship, we met and were accepted by each other's children and ex-wives. The fact that we became members of, and participants in, each other's family has been a great source of joy to us. John's sons live in California, however, and Fred's children live in New York state, so that our progeny, alas, have yet to meet their "stepsiblings."

Our marital backgrounds had given us a lot of experience in longtime companionship and in its necessary give-and-take. It is the latter that we especially recognize as the key to our longevity as a couple, for we soon discovered important differences between us, and not just our age gap. For example, even our intellectual orientations are different, Fred's being more arts-centered (he was a high-school English teacher) and John's being more science-and-technology-centered (he had been an atomic physicist, documentary filmmaker-lecturer, and computer programmer). And almost as a corollary of this, our basic personalities differ as well. But instead of trying to make each other over, each has accepted the other as he is.

Thus even our day-to-day routines quickly fell into place with a minimum of conflict. It would be tedious to go through the minutiae of our household management, but there are some general features worth noting. First, because as fathers we're not each other's financial heirs, we have separate bank accounts and separate money; each keeps track of the outlays for mutual expenses that he's made, and at the end of every month the balance of payments is evened out. Second, there is no sharing of responsibilities. Each of us had acquired, by necessity or inclination, his own set of tasks, so there are never any arguments about whose turn it is to do what. For example, John, who likes to cook, buys the groceries and prepares our evening meals; Fred is happy to lessen that burden by buying all the milk, juice, and soda and by doing all the dishes. Third, we recognize our similarities and differences in the areas of travel, culture, and social life by acknowledging a right of first refusal. If, for example, Fred is interested in seeing a particular play, he'll ask John if he wants to go and will get one or two tickets accordingly. Neither of us has ever felt that all activities must be shared, and indeed we do as much separately as we do together. This is true of our friendships as well. We know virtually all of each other's friends, old and new, in the same way that we know each other's families, but not all are shared. On the other hand, we also have many friendships that we've made as a couple. So we socialize both singly and jointly. Fourth, as an outgrowth of this and, even more, because we do not feel that we own each other, from the very beginning it was understood that our sexual relationship would be an open one. We both exercise this option to see others, but only occasionally and irregularly, for we've realized that other men are "a nice place to visit, but we wouldn't want to live there."

After more than thirteen years, we've come to the conclusion that what has kept us thriving as a couple is not just sex or even love alone. It is also a good-humored tolerance of weaknesses and an affectionate respect of strengths, and apartness as well as togetherness. In political terms, we are two sovereign states united in the federation that is our enduring relationship.

New York City

Okinawa Honeymoon

Stan Isaacs with Bruce Brewster

Bruce and I have been together forty-seven years. July 7, 1997 marked that anniversary.

I cannot remember Bruce ever saying he had any guilty feelings about being attracted to his own sex. *I* never did. I remember a very exciting awakening to my feelings, and always thoroughly enjoyed the physical part. Of course, I'm not sure what my family would have thought of this; but my mother did know eventually and took it quite well.

Bruce and I met in Okinawa, after World War II. We had independently decided to give the service another try. I had previously served five years in the infantry. I was separated from the service in 1946 as a first lieutenant, complete with a combat infantryman's badge and a *cute* bronze star medal!

My dream at the time had two parts: I had always wanted a monogamous relationship—a lover for life; *and* I wanted a pet, because my love for animals is very strong. When we met, Bruce stated that he was not interested in long relationships. (After forty-seven years, I guess I can claim to have won *that* one!)

My duties on Okinawa were in Special Services, and since I was an amateur pianist, I traveled around the island playing and singing with native talent. Bruce was an operations sergeant in G-3 of the Ryukyus Command (Rycom), and in his spare time he instructed enlisted staff in basic infantry drill and manual of arms. We met at the Sergeants' Club, since I was a staff sergeant and Bruce was a sergeant first class. After a few drinks (and when I'd finished my turn at the piano) we went to his barracks, where enlisted men of higher rank had private rooms. It was there that we consummated our love—or, to be more exact, *my* love, because even though we had just met, I knew this was It. Bruce, as I've said, wanted no talk of major commitment.

Not too long after—if I may inject a bit of vulgarity—the shit hit the fan. We were again in the barracks where Bruce had his room and were a bit high from several drinks in the common room, and after conversation with other guys who lived in the barracks, we went to Bruce's room, stripped, and started making love.

There was a thud at the door, it burst open, and in stalked a young GI, rifle in hand, with other soldiers behind. The lead GI looked very troubled.

We were escorted to a jeep and driven to the island lock-up—in separate cells. The next morning we were driven to our respective companies. I remember my company commander was quite calm and even remarked something to the effect of: "Who's to say if this is improper conduct?"

But there we were, stuck in Okinawa for several months while the powers that be processed us for discharge. There was no contact between us for several days. Finally, I went back by bus to where Bruce was stationed. On our reunion, I can remember him saying only one word: "Well."

We had complete freedom on the island during these months—no guards, no reporting to anyone. So we had dinners at several Chinese restaurants and even frequented several sergeants' clubs. Although word of our being caught in the act must have swept the island like wildfire, we were not known by sight to any but a few GIs. So we would have a leisurely bottle of champagne, leave the club and, before heading for buses to take us to our separate companies, we would find a dark spot off a dark road and proceed to make love. After adjusting our uniforms, we would walk to the bus stop— sometimes laughing hysterically at our ludicrous situation.

Finally, the day arrived when we boarded our ship and sailed away from Okinawa. Though our futures were uncertain, to put it mildly, I can remember thinking, as the island faded into the distance above the ship's wake, "Wouldn't it be wonderful if all this were the *start* of a life together, rather than just the end of our military careers?"

We had a grand time on board. I entertained the troops—on the piano, I mean! As I've said, I already knew I had my dream man— and we helped one officer conduct bingo games on the upper deck, dining fabulously after the games, with the officers and their wives.

Surely many of our fellow passengers knew about us, and why we were heading for San Francisco; but no one on board seemed to care. One officer even lent us a small sum "to get us started." When we repaid it to his home address, he had to have known he had done just that—helped "to get us started" as a couple. At a time when homosexuality was generally looked down on, he had made an extraordinary gesture.

On docking in San Francisco, Bruce left to see his family (elsewhere in California), and when he returned to San Francisco we headed for New York together. Bruce had bid his family farewell, merely indicating he was through with the military and was off to launch a new career. I wrote my mother I would be living in New York City with a friend I had met in the service. Neither Bruce nor I confessed to the "shameful" circumstances. Our discharge from the service was not honorable, not dishonorable—just "undesirable," so I'll say now (as I said then)—fuck them—the military establishment, that is.

We arrived in New York, registered at a hotel, and I phoned a landlady I knew who managed two brownstones with rooms and small apartments. She told me she had a room with a double bed and a three-burner stove—but the bath was one floor below. I said I'd take it—at seven dollars a week. (This was 1950.)

Now I must confess to the first of two unpardonable things I did that jeopardized our relationship. I told Bruce I would go take a look at the room to see if it was livable, took my luggage without telling him the address of the brownstone—and flew! I spent that day in the room, in panic; late that night I wrote him a letter, telling him I had at first decided never to return. "Please forgive me," I wrote, giving him the address. I mailed it to the hotel--and waited.

Bruce showed up the following day (this was 1950, when next-day delivery of mail was taken for granted). We both shed some tears, and he went back to get his luggage and check out. I can't explain my behavior to this day. Perhaps it was the responsibility I felt for forcing a permanent relationship on him.

Bruce got a position at Manufacturers Hanover Bank, where he stayed for twenty-two years, advancing to officer position until we left for California. I, meanwhile, secured office work at *The New York Times*.

Though our beginners' salaries were not large, combined they made it possible to settle into comfortable domesticity. There was enough left (after rent and groceries) for an occasional evening out, and we developed a small circle of friends. The sexual aspect of our relationship continued to delight me, and I never heard any complaints from Bruce!

By 1955 we had moved to the borough of Queens—actually an area called Sunnyside. And we had acquired a most lovable black dog from the Humane Society that we named Binky (she lived to be almost seventeen). I had fulfilled my dreams: a picket fence around Mr. Right—plus a pet!

After five fairly uneventful years in Queens, I thought I would like to try making my living as a pianist-singer in small clubs. I resigned from the *Times*. I had to secure a union card from Local 802, the musicians' union. I couldn't read a note of music—I had always played by ear. The union required a year's residence in New York, so I qualified there, and could apply for a card. They placed a sheet of music in front of me, some popular tune; I faked it and got my card.

Several jobs came my way, playing and singing in various clubs—really just bars. This went on for several months, and one night Bruce came into one of the bars where I was working. He stayed a couple of hours, and when he left, I was jealous. What I really wanted to do was to go home with him to Queens, to our apartment and dog. The thought occurred to me that I really didn't want to continue this life: six nights a week away from home, one night off, on Mondays. I wanted to be with Bruce more than that.

But before I stopped this insane schedule, I accepted one last engagement at a gay bar at Eighty-Eighth Street and Broadway. Here was where I committed a second unpardonable act that nearly destroyed our relationship.

Into this gay bar, among the customers, came a sailor, who was billeted in an apartment a few blocks from the bar. (Military men who work in large cities are often given an allowance that enables them to get room and board in a civilian establishment.) Foolishly, I went home with him that night and spent three days. Bruce had no idea where I was. The sailor was good-looking; however, outside of love making, we had nothing in common. Excuse the abusive remarks: he was stupid; I was even more stupid. (Was this temporary insanity? No. That's too easy an excuse.) Why did I do it? I do not know!

Back to Queens I went. I arrived home in the afternoon, greeted Binky, took her for a walk, and waited. To say I was upset—tears, the whole bit—is putting it mildly. Then Bruce arrived home. "I'm leaving," he said. He and a friend of ours, novelist John Weldon, had even reported me missing. Oh, God, I must have been mentally deranged. I'm confessing. Neither Bruce nor I can remember anything that was said that day. Perhaps it's just as well. Our relationship survived. Never, never again did I do anything to destroy the life I had always longed for. Again, forty-seven years together—our relationship survived.

For the remainder of our time in New York, Bruce stayed on at the bank, progressing to a very responsible position, setting up one of the first bank-card systems, which quickly became universally popular. It might be said that everyone of us carries a bit of Bruce in his wallet. I worked for a series of publishing companies and advertising agencies doing a variety of jobs. I had always loved opera and was thrilled to have the Metropolitan available to me. Two or three times a week, during the season, I would join friends for supper after a long day's work, and then buy standing room at the back of the old house. This was not an enthusiasm shared by Bruce, and the old Met (before the transfer to Lincoln Center) had something of a reputation for hanky-panky among the gay standees. But after my affair with the sailor, I went there only for opera, and I always let Bruce know in advance, either before we left for work or, if a sudden impulse for art hit me, by phoning the bank from my office. Bruce had become the cook in our household and I didn't want him holding dinner—or calling Missing Persons!

Often, on weekends, we would entertain a circle of mutual friends, including several lesbian couples we had met. And once a week we stayed in Manhattan to dine together at a favorite French restaurant. These years were a happy, domestic time for us. Bruce enjoyed playing chef while I bustled about replenishing drinks and hors d'oeuvres (the latter of which Beggin' Binky helped diminish as each new platter was placed on the coffee table). Every New Year's Eve we gathered much the same group in our apartment—

feeling a bit guilty, frankly, as they then straggled off into the wee hours of a new year to make their separate ways home to Manhattan (not a quick-and-easy journey via subway on early-morning holiday schedule).

Ultimately, in 1972, we decided to move to California. Bruce had always been eager to settle down where he was born. He had earned a pension for his service to the bank. (Binky had to be put to sleep because of several illnesses brought on by her advanced age.) Our French restaurant threw us a farewell dinner party.

Leaving New York City, where we'd had so many good years, was made easier for me by the fact that several of my career moves had petered out. A magazine I had long worked for was sold out from under its staff (to Midwest Mafia, which promptly killed it—maybe for a tax write-off?). . . . The international agency where I found my next job quickly promoted me to a communications post (I enjoyed conducting all the global teletype conversations), then refused to hold my job while I was hospitalized for a couple of weeks. There I was, left without *any* retirement benefits from a spotty career, and wed to a man who had worked steadily up the ladder at a single company and had retired with major benefits. I saw my bargaining chips were few and quickly warmed to the prospect of a fresh adventure.

We jumped on a plane and beat our moving van to the small California town where Bruce had been born. It was a bit of a culture shock for me, but I soon adjusted, relying more and more on the opera albums I had brought west (plus the Texaco broadcasts) to keep alive memories of the many Met performances I had stood through.

*   *   *

Here, in California, Bruce worked for a liquor store, and I secured a state government job with the Department of Motor Vehicles. Finally, after twelve years, I was eligible for a pension, Bruce stopped work, and we both retired.

Now, we enjoy the benefits of Medicare, our pensions, very good health insurance (from the bank for Bruce, from the State of California for me), and we have a great HUD apartment in Santa Cruz.

Our apartment was built as if it were a condo, atop the trees, so to speak, with beautiful redwoods outside our living room window.

We share the apartment with two wonderful, lovable indoor cats named Mimi and Trudy. Trudy was adopted from a veterinarian, but Mimi just arrived at the back door, determined to find a home. She was three months old at the time and has been with us ever since—she's sixteen years old now. So, there are three matriarchs living here: I'm seventy-six and Bruce is eighty.

I'm so glad we found each other forty-seven years ago. Not everything has been smooth all the time, of course, but on the whole it's been wonderful. And with the inevitable diminishment of age, how comforting to know that one's life partner is there in a health emergency, to see that one gets the medical attention one needs! I feel very lucky that my dream on long-ago Okinawa has been so fully realized. I wouldn't change a thing. And I'm glad, *glad* to be gay. I would like all the right-wing fundamentalists to know that!

Santa Cruz, California

Across Boundaries

Tracy C. Perreault with Grover L. Harrell

This is a story about how two gay men of very different backgrounds and with no experience in the gay world have managed to love each other and have a monogamous relationship for seventeen years. Grover Lawance Harrell is an African American from the South, tall and muscular and dark; and I (Tracy Charles Perreault), am a white of French-Canadian and English extraction from the North, olive-skinned and with a small swimmer's frame. The two of us met when we were twenty-one years old. It was our good fortune that we were able to come together first as friends.

The bars and the gay scene were not ever in the picture for either of us, mostly because no one we knew was gay and we both tried to act straight.

GROWING UP APART

Grover's background centers on his extended family and community. He grew up in Columbia, South Carolina. For twelve years he lived in a small rural subdivision called Piney Grove. Grover never knew his father, but his mom, Rhudine, remained devoted to her children and lived in the Piney Grove community until her untimely death on February 11, 1991. At first, Great-Grandma Josie, in her old farmhouse, looked after Grover, along with his older sister Vanessa, younger sister Rosalin, and younger brother Odell. But when Grandma Josie became too frail to care for the kids, Grover moved less than a quarter-mile down the road to his Great-Aunt Velva's; the other kids lived nearby with Rhudine and *her* mother, Catherine.

Grover had a well-disciplined life, between Aunt Velva and Mom and Grandma; he learned to behave or face punishment. The thought of being gay—let alone show a sign of it—would never occur to him until he met me in 1980. He had only a very brief encounter with a female in high school and one other time—after we met and moved in together.

My hometown had been Schenectady, New York—until the summer of 1980, when my dad, with his Marine Corps background, accepted a promotion and transfer to Columbia, South Carolina; so my mom and my younger brother and sister and I became transplanted Yankees (and I became known by some as Snow-Bunny).

Prior to moving south, I was due to graduate from high school in 1979, but because of lack of application on my part, I dropped out late in my senior year. This was a low point for me and my family. I'd had a regimented upbringing, and my dad, especially, saw my dropping out as a real failure. It would take four years and a move to my new home to make me realize that getting a high school diploma was a goal I needed to accomplish. I set out to get a GED in South Carolina in the fall of 1984.

GETTING TOGETHER

Back in September 1980, Grover and I had met working at a local furniture store; we were assigned to do daily deliveries. Normally, Grover did most of the driving because the area was unknown to me and map reading would help me become more knowledgeable about local and out-of-town geography. (My sense of direction *has* improved over time.) Although our working relationship ended in 1981, we remained the best of friends, but never did we give each other a clue to how we felt about one another.

About a year after we met, we took on an adventurous challenge, one that helped shape our relationship. On the day we were let go from our jobs, we agreed to move in together, sharing a two-bedroom apartment in the St. Andrews area of Columbia. So, in the early fall of 1981, Grover set out to try to live with what he thought was a very straight-looking and straight-acting white guy.

The first months were a shaky time because Grover wasn't getting other job offers. He proved to me during this early period that he was a man of determination and showed great character in spite of storm clouds over us.

Restaurant work—a career that I have followed to this day—was my work of choice during the years 1981 to 1985. I was employed at a downtown private club—a place which was full of that old money of the South. This was a real opportunity; I advanced from banquet waiter to assistant bartender and developed good rapport with co-workers, managers, chefs, and club members. Working at the club also put me in contact with other gay men—for the most part, the wait staff.

The schedules we kept were mostly opposite. Grover, who had finally received a call to return to the furniture store, did deliveries and managed inventory and delivery personnel from 9:30 to 5:30. As for me, anyone who has been in food service can tell you that working odd hours and weekends is part of the job. Monday to Friday, I worked an 11:00 to 3:00 shift and then from 5:00 until closing—often in the wee hours. Sometimes, after closing a few of the wait staff would go over to a local gay dance club, and I would go along. That was before Grover put the move on me. And I still didn't think I might be gay.

A WALK ON THE WILD SIDE

We became more sexually interested in each other as time passed, but we didn't do anything about it. One evening in late November Grover and I would get to know each other in a very intimate way. The first move was made when I gave Grover a shoulder-and-neck rubdown. That led to our staying up all night and making love in a way neither of us had experienced before. This new attraction to each other was our first challenge—to see if we both were gay or if this was a passing fling.

As our intimacy developed, Grover wanted me to come home after the job, but I had other ideas—for a little bit. Then I got a short but sharp lesson when I stayed out one evening after work to go to the gay bar. After a few drinks, I arrived home late and Grover was less than happy with my conduct. I was confronted with another challenge in our first fight; Grover told me that he was the only man that was going to have me. Once we had this out, I felt a stronger bond to him. I wanted to build on the fact that he showed such concern for me.

Because of our schedules, sometimes we would communicate by writing notes to each other and placing them on the refrigerator. In the early part of our relationship Grover was always on the lookout for my mood swings. I was at times unsure of myself, and in notes and in person Grover always tried to show his confidence in me and to build my own self-confidence. He helped give me an outlook on life that no one had ever instilled in me. "Tracy, you are a fine person and you have nothing to fear." It would take this reinforcement to put my mind at rest and convince me that I should not be self-conscious about my looks and should be proud of myself. The confidence he gave me added support when I eventually came out to my folks years later.

THE CAREER-PATH YEARS

During the period 1981 to 1985 Grover and I remained inseparable, but in the early spring of 1985, I decided to attend Johnson and Wales University in Charleston, South Carolina, to get an Associate of Science Degree in the Culinary Arts. I would start my freshman year in the fall. This change meant that Grover and I would no longer be living under one roof. Grover now set his sights on moving into a two-bedroom house in another part of town. What I failed to realize at the time was that this was not an ending but a new beginning for the two of us. I helped Grover get settled into the new place. Then it was my turn to get established in a new environment.

My dorm was a two-bedroom apartment that I shared with three other guys. It was a lot for me to get accustomed to, living with three men from very diverse backgrounds. I tried to take it all in stride. This was college, and my main focus was to get through the next two years and finish my degree.

Grover and I could now see each other only on weekends. Depending on my class schedule, we would hook up on Friday and spend Saturday and Sunday together. While I studied and did homework, Grover worked on projects around the house. This left me the time needed to complete the material for each lab assignment. In my two years at J&W U, we missed seeing each other only during a brief three months while I was in Providence, Rhode Island. As a requirement of the course schedule, everyone in the second year had to work and learn at the J&W facilities in Rhode Island and Massachusetts. The scheduled time for me was late February through early

May 1987. After that, I would graduate with honors. When I reflect back, I realize we really relied on the cards and letters to help pull us together during our weeks apart.

Grover flew up (his first plane trip) to be with me at the end of the semester in Rhode Island. We drove home together, and our reunion was delightful for both of us, because each was focused on the other. And we never once lost our way.

THE MOVES

Grover's Aunt Velva had passed away a few months earlier and he became executor of her estate. After working on the homestead (prior to my graduation), Grover moved in—and he has occupied this residence ever since.

Having graduated, I began to look for the right job, location unknown. I was fortunate to find a position at a brand-new retirement community in Charleston. This job would help advance my career and give me motivation like never before. Doing extensive marketing in and outside of the "Holy City" (Charleston's nickname), drawing on my degree in culinary arts, and learning how to manage an operation—all this would consume most of my time. Now Grover made the effort to visit and reunite us on the weekends. Grover helped me get settled in my two moves in Charleston.

After about eighteen months, a better position opened up in another new facility in Augusta, Georgia. Leaving Charleston was difficult. Altogether, with attending college and landing a job there, I had lived, worked, and played in Charleston for almost four years. Again, the move placed a new challenge before us, but the story does not end there. Over the next seven years, with Grover's help, I moved four times.

In my view, my career path has benefited us, because I feel that each time we are together we affirm our sharing. My jobs have given me a chance to see different areas of the country. Although we have lived at times 150 miles apart, we continue to make time together on the weekends. The temptation to seek out other gay men was not a concern, due in part to the small communities in which I lived. I had to try to fit into each setting. But my current status is that I'm a lot more open and relaxed about who I am.

One thing I've learned from our situation is that we need to have faith. Living within ourselves is barren and shallow, lacking in warmth and understanding. But when we can be outgoing and giving, the importance of others becomes doubly strong.

THE QUEEN CITY

Both my parents now know of my relationship with Grover. Because of my awareness of my dad's disappointment in me, we had grown apart. To celebrate his sixty-fifth birthday this past June, I proposed we attend a Promise Keepers conference in Knoxville. I just felt it was time he and I share a spiritual bond, after letting too many years pass us by. That's what the P.K. organization is all about—establishing or reinforcing male bonds that will help guys deal with personal problems.

Dad picked me up for the four-hour drive over to the Tennessee Bowl. Those drives over and back were nearly as valuable as the conference itself. Showing a lot of emotion is not something my folks shared with me, growing up. Sometimes I get a little oversensitive about it. But this time alone let Dad and me do some catching up.

The event itself was impressive. The stadium seats 60,000 and it was nearly full to the rim. A huge TV screen and good PA system let us all see and hear the dynamic speakers, who gave us a worldview of the need for human understanding. I would guess the interdenominational event was sponsored by Knoxville churches, so you might call it a revival—if so, the first I've ever attended. But it obviously meant a lot to men around us, from all walks of life. While there seemed to be other father-and-son pairs, there were many different bondings—such as between young husbands who were pals and pledging to be better heads-of-household.

Although one of the speakers made it obvious the P.K. organization is against homosexuality, I'm not an activist, and I can take what's good from their program and ignore what isn't. Anyway, this conference and those drives back and forth helped to promote a real reconciliation between me and Dad. I feel, at thirty-seven, it's about time.

My mom is less understanding about my relationship with Grover. She thinks that my growing up was very normal. And it was. "So why have you turned out gay?" she says. Yet when she needs to bend someone's ear, who do you think she calls? That's right—Number One Son. As for my sister and brother, I don't have any contact with them, unfortunately.

Grover has never come out to his relatives, but they know me, and his sister treats me like one of the family.

Despite our living apart, we do have mutual friends, including some gay ones in North Carolina, where I now reside. As a biracial gay couple, we truly have not encountered serious negative reactions. Our straight neighbors in Columbia accepted us. To me, people in the South are more cordial and gentlemanly than those in the North. Yes, some people have had a problem with our situation, but we try to deal with it in a positive Christian way. (I am Episcopalian and Grover belongs to the African Methodist Episcopal Church.)

This short overview of the lives of Grover Lawance Harrell and Tracy Charles Perreault shows that a little persistence can pay off. All a person needs is determination to make a situation or opportunity work out. The world may be deluged with problems, laws to live by, formulas, fear, conflicting faiths, and the everlasting struggle to survive in the face of others, but it is necessary to share laughter in happiness, to know God in a sunset, and to feel joy in a sunrise, all the more beautiful because of others. Victor Hugo wrote that the greatest happiness in life is in knowing that others love us for ourselves, or rather, they love us in spite of ourselves.

For now, I plan to remain with my current employer. I manage a large production kitchen that provides around 500 meals daily, and I reside in Charlotte, North Carolina, known as the Queen City. Grover continues to live and work in South Carolina. He has been with his employer, the Whit-Ash Furniture Store, for the past sixteen years. He is willing to move to live with me, so we are looking to buy a house in North Carolina, maybe within a year. Until things change we will make every effort to see one another on the weekends. Just to get us under one roof together would enable us to stand as a unit, partners for life. If this sounds like the goal we have set ourselves, it is.

Charlotte, North Carolina
and Columbia, South Carolina

Lives Long Entwined:
Comments (at Forty-Seven Years)
on a Committed Relationship

Alfred Lees and Ron Nelson

LIFE DOESN'T BEGIN AT FORTY
(BUT IT STARTS GETTING BETTER)

by Al

When I turned forty (in 1966), Ron and I had already been in a monogamous relationship for fifteen years. (Ron's roughly two and a half years younger than I—a gap that has, as we'll relate, proved significant at times.) I was pursuing what proved to be a successful career as an editor of do-it-yourself (hereinafter DIY) features on national magazines. Ron had an important post with a major publisher of college texts. Ron's racket was a good deal more gay-accepting than mine. My byline appeared on several articles each month directed specifically to U.S. males (most of them in middle America) who had basement workshops full of power tools. I would guess that the majority of my faithful readers would (had I announced I was gay) have run me through their radial arm saws or turned me on their lathes. By *not* shoving my sexual orientation in their faces, and by continuing to be the "regular Joe of DIY" I had long considered myself, I not only worked my way into an honorable early retirement, but graduated into the presidency of a national writers' association.

Note: Each of the sections is "bylined" Ron or Al, indicating authorship of the main text; any "marginal comment" is by the opposite member.

Not for a working minute did I feel the least apologetic about my personal life. Indeed, I've always felt that my long and stable rela-

> RON RESPONDS:
>
> I can echo that.

tionship with Ron is the single achievement in my life of which I'm most proud. In total contradiction to what ACT-UP et al. insists, my "coming out" publicly in the 1950s or 1960s would have accomplished absolutely nothing but the destruction of a fairly illustrious career.

I never considered myself "in a closet" of any kind. I never made up a "supportive little woman—conveniently infertile" when colleagues at lunch presented their baby pictures; I never countenanced gay-bashing jests in my presence. I simply evaluated my working environment, saw it to be totally straight, and adjusted to it. When books based on my DIY articles began to be published (there have been a half-dozen—all, happily, successful) I frankly acknowledged my debt to my project partner—indeed, openly dedicated two of them to Ron.

Each individual must, of course, make his or her own accommodation to the straight majority, but I've long felt annoyance with today's aggressive young bucks who haven't a clue about the realities of professional life in the 1960s and who make absurd claims (which often cost them little) of being Out and Proud. The simple fact is, chums, that one can be damn Proud without being in-your-face Out. In fact, even today (when things are infinitely more free and accepting), to insist on total endorsement of one's homosexual orientation—and even one's lifestyle *choices* (two very different things, by the way)—from people who've been raised to think sex exists only in the missionary position for the purpose of procreation, is not only futile but infantile.

Ron and I are living proof that a sensible and sensitive approach to social integration not only works, but keeps everyone happy—the very *last* thing today's scruffy activists wish to achieve, of course.

(I'll voice one reservation about Ron's social integration in our "Problems?" section.)

> What might that be? I can hardly wait.

I would never let an injustice based on sexual orientation go unchallenged. On the other hand, I hold that Queer Nation's insistence on total acceptance of leather fetishists, drag queens, and NAMBLA members is not only unrealistic but counterproductive. These "variations" have little to do with sexual orientation. They are clearly lifestyle choices, and middle America's alarm at their being presented as civil rights is quite understandable and often justified.

Gays can never hope to achieve Bruce Bawer's "A Place at the Table" if they insist on dragging the lunatic fringe along.

That said, dear reader: If you'd welcome a bit of insight as to how two products of a benighted past have managed productive careers and happy lives for forty-seven years of "wedded bliss," read on.

Going back to the sexual beginning, I don't ever recall sharing the standard gay-autobiographical complaint of feeling I was the only homosexual in the world and must suppress my unspeakable urges at all costs. I was raised in a fairly strict Presbyterian parsonage, and Lord knows there was scant opportunity for boyhood experimentation. But I think I realized fairly quickly that, though most of my pals were neighborhood girls, I dreamed of someday making a life with *Mr.* Right.

Though I never felt this made me unique or peculiar, I was not at all happy with my early sexual experiences, which I quickly saw were mere desperate venting of strong sexual urges and weren't likely to be of any long-range value. I despised promiscuous grop-

By *my* early teens, even by age nine, I was at some level pretty sure what my sexual orientation was. I realized that the sexual play boys indulge in clearly meant to me something different from what it meant to my playmates. But I had a long adolescent anguish about integrating that central aspect of my life with what I felt family and society expected of me. Still, the pressure to *perform* was so much less then. Young people today probably can't imagine the sociosexual situation a half-century ago. Most of my schoolmates—male and female, straight and gay (whoever *they* might be)— were virgin by the end of high school. And many still were at college graduation (unless they had been in the service). My own sexual experimentation had not been very satisfactory, and I couldn't find a comfortable niche in the sub-rosa gay society of Seattle in the early 1950s. But I was very uneasy about Al's proposal that we link our lives. There were *no* role models to follow, no societal guidelines, no support groups, no handbooks. We had to hack out our own path.

ings from the start. I recall flinging Gore Vidal's *The City and the Pillar* against the opposite wall when the protagonist rhapsodized about how "clean" he felt after anonymous one-night stands. This was so counter to my own experience I felt it was, at the very least, irresponsible reporting.

So I guess it was inevitable that I would be a slow starter. My initial coupling was with an Air Force officer with a yen for boyish cadets (in photos taken on my Arizona base, I look all of fifteen). It wasn't the worst possible indoctrination, but I was guilt-ridden—not because I was having sex with a man (anything else would have been grossly unnatural for me) but because I was acutely aware this was not a proper search for Mr. Right.

That was to evolve—slowly—during my college years after the service (and thanks to the GI Bill, made possible *by* the service). I had volunteered as an air cadet shortly after graduating from high school. I was bright enough to be scared to death of combat, but righteous enough to see the Axis as an Evil That Had to Be Conquered (any youngster today who questions the necessity of World War II should be treated with sheep dip or an escorted tour of the Holocaust Museum).

I certainly didn't enjoy my year in the Air Force, but it wasn't traumatic either (even that seduction by an officer left no permanent scars). And I'll always be grateful that the GI Bill allowed me to apply to Stanford—a university that would have otherwise been out of financial reach. Had I not enrolled there, how would I ever have met my Mr. Right?

In truth, I'm much more of a romantic fatalist than Ron. I insist that we were *destined* to meet and fall in love. He rates it as fortuitous circumstance. We can agree that our being classmates at Stanford certainly simplified matters.

> Though it took us four years to connect!

At any rate, from the vantage point of forty-seven years together, I can unequivocally state that, challenging as the early years were as we forged our lives together, the years since—and especially these years since forty, with the scramble to establish viable careers behind us—have gotten steadily richer.

One of the most significant (and felicitous) corrections in the history of human ceremony was the substitution of "cherish" in the vow for "love, honor, and *obey*." That final draconian pledge has nothing to do with marriage. But even though Ron and I have never had the opportunity to exchange formal vows, we do truly love, honor, and *cherish* one another. (I often turn that lovely word over in my mind as he sleeps in my arms.) And thus do the two of us celebrate belonging. For, from the start, that's what our nonformalized pledge to one another was all about: we belong together, and truly belong to one another.

It took us a while as a couple to recognize the full responsibility of that fact, and the infinite trust it must involve. But an "open marriage" is no marriage at all; at its best, it can only be a contract of convenience and, as such, may be a workable arrangement for some couples (gay or straight). But since it lacks the total commitment which must be the basis of any true marriage, it must be considered on less demanding (and far less rewarding) terms.

I'm not temperamentally disposed to formal vows. One can be a patriotic citizen without wrapping oneself in a flag, one can be a moral person without flaunting a religious label, and one can be a committed lover without undergoing an official ceremony. (It goes without saying, of course, that nontraditional couples should have the same rights and privileges—and obligations—as conventional couples.) But I am disposed to our belonging together, and on that point we can certainly agree.

THE STANFORD START

by Al

In the fall of 1946, freshly discharged and buttressed by the GI Bill (one of American society's most sensibly generous provisions), I presented myself in Palo Alto, California, scarcely able to believe my good fortune at having been accepted by Stanford University.

Stanford aspired to be the Ivy League college of the West, and thus had a reputation of being elitist. As a private school, its ratio of students to faculty was much lower than at state universities, and its tuition was already high (though it has since soared through the ceiling). Stanford had been a school for pampered rich kids, but the GI Bill was about to change all that. With the influx of all us ex-GIs, Stanford got its first taste of a broad-based, democratic student body. It also got its first freshman class with a major age spread: veterans in our twenties were tossed into dorms with kids fresh out of high school. Remarkably, this all worked out to the benefit of both.

The Stanford campus, nestled into the "dry-side" foothills of the Coastal Range that runs like a spine down the peninsula south of San Francisco, was unusually handsome. The school had been endowed by a millionaire couple in memory of their only child—a promising lad who died short of college age. Architecturally, it was California Mission style, with sandstone red-tile-roofed buildings wrapped around an Inner Quad centered on a magnificent mosaic-faced chapel. I spent my early days wandering the campus, mouth agape and a bit intimidated by the intellectual prowess of my younger, well-to-do classmates. Most of them had graduated (with honors) from urban high schools of a sophistication far beyond the small-town schools I had known. And thus, though I was older and had greater "experience of the world," I quickly saw that I was less well-read and socially adept than my young peers. I had grown accustomed to top grades and easy superiority in grade- and high school, but I now saw I would have to hustle to compete, here. The challenge was stimulating but stressful.

Though we shared a large freshman dorm on campus, and (as it turned out) even had mutual friends, Ron and I never met during our first Stanford year. We returned as sophomores to a harsher reality: campus housing was inadequate for the GI-swollen student body and those of us who weren't fraternity pledge types were relegated to a community of recycled army barracks in an adjacent town.

> **RON RESPONDS:**
>
> I was one of those fresh-out-of-high-school kids—was that after the summer I worked in the cemetery or the lumber yard? With breathtaking naiveté, or chutzpah, I had applied to only one college—Stanford. Luckily . . . the annual cost then—tuition, room and board, books, clothes, hamburgers, records, transportation—was under $2,000, a lot at that time.

> I came from a small, suburban school—top of the class—and the shock to me was not just the brightness of the other students but also the motivation and relative sophistication, largely because of the older vets. Despite some appalling grades during the first quarter, by the end of the year, I was holding my own.

By chance (as Ron would have it) or by destiny (as I prefer) Ron and I were assigned to adjacent cubicles (separated by shoulder-height partitions) in the same hall. Each cubicle held a pair of double bunks and desks for four. Ron and I established social contact at once and moved largely in a shared circle of friends (with mutual disdain for the rowdier element in the barracks that would stagger back from beer-busts to vomit in the lavatories).

Ron had reached Stanford directly from a suburban high school outside Tacoma, Washington, yet we had a surprising number of things in common. I was soon having him sit, shirtless, for a water-color portrait of bizarre aspect. We still come across it occasionally among keepsakes. The subject crouches over the top of his own skull, neatly sliced off and placed on a table before him, and threads searching fingers through its crop of red hair. Of Scandinavian descent, Ron had pale skin and that remarkably fiery thatch. He favored the campus costume of a pullover sweater and tight jeans—attire particularly fetching on his tall, broad-shouldered frame.

> Al was darkly and sensually attractive—Italian genes mixed with those from Britain—and had an intense, dramatic manner. I recall two predictive events. One Christmas break, with two other students, we drove north for the holidays. Al and I shared a motel room, when we had to stop because of snow. I recall the rush of inexplicable, intimate feeling I experienced. And one afternoon at the village, I came upon him sitting naked on his bed, fresh from the shower, and I thought, *that's a very interesting penis.* But I put these impressions in my memory bank.

Though close friends for our three remaining undergraduate years, we never roomed together. In fact, when we returned to Stanford Village (as the barracks community was called), it was to private rooms on opposite sides of that complex. And we had almost no classes together, my major being rooted in Stanford's Creative Writing Center while Ron pursued an academic career in the History Department.

Our student lives became more closely entwined when we returned as seniors to move back onto campus into a newly-built dorm called

> We had one rift, a "lovers' quarrel" (though we didn't know it); I have no idea what it was about, but it was defused, I think, by shared theater tickets, to Martha Graham!

Stern Hall. (Current Stanford students report it's now regarded as the pits, but it was then fresh and exciting, in welcome contrast to those distant barracks where we had spent two years of exile.) Ron and I (though sharing rooms with other friends) began to spend more time together, venturing to concerts in San Francisco or simply heading off for those late-night snacks so dear to stressed-out students. We even began to plan a mutual graduation present: after accumulating summer-job earnings, we would head off for a bicycle tour of Europe, come October.

> This mutual adventure was taken as perfectly natural by our friends.

In all this growing intimacy, however, there was nothing sexual. As the older, more experienced male, I sought release only in anonymous encounters—not difficult to tap into on a campus of horny youths under a good deal of academic tension. In fact, the four corners of the Inner Quad offered men's lavatories—small separate buildings housing stairways that descended into a sort of dank underground hell. Some regular visitors would have characterized these as heaven, I suppose, since on most evenings you could make contact with an equally desperate student in an adjacent booth—if not in

> I was in deep denial, or at least resistance, surviving on masturbatory fantasies. I had tended, starting when I was nine, to develop crushes on couples (heterosexual ones, of necessity; I didn't know any acknowledged male couples): family friends, neighbors, older students. I realized later, of course, I was only interested in the male of the pair. My last such crush focused on my junior-year roommate and his fiancee. He was a graduate student, seven or eight years older, vigorously athletic, notably well-endowed, and emphatically heterosexual. It made for a frustrating year.

this particular facility, in one of the other corners, visited in sequence.

Some of the lads (or off-campus adults with no connection to the school who also haunted these johns) would be desperate enough to perform on the premises, using the glory holes that paired at least two booths in each subterranean corner. But most of us would exchange notes beneath the partitions, glad if this night's stranger had a room or a car where emotionless intimacy could relieve sexual tension. Sex and *affection* (I dared not dream of love just yet) were still very separate things in my life.

And remained so until fateful circumstance intervened. The Dean of Men became abruptly exercised over Stanford's subterranean homosexuality, and a witch-hunt was launched—of which I only became aware when I was summoned to his office (in a recycled quonset hut tucked well behind the Quad).

Sucking on a perpetually unlit pipe, this worthy informed me that I had been charged (by a fellow miscreant under the lash) with behavior warranting expulsion. Since my contacts were nearly always anonymous, had been both infrequent and discreet, and since I was not part of any "queer" clique on campus (I doubt any such existed) this news came as a total shock. In a strictly Presbyterian sense, I may have felt this humiliation was "just desserts" for shameful indulgence. Still, I was stunned. I loved this school and greatly valued the diploma that was only a few months from my grasp. My parents valued it, too, and would find my abortive departure inexplicable.

In desperation, I confided the horror to my circle of friends, assuring them it was all a misunderstanding arising from research I had undertaken for a creative writing project —a story in which a major character was "queer." I despised this subterfuge, feeling I had doubly demeaned myself—first by associating myself with these sordid pursuits, then again by lying to my friends. But I was heartened by their loyal response. The circle closed protectively around me and filled the anteroom of the dean's office, demanding to testify in my defense. All these young men were, so far as I knew, straight; yet all—Ron prominent among them—were outraged by what they saw as an injustice.

> I remember the scene in the anteroom—we were all prepared to come to Al's defense—but I don't really remember what we thought or if we believed his cover story. It all seemed ludicrous and unfair. The dean was not well regarded, and anyhow, students are always at odds with a school administration.

Their mere presence in that anteroom—the sheer force of their numbers and their indignation—turned the tide. No "character witnesses" were called to testify. While they waited, I had a final session with the dean. I vividly recall that when he asked about the pierced partitions in those subterranean johns, I told him that one of their regular patrons had told me (in a research interview, doncha know) that the glory holes had been there so long all their users assumed they had the administration's blessing—that it was university policy, indeed, to relieve student sexual stress. The dean's cold fury at such a suggestion caused him to bite through the stem of his ubiquitous pipe. He was picking fragments from between his lips as he gestured me out. I recounted this incident to my waiting friends as I ushered them out with me.

Needless to say, workmen were summoned the following week to bolt sheet metal to both faces of all pierced partitions. And, soon after, the dean himself was summoned to a new project—as chancellor of the University of Chicago. I've often wondered if his first official act, there, was to inspect all the men's rooms for glory holes.

In the spring of 1950 we all donned robes for an outdoor ceremony. Ron's parents drove down from Puget Sound. Mine hopped over from the San Joaquin Valley (where my father had accepted a pastorate, having fallen in love with California through visits to Stanford during my four years there); one of my Minnesota sisters buzzed in, as well.

So the two sets of parents (both Ron and I were products of stable unions—raised in the faith of faithfulness, you might say) met for the first and only time. How would they have greeted one another had there been any presentiment that their only sons would soon be life mates?

> Need you ask? In the 1950s? They wouldn't have been able to conceive of the relationship, and if they had, they would have been unhinged.

But then, neither of *us* had any suspicion, at this point. I enjoyed Ron's company and liked discussing everything with him (well, nearly everything; we never spoke of sex). And I greatly looked forward to the Grand Tour we were planning for the fall.

Happily, those plans kept us in touch all summer, though I was perched high atop a peak on Washington's Olympic peninsula, as a fire lookout. *Un*happily, our plans were thwarted by the Korean War. Ron was vulnerable to the draft, so to maintain his education deferment he would have to enroll in

> I went to see him on the *one* day I got off from the frozen food plant where I was working. My parents drove me to the trailhead seven miles off the highway, then I hiked seven miles farther up (facing a fourteen-mile return trip). There must have been something drawing me to the top of that mountain peak.

graduate studies at the University of Washington.

So down I came from my mountain at summer's end, and off I went alone to cycle across Europe. And gradually it struck me: I was not simply missing good companionship—I was separated by the Atlantic and the U.S. continent from the man I loved! Once the revelation hit, it seemed both natural and inevitable.

But dared I hope Ron felt the same about me? I wrote him in some trepidation, explaining that only the separation had let me see my deep disappointment for what it was: frustrated love.

I continued to press my suit in letters from New York City, where I settled (temporarily at least) on returning from a great—if lonely—

> I was feeling very sorry for myself, indeed. But I finally admitted my homosexuality to myself, and on the night I had hoped to be sailing for Europe, I went to a hotel bar and got picked up, by an airline pilot. I still didn't think of Al as being "that way" and didn't think I knew anyone who was.

cycle tour of western Europe. By now I was certain I wanted to spend my life with this man. Memories of him in his campus uniform drove me wild with frustration; those jeans got tighter, those sweatered shoulders broadened in reverie.

But I got little succor from his written responses. He was "not sure what love was," doubted he was capable of it, felt unworthy of my devotion. He had taken up with a shallow, flippant homosexual fraternity at the U, and seemed resigned to a life of pointless promiscuity.

Each of his letters was like a fresh wound, but I persisted through that New York winter and spring, laboring at temp office jobs until

> For a number of reasons, this was a low point in my life. Some years ago, I happened to come across some letters I wrote to other friends at the time, and I was stunned by the deep despair they expressed. So my responses to Al were part of a pattern.
>
> It was a fraternity only in the sense that it was a male group, mostly students, centered on bar-hopping (not hard to do since there were so few bars).

the main thrust of my life was resolved. Finally I wrote that I had reapplied for my previous summer's job as a fire lookout and would soon be coming west to beard him in his own den.

He had moved back to his old room in his parents' home for the summer by the time I arrived to report for my job. The room had stacked bunks and I would murmur down to him in the depth of night, pleading for a chance, promising I would do anything to convince him we were meant to link our lives . . . that when he returned to the U in the fall I would find a job in Seattle so we could live together.

When properly motivated, I'm a persuader—and I well knew that my very life depended on being able to win him over.

Had his parents had any in-kling that the sole purpose of my visit was to woo their son, I doubt they would have been so hospita-ble, but at last Ron took pity and

> Al seems not to remember our being entwined on the stu-dio couch in the living room, when I confessed to him, "I love you; I know it now."

reached up a hand in the dark and we were at last joined. I felt I never wanted to release my grip on that hand; and the night before I was to report to my mountain we—at last!—kissed. And he assured me that as soon as he could take time from *his* summer job, he would hike the seven miles up the steep trail to spend several days with me at my lookout.

I *flew* to my mountain peak! I had never felt so relieved and re-warded. I could now see a life ahead that made sense—a life of promise and pride; a life of love. Our mountaintop honeymoon was sheer bliss—until he had to leave. But we had now plighted our troth and would soon be sharing a home.

> This time an old high school friend drove me to the trailhead; the two of us carried a couple of heavy backpacks of food for Al, but my friend's pack broke so I ended up tot-ing the whole mess. Late in the day, my friend left, and left us alone, as alone as we had ever been.

Living together! I could scarcely believe my good fortune, and willed the summer to pass quickly.

And at last I traced his steps down the trail and signed off my mountain, for good. And we were searching for our first home. And, wonder of wonders, found it in a cozy houseboat, docked just across from the U of W campus.

> The houseboat was a truly romantic way to start our lives together, a commitment we both took for granted would be for good. The boat rocked in the waves from passing lake traffic; it was remote, even though in the city; the quarters were intimate; there were stacked, narrow bunks, but except when friends or rel-atives came to stay, we only used the lower one.

We began making a life together—without (as Ron has already written here) the benefit of role models, without being certain anyone had ever managed to do this before. But—what bliss!—knowing from the start with absolute certainly that this was to be 'til death us do part.

CAREERS AND FINANCES

by Ron

When we started living together on the houseboat in Seattle, neither of us had a career or any finances. Because we didn't have any money and because we had committed ourselves to each other, we integrated our finances from the beginning. I got through another year of graduate school, working at the University Bookstore. Al got a job with an airline that flew to Alaska, working erratic and sometimes awful hours. We felt deprived of our trip together to Europe, so when I received the payoff of a small insurance policy—a grand $500—I thought it would be appropriate to use it to go to France to pursue my graduate studies at the Sorbonne. Somehow we had accumulated enough money to cross the continent, take an ocean liner to Italy, and then try to settle in Paris. With astonishing innocence, we thought we would be able to get work in Paris. This adventure was not a great success, academically or financially, though we did salvage a memorable trip to France, the Lowlands, and England.

We returned to New York, discouraged and financially depleted. We got through the holiday season

---

AL RESPONDS:

The one positive note in the Paris fiasco was the confirmation of our commitment to one another. We were innocents abroad and were badly taken by less-than-ethical Parisian agents. I remember our meeting on the Opéra steps after separate but equally futile errands to retrieve deposits we had trustingly left with agencies who had failed to provide promised services, and I thought, in disgust: "Lifemates should offer compensating strengths, but *we* seem to reinforce each other's weaknesses!" I think we both realized, however (if not on those Opéra steps, soon thereafter) that if our relationship survived this miscalculation of trying to live abroad, we could weather anything the future held.

with Christmas store jobs. In January 1952, I was invited to apply for a government job in Washington, DC, one that would make use of my years of studying Chinese and Chinese history. I bused down to Washington, had an interview, and was given a translation test. That must have gone well enough because they asked me to stay over for another interview the next day. I couldn't afford even the Y, so I sat up all night in the bus station, and presented myself unshaven and bleary in the morning for what turned out to be a security evaluation with lie-detector test. This was one of the iciest periods of the Cold War, the Eisenhower Administration was about to take office, and Senator McCarthy was in his heyday. Homosexuals and Reds were the demons of choice. Strapped into the lie-detector machinery, I was, of course, asked about my sex life. Even today, it is hard to comprehend my stupefying naiveté. I actually thought they were only worried about people who could be blackmailed. I figured that they would have nothing to worry about if I told them the truth. So I told them the truth. Oddly enough, I was not offered a position with the NSA.

Back in New York, Al justifiably insisted that it was his turn now. He had set his sights on a career in magazine publishing. He got a job with a bimonthly called *Home Craftsman*, thus launching a distinguished career in the do-it-yourself field. He stayed for several years—honing his skills in expository and instructional writing, expanding his knowledge of the field, developing contacts, and

> I stayed at this first job too long—seven years—trapped by a clever and appreciative publisher who timed unsought raises to my periodic resolves to move on. Then finally he made a foolish, greedy sale of the magazine to Midwest Mafia, who promptly killed it for a tax write-off.

also writing the first of his several books on do-it-yourself topics— until the magazine was sold. In the meantime, I worked, ironically, for a reactionary political propaganda outfit. After some abortive attempts to get a job in book publishing, I finally got a low-level job at Prentice Hall, in educational publishing, the only connection left with my years of college. At one point, I recall, Al was making $100 a week; this seemed an unimaginable goal for me (we're talking mid-1950s). We did manage to live comfortably in New York, taking as much advantage as we could of the cultural life, upgrading our apartment from time to time (a kind of classic pattern: Upper West Side brownstone, Village garden apartment, Upper East Side walk-up; later we moved to an elegant Mies van der Rohe apartment in New Jersey, and finally returned to a downtown co-op in Manhattan).

Al's career flourished; after a stint at *Family Handyman,* he got a welcome offer from *Popular Science.* This was a particularly satisfactory period for him—a congenial and admirable group of co-workers and his own growing prominence in the field. Changes in *PS* management coincided with a job offer from a competing publication, *Popular Mechanics,* so he switched over. Subsequently, the editor in chief he had not respected at *PS* moved over to *PM,* so Al jumped at an unexpected opportunity at *Woman's Day* to head up their shop, which created fancy projects for publications and built the sets for photo shoots: a different challenge and a lot more pay. This turned out, however, to be a weird experience, and his dealings with the emasculating Amazon editors were touchy. After less than a year, he was happy to accept an invitation to return to *Popular Science,* where he stayed until retirement. In time, he became the group editor in charge of all do-it-yourself material, and for a number of years was delighted with his job. The last part of his career was marred by a destructive and vindictive editor who was oddly determined to eliminate the section that Al edited. But by forging an alliance with the president of the magazine division, he was able to carry on until he stunned them by taking early retirement.

I was more or less developing a career, though unlike Al's, which was goal-oriented, mine just sort of happened. I worked in editorial

One way I knew I was in love with Ron was that I was willing to pool financial resources. I had been raised in genteel poverty—the third child on the salary of a small-town pastor—and had learned early to be careful with money. But once I had wooed and won the man I fully intended to share the rest of my life with, keeping strict separate accounts seemed pointless. (In fact, we snickered at other male couples we knew who would squabble in restaurants as they jotted down meal-item costs for later settle-ups: "But you had *two* drinks"; "Well, your entree was $1.50 more than mine.") But Ron's right: With our disposable incomes now cut in half, we've had to become less casual. I don't *like* our current accounting sessions, but I recognize their necessity.

development of textbooks, eventually heading up the department responsible for that function. In 1970 I moved to John Wiley, in Manhattan, in a similar position; along the way I also became editor of foreign language texts (no Chinese, though), until I took early retirement.

I finally caught up in salary with Al, and for a number of years, we had virtually identical incomes; one of us would advance, and then the other. This continued until the last few years of Al's working life, when the antipathy of his boss meant unfair, small, and spaced-out increases. We maintained separate checking accounts (except for one brief, disastrous attempt to manage a joint account to pay bills associated with our co-op). We each had our own retirement accounts, CDs, and investments (with the other as beneficiary), but we have had some joint saving accounts. We always tended to share household expenses rather loosely, though now that we're on fixed retirement incomes, we're rather more careful about the division of the costs.

Did our sexuality have any effect on our careers? We were lucky, I suppose, to be living in New York and to be in publishing. We certainly never had a problem in getting jobs because of our sexuality. In my case, there were no obstacles to advancement; any barriers were my own (for instance, I wouldn't leave New York and turned down lucrative offers in California). Book publishers on the whole are indifferent to employees' private lives; besides, there are lots of homosexuals in the industry. Al's magazine world was more conservative, but he didn't encounter any discrimination; talent and application were what counted. Neither of us was aggressively "out"—remember, we're people of

> The only wince-moments I ever had were during lunches with the *PM* execs. They had all just been transferred from Chicago when the magazine was bought by Hearst (which wanted it published in Manhattan, like their other magazines). These men and their families had been uprooted from suburban communities where whispers or sneers about urban "lifestyles" were common. They brought some of this to Manhattan, and I *hope* I helped them realize it was inappropriate here. (They all, of course, settled into suburbs as nearly identical to those they had left as possible, and never stayed after work to sample what Manhattan had to offer—any more than they had taken advantage of Chicago's riches.)

the 1940s and 1950s—but neither of us made any effort at conceal-ment. Because of the nature of book publishing, I could afford to be somewhat more open with colleagues than Al.

Paralleling our good luck in employment was our good luck in housing. We never encountered a problem, from our first rented fur-nished apartment (two attractive young men in their early twenties and one bed) to our purchased co-op (the co-op and Citibank were only interested in whether we had the money). New York gets a bad rap from many, but not from us.

CULTURAL PURSUITS IN TANDEM

by Al

Okay: opposites may attract, but how good are they for the long haul? Happily, I'll never have to find out, because Ron and I have remarkably compatible tastes in all the arts that are vitally important to us. And many *are*, which is why we live in New York City.

We've often wondered why anyone who isn't interested in the city's unmatched cultural riches would choose to live here. Other cities are more gracious, more architecturally distinguished, more functional, less stressful, less filthy. But perhaps no other city in the world (we've visited most of them) and *certainly* no other city in the United States offers New York's perpetual smorgasbord of the arts. That it reigns supreme in the vitality and variety of its perform-ing arts goes without saying. There's more theater (on Broadway, Off Broadway, and Off-off) than any smaller city could support; there's far more dance, a broader spectrum of music—symphony orchestras (resident and visiting), opera companies (ditto), chamber and jazz groups—than anywhere else. Any New Yorker has access to more top museums—and even a broader range of movies—than any other urban American.

And both Ron and I recognized early on that cultural input is our lifeblood. Art is, quite literally, our religion (and sometimes our politics). We began life together on that houseboat before Seattle became the swingin' Northwest Capital it is today, and quickly recognized the city as too limited, too provincial to sustain us.

So, Manhattan beckoned, and for years we've taken full advantage of its ever-renewed wealth. Our friends feel we're obsessive about it, and statistics tend to bear them out. In recent years, we've maintained subscriptions in five theater clubs, five concert series, four dance series, and two opera companies. In addition, we regularly sample the wares of a half-dozen summer festivals.

Just juggling all these performance dates keeps us on our toes—and to carve out enough uncommitted time to take a major trip calls for acute surgery (some subscriptions let you switch dates, some don't). And in addition to all

> **RON RESPONDS:**
>
> Not to mention memberships in two museums and, through retained employee benefits, free entry into several others.

these subscriptions we must work in individual performances of independent companies and schedule visits to special museum shows.

Just recently we finally remodeled one long wall of our lower-Manhattan loft, installing shelving with many cubicles to take our chronologically stacked theater programs. Alas, as a high-schooler I began to save programs from every professional performance I attended—every play, opera, concert, or dance group. My earliest program is a fragile yellowed sheet dated "ONE NIGHT ONLY: March 25 '43" (Boris Karloff in the road company of *Arsenic and Old Lace*). This is not a collecting obsession I can recommend—though if any question about a performance in the past fifty years arises, it need not be left to arguing—I can research my wall. Problem is, fifty years of consistent theater- and concert-going adds up to thousands of programs. The accumulation threatens to crowd one from one's home, yet the chore of packing and reshelving the collection discourages moving to larger digs. I sometimes envision Ron and myself inundated in toppled stacks of programs, like upscale Collier brothers.

All of this is background for my contention that our similarity in cultural tastes and energies has contributed to the stability of our partnership (oh, hell: let's call it what it obviously is—our marriage). We've known couples who shared few enthusiasms—where one partner hastened off several times a week to join pals at an opera performance while his mate was content to linger late at his office and then fix himself a solo dinner. We've even known pairs who rarely agree on which movie to catch, with the result that the one who "gives in" takes out his resentment on the film he had no interest in seeing. Such marriages of accommodation often survive nicely (I would guess several are represented in this book) but how infinitely more rewarding when partners in life are also full and enthusiastic partners in cultural pursuits!

For a decade, Ron and I published and distributed, each January, a comprehensive listing and evaluation of all major films we had seen the previous year. Several times we included critics we admired in the mailing. (Judith Crist responded by arguing for favorites of hers that we had dismissed.) Only rarely did Ron and I widely disagree, though at times our enthusiasms varied. On the whole, though, we were doing the "two thumbs up" routine long before Siskel and Ebert.

This unanimity of taste extends to other visual pursuits, as well. Ron and I shared a laugh of recognition at the beach scene in the film *Longtime Companion* where two older lovers, sprawled to survey the parade of flesh, are mutually disturbed as an exhibitionistic hunk passes. We often find we must take care not to swivel *our* heads in tandem at a passing Adonis. Observing natural beauty (landscape, flora, and especially fauna) is a cultural pursuit too, and the visual delight we take in men is remarkably parallel. I've often been glad our relationship is an exclusive one, else we would have been in frequent competition.

Though we've shared enthusiasms for favorite performers over the years, neither of us has ever been a "fan," fixating on an

> Well, once I did send flowers to a favorite dancer on the occasion of her retirement.

individual obsession or attempting to make personal contact—even as pathetic a one as seeking an autograph. In a life of active pursuit of the arts, I can recall only one personal encounter with an artist I admired: composer Ned Rorem once proposed to take me home from an all-male party in Greenwich Village in the late 1950s. Considering Rorem's self-confessed lifestyle at that time, I don't guess that gives me much distinction. (Anyway, I had brought Ron to the party and my leaving with someone else was hardly an option.)

We were both recruited by listener-sponsored radio stations in the 1960s to review the arts. Ron covered theater (mostly Off Broadway) while I reviewed current films. My greatest reward from this decade of effort was getting a line from my rave for *Easy Rider* quoted in newspaper ads. I've always felt one can best appreciate performance arts that one had tried oneself—and this includes criticism. I once hosted a radio show called *Before You Trust in Critics* in which I interviewed the leading theater and film critics of the day, probing their qualifications and motivations, and have never ceased to be wary of lax criticism. Along

> This was one time when our interests diverged. My tolerance for the experimental production and the fringe event and the out-of-the-way venue exceeded Al's, so I usually went alone. Recently rereading scripts of my reviews, I was amazed that some works remained so vividly in my mind and that others had left not a single neural trace.

similar lines, only someone who has experienced stage fright can truly evaluate an actor's skills. I had appeared in a dozen amateur and semiprofessional theatricals—starring in the high school plays but getting only minor roles at Stanford or in community theater. I did have a chance to work closely with professional actors in the latter two, however, and have never lost my admiration for quality performance. Anyone who thinks it's easy to hold a large audience simply hasn't tried it.

The cultural pursuit where Ron and I most diverge is reading. On those occasions when we *do* manage to read the same book, we enjoy comparing notes, but our tastes differ here. I'm likelier to read biographies of creative giants (especially of men with gay proclivities, such as Bernstein, Olivier, and George Cukor) and novels and essays by gay writers (Bruce Bawer, Randy Shilts, David Leavitt, Paul Monette;

> After college, I retained a very studious approach, using systematic lists of serious works, carefully balancing fiction (domestic and foreign) and nonfiction (science, history, and so on). I got over that long ago, but there's a residue, a tendency to tackle large, "important" works. The rest of *Remembrance of Things Past* sits on the shelf, admonishing me for my sloth. Maybe *next* winter.

I can't abide Edmund White, Andrew Holleran, or Armistead Maupin) and I'm likely to drive Ron to distraction by reading aloud favorite sections.

Neither of us is a culture snob. We're as likely to wax ecstatic over a musical as an opera, a good film as a Shakespeare play. I write this from the perspective of a season in which running concurrently were Sondheim's *Passion, Kiss of the Spider Woman,* and stunning revivals of those twin pinnacles of the Broadway musical, *Show Boat* and *Carousel.* It might be said that these are all serious works with something to say—in a theatrical form oft noted for its frivolity. I would even state that anyone who hasn't caught these productions is the poorer for not having experienced them. Ron and I enjoyed them all—together   even flying to

> Here's an area where we might be accused of snobbery. We can't bring ourselves any more to undergo Andrew Lloyd Webber or his imitators. We haven't seen *Phantom* or *Miss Saigon* or even—we'll probably be drummed out of the brotherhood—*Sunset Boulevard.* Shows famed for their sets and endlessly repeated whining themes do not appeal.

Toronto for an early view of *Show Boat.* (It should be admitted we mutually enjoy the more frivolous ones, too; we just don't work as hard—or invest as much—to see them. Our tastes, here, too, are matched: we found the revivals of *Guys and Dolls* and *She Loves Me* charming, but are bewildered by the interminable run of *Cats* and the popularity of *Beauty and the Beast.* The latter was delightful as a Disney cartoon feature—but why would anyone want to see it in "live performance"? It's like those bizarre skating shows that feature "Hamlet on Ice." Recycling art into inappropriate forms inevitably diminishes it.)

The special reward of sharing all these pursuits has never diminished for us, and even when I go solo (as I frequently did during business trips and still do when Ron travels) I'm taking mental notes toward sharing the experience with Ron when we're together again.

I recall an incident—several years ago, now—that brought the esthetics of sharing into focus. Ron and I split responsibilities for contributing to cultural institutions (he handles the Metropolitan Museum and New York Philharmonic; I support Carnegie Hall, Paul Taylor Dance, etc., etc.—you can tell we're pretty mainstream), so we receive quite a number of invitations to receptions, rehearsals, and members' previews. We were previewing one of those blockbuster shows at the Metropolitan—the kind that go on for gallery after gallery. (It was probably their mammoth show on Mexico—a country we've explored a number of times.)

The galleries were fairly crowded with "first nighters"—all contributors—enjoying one of the civilized privileges of having "made it" in New York City. Ron and I were moving with the flow and, pausing to read the placard posted near an historical artifact, questioned the chronology. Resolving the matter involved retracing steps to a prior gallery, and Ron volunteered to go back to check the earlier reference.

I stood studying the object in question, then glanced toward the connecting door as he returned. And was unexpectedly seized with a palpable sense of wonder and gratitude that this attractive man—his face lit with pleasure in the information he was eager to share—was coming to *me*. Out of that whole crowd of intelligent, sophisticated people this loveliest of men was singling *me* out to share his pleasure with. I've never (until this writing) told Ron of this moment, but have often recalled it, since, under similar circumstance.

The simple fact is, there is *no* cultural pursuit I enjoy (and that, as I've indicated, takes in a very broad range) that I don't enjoy *more* if it's shared with Ron. I love good films and will go alone if circumstance dictates, but I far prefer to go with Ron. The same holds for theater, concert, and dance performances. I applaud friends and family who seek out such pleasures alone (whether because they're single or are stuck with a spouse who doesn't share their enthusiasms) but I'm eternally grateful that Ron and I have much the same interest and taste in things of the spirit—for that is what the arts are to me. I find this essential for our relationship since, as I've said, art has pretty much become my religion. (Ron and I do *not* share religious beliefs. Raised by a Presbyterian minister, I accept the basic tenets of Protestantism, but if I were intense about it I can see it could produce friction between us. Were I heaven-obsessed or just dogma-obsessed, it would trouble me that Ron does not consider himself a Christian and is not comfortable in any church below the order of Monumental Cathedral—we both love exploring the world's great temples.)

But art, happily, remains the focus of our lives, and here we are attuned as well as entwined. As I said at the start, it may be true that opposites *attract*, but do they cozy up for the long haul?

This truly is a potential advantage of same-sex marriage. I'm sure we've all known devoted heterosexual couples who've become inseparable, sharing everything—including, eventually, physical characteristics! But gender differences inevitably make it less likely that a man and a woman will have identical (or even compatible) interests and aspirations. In a pairing of two men or two women, on the other hand, such fortuitous similarity in outlook and enthusiasm should be far more common. Or am I just prejudiced toward that view by my precious good fortune?

Of course, I have to keep reminding myself that the arts aren't of major concern for many Americans. When I was interviewing those critics, one told me (in his best off-the-record, off-mike eloquence) "There wouldn't *be* Manhattan theater if it weren't for the

> Just consider those pathetic congressmen who never met a gun they couldn't like but never met an artwork they could deal with. Art is life-enhancing, but it's also challenging. In that sense the religious right *should* feel threatened.

queers and the kikes." Certainly gays and Jews are a prominent *part* of the theater audience (and obviously both contributed to the success of Tony Kushner's *Angels in America*) but if they constitute theater's *chief* support, how can one explain the short runs of plays addressing their vital concerns, such as *Twilight of the Golds* and Arthur Miller's stunning *Broken Glass*?

Several of the theater clubs we support offer a Gay Singles Series, with performances linked to a "mixer." We've never signed on to these for several reasons: (1) We hardly qualify as singles! (2) This seems another example of gay ghettoization; are gays really such a separate class they can't even enjoy theater with straights? (3) We don't attend theater to socialize.

Early on, in New York, we *did* try to share our theatrical enthusiasms with friends, organizing evenings of dinner and the theater for a batch of gay male couples. Such evenings were enjoyable, but we came to realize that most of these friends were indulging us. They didn't participate out of any personal *need* for theater art—and not one of them ever reciprocated by initiating such a group outing.

So our cultural pursuits are now our private concern. As I've indicated, few of our friends can comprehend the energies and cash we invest in these pursuits. As I grow older, I've had to learn that art means little to most Americans—straight *or* gay; they happily live without it, perhaps venturing to the theater or a concert for annual special occasions. And in the rare instance they even go out to a movie, they search out the most mindless trash available (how else to explain that at this writing the top-grossing film in the United States is *Dumb and Dumber*?).

I seem never able to communicate to such folks that I am every bit as astonished at their *lack* of interest as they are at our "excessive" devotion. And I've given up attempting to proselytize.

But can you wonder that I say a daily prayer of thanks to Apollo for having mated me with a fellow disciple?

HOW MANY CORNERS ON A GLOBE?

by Ron

Another shared enthusiasm, if not obsession, has been travel. This interest was a natural development. After all, our first romantic adventure was to be the post-graduation bicycle trip in Europe. As circumstances developed, Al went on the trip and I went to graduate school. But he sent me frequent, almost daily, cards and letters, recounting in charming detail what "we" had done that day. In one of those letters, a birthday greeting, he first raised the possibility of a sexual element in our friendship.

Al had spent his childhood and adolescence traveling around the United States with his family. I had the fantasy if not the fact of travel: the attic playroom was filled with *National Geographic* magazines, wall maps, and a cherished large aerial photo of New York City— obviously a portent. At ten, I was given the treat of a trip to San

> **AL RESPONDS:**
>
> When a longtime friend (who has a collection of our postcards from every corner of the globe) learned we had been asked to provide an essay for this book, he wrote the editor to say: "Be sure they include their world travels— this must be the most peripatetic gay couple in America." While I doubt we qualify as *that*, since I'm sure other mates devote more of their total time to travel, we *have* been at it for forty-seven years and have reached the point where it's easier, when people ask us to list the places we've visited, to tell them where we *haven't* been: Argentina and Chile, for starters; Russia (soon to be remedied) and Eastern Europe (except for Yugoslavia—happily before its peoples became determined to destroy it); sub-Saharan western Africa, Israel, and (to Ron's impatience) Japan. We do not lack for future goals.

Francisco (another portent?), accompanied by my grandmother. (A lively lady, she stunned the family by taking me to see the Folies Bergères and Sally Rand.) That trip hooked me on travel and cities.

After our houseboat honeymoon, Al and I decided to take that joint trip to Europe. Al, being somewhat more practical, was probably indulging me, but, as mentioned earlier, I intended to continue my graduate studies at the Sorbonne. We went from Seattle to New York, via San Francisco and Los Angeles, where Al's parents lived; we answered a newspaper ad to share expenses on a cross-country drive, paused to visit his sisters in Minnesota, and finally got to New York

> We had made the youthful mistake of trying to *live* abroad. We've since come to love Paris —and to confirm that Paris is for lovers. Last time we were there was to help them celebrate their bicentennial. Having just retired, I was able to tag along as Ron covered a business convention. Suffused with (happy) guilt, I spent my days exploring the museums while Ron manned a booth. Obviously at least one more trip together is required.

to take passage on the *Conte Biancamano* to Italy. Many aspects of the trip were memorable and delightful, but the Paris experience was defeating. So by Christmas, we found ourselves back in New York.

We were still determined to travel. Our limited vacation times had to be apportioned; we each had family obligations. But we tried, insofar as possible, to balance domestic and foreign travel, as finances would permit.

We are, I think, remarkably congenial as traveling companions. We've certainly agreed on destinations. For the vast majority of our trips, we've traveled simply as a duo. We worked out our own itineraries. In the early 1980s, out of necessity, we took a group tour to China—fortunately, a generally affable small group. Subsequently, we lucked out, in India and Egypt, on "tour groups" that consisted of the two of us, combining the logistical advantages of an organized tour and the freedom of independent travel. In going to several Olympics, because of the way tickets are sold, we've had to buy packages. We've also taken a couple of well-managed tours, to Bali and China, sponsored by the Stanford Alumni Association. In all these cases, we were the only male couple. Never for one instant did we encounter any problem or prejudice, and in fact we've made friends on some of these trips. In North America, we've traveled with friends, a few times with another gay couple, more often with straight friends. Was there any difference? Since in all cases the purpose of the trip was the focus, all were equally congenial. Sure, with another gay couple we might make in-jokes or express an evaluation of some fetching fellow traveler or waiter or hiker, but those were passing moments.

For many years, one of our pleasures was making a movie record of our travels, carefully edited, titled, and sound-tracked. We gave that up for two reasons, the increasing cost and unavailability of film, and the gradual loss of audience. So for a decade, now, we've confined ourselves to color slides. We can still offer a pretty good show, if we can find anyone to watch.

Since we were committed to our relationship when we started our travels, we have no titillating tales to tell of encounters with gay life

> It's long been a contention of mine that American travelers one meets in exotic ports who brag they know little of their own country are reverse chauvinist snobs. A woman aboard a Yangtze steamer recently confessed to me that she'd never set foot in a U.S. National Park. "Too busy seeing the world!" she crowed. "Ah," I responded, "saving the best till last, when you'll be too feeble to explore!"

> I had best not attempt to articulate my contempt for those who eagerly embrace that American cliché of "sophistication": raising an eyebrow toward sharing the record of a friend's travel experience. Except in truly rare instances of gross ineptitude, both Ron and I are delighted when any friend compliments our intelligence by wanting to show us photos he or she has taken of a trip that has meant much. When we offer such a presentation ourselves, we're scrupulous to make it professional. As to audience, confirmed peasants need not apply.

abroad. If I rack my brain I can recall, say, a Neapolitan youth who, having failed to interest me in either a cameo or his sister, offered himself; a handsome college-student tour guide in pre-Castro Havana who invited us to his downtown room, for "wild things"; aggressive teenage hustlers in Rhodes and Katmandu; a hypersexed Yucatán guide, father of nine, who somehow maneuvered himself into our hotel and onto—*not into*—our bed ("You'll really like my chicken," he had announced with a slight mistranslation), assuming that, since he had partied the night before with two other American men, we would be happy to oblige him, too. Obviously (since we demurred in each case) there's little gay spice to report from all our travels. Gosh, we weren't even propositioned in Rio!

The other day, an article in the *Times* reported on the flourishing trade in gay travel and the rise in *exclusively* gay travel (as well as places that are hostile to gay men and lesbians). I must admit that gay-ghetto travel lacks appeal. I'm not sure what the attraction is. We're perfectly happy to go to, say, Key West (we'll be there a couple weeks from this writing), and we often search out gay B&Bs, but destinations are what draw us, not the social life. For those who want an all-gay cruise, I'm happy they exist, but we won't be signing up.

There has to be a point to this expenditure of time, energy, and money. *Why* did we want to see all the places we've seen? Curiosity. Curiosity about the many ways people have devised to get through life on this planet. Curiosity about the amazing art and architecture and artifacts people have made. Curiosity about the astonishing variety of natural wonders that Earth has to offer. It's one thing to read about and see pictures of a voodoo

This may be our most valuable eye-to-eye re travel. I'd say we both find "married couples" who travel in search of extracurricular sex (either independent or shared) downright weird. These are likely to be tourists in the worst sense—out to exploit or corrupt any foreign culture they encounter. Travel in itself is sufficient stimulus for us. And I confess it often contributes to especially good sex—between us.

I would be less than truthful if I didn't admit I'm looking forward to the "clothing optional" all-male guest house in Key West—doubtless more than Ron is. At my age, the impulse toward exhibitionism is long past, but I remain a very visual type. However, I agree that Hanns Ebensten will have to manage without us. He doesn't need us; we don't need him.

I suspect Ron's grabbed his key word from a woman friend who recently remarked to us: "You two exhaust my husband and me with your travel plans! We lack your curiosity." An accurate self-analysis—and this academic couple has a happy life without travel. They've also refused to have a TV set in their various campus homes since their kids left the nest. While Ron and I watch little television (no time!), denying ourselves the option would never occur to us. Yes, our curiosity quotient *is* high—and ceremony by a waterfall in a Haitian jungle, or a group of Tibetan Buddhist monks in Shigatse chanting and praying, playing gongs and shell horns, suffused in the scent and light of yak-butter candles, or a dancing-and-drinking Mother's Day party in a hut on stilts in the Amazon; or an elaborately carved marble Jain temple complex in the uninhabited wilds of Rajasthan, or the shimmering jewelbox of the Sainte-Chappelle in the heart of Paris, or the awesome corridors and statues of Luxor and Karnak;

(thank God!) shared. And so, tomorrow: off to Rome! TWA made us a fare offer we couldn't refuse—*if* we bought our tickets the day after the ad appeared. Ron turned to me and said: "Isn't the flexibility to grab something like this exactly what we envied before we retired?" Well, yes—though we're not *that* flexible. To create this travel window we've had to switch performance dates on three different series. But had we *not* grabbed the offer, our curiosity about the restored Sistine Chapel would have gnawed at us!

or the stupefying succession of cascades and falls at Iguaçú, or the ranks of mist-shrouded conical peaks of Guilin, or the colorful and elusive underwater world of the Great Barrier Reef—but it's an entirely different order of experience to witness them firsthand. That adventure has been the point of our travel.

FRIENDS AND SOCIAL LIFE

by Ron

Here's a tender topic. Although we've had many friends and a once-active social life in our forty-seven years together, the fact is, we now find ourselves without a single joint friend in New York. Departures, deaths, and fallings-out have all taken their toll. I am amazed by some of my relatives, who have friends they still see regularly that they've known since grade school. (Granted, they've never moved far, if at all, from their childhood homes.) Straight women seem to have an admirable capacity for maintaining long-term friendships, to judge from some women I know (family members and not). And I've been impressed by the intense friendships demonstrated in the gay community since the onset of the AIDS crisis. Neither of us, in contrast, has ever had much social skill in making friends, and we obviously haven't done very well at keeping them. In years past, however, it all seemed very different.

When we started life together on the houseboat, we had some mutual friends from college days, but they were scattered across the country. I hadn't made any friends in the Seattle gay community, and had amicable relationships with

> **AL RESPONDS:**
>
> I agree neither of us makes friends easily. Ironically, the Big Apple seems the worst place on earth for establishing "meaningful relationships."

only a couple of people at the university. But we were young and in love and didn't feel the need of a social life.

In New York we very slowly met people, almost entirely through work. Our first New York friend was an elegant, knowledgeable, gay Negro (that was the term of choice then), whom I met in a bookstore where I worked briefly. He introduced us to aspects of life in New York, including the Village. Al met a gay couple through work, I met another the same way. And there were single-gay-male and nongay relationships as well. Some of these led to non–job-related friendships. In looking through old journals and calendars while preparing this piece, I was astonished to note how often we were seeing people—for theater or movies, at parties, for dinner at our home or theirs, taking trips together.

For a long time, we certainly seemed to be able to find amusing ways to assemble groups. In 1962, we undertook a project that involved a large array of friends and acquaintances: we made a movie. It was a free-form parody of an arty and mysterious French film, *Last Year at Marienbad*. Ours was called *Next Year at Tranquility*. A friend from Stanford was a recruiter for a New Jersey college and was living in lonely splendor in a large former inn in Tranquility, New Jersey. It was imposing, with lots of rooms, and gave us the idea for our film. We started shooting in the fall, and throughout the winter and spring we subjected friends to endless shooting and recording sessions—in their homes, in a motel, in a cemetery, and at our apartment. We had a huge party to which everyone was requested to bring an idea for a sequence. So, in addition to *Marienbad* we had miniparodies of scenes from *Psycho*, *Lolita*, *The World of Apu*, the Melina Mercouri/Anthony Perkins *Phaedra*, *La Dolce Vita*, and on and on. Our victims were amazingly willing and cheerful about it all, especially since the visuals and sound-track were wildly unrelated, and only we had any idea of how it would all come out. After an enormous amount of editing work, done at home, we finally completed it and had a gala premiere party. Everyone had a grand time. Twenty years later we were able to assemble a large crowd, many of the cast and a number of newer friends. Again, it went over well. (Today, I doubt that we could gather a crowd of three.)

I had forgotten what imaginative parties we threw. Scattered friends flocked to them from Princeton, DC, Boston— and talked about them for years after. "*Please* revive the Twelfth Night party," was a plea from many quarters.

By contrast, the standard "Eastern Corridor" cocktail party is an expendable form. Hosts concentrate on ordering in generous supplies of booze and nibbles, but give nary a thought to their party's *purpose*. Few parties have either structure or theme; they consist of tossing ill-matched people together in hopes that enough drinks will grease the social skids. I prefer dinner parties: anyone who's going to the trouble to *feed* guests is likely to prune the list and give some thought to compatibility.

A few years later, not having learned our lesson the first time, we undertook another movie. The inspiration for this one was a pop psychology book, *Games People Play*. We started during a weekend trip to Martha's Vineyard, with two other gay couples and two singles. The movie was a murder mystery, but the tensions that developed in the group were often more dramatic than the series of murders in the film. This was a much more ambitious undertaking. We had a script (much of it, admittedly, written on the drive to the Vineyard and on the spot); we did a lip-synchronized soundtrack (sheer agony with our primitive editing techniques and our non-professional cast), with an ominous score lifted from Béla Bartók. Once again, there were postlocation shooting and recording sessions. But we got it all together, and had our premiere, with another huge party.

In this same era (the 1960s), we even arranged an enormous bon voyage (or *buon viaggio*) bash on the Italian liner *Raffaelo* when we embarked on a long European venture. And for a number of years we held an annual Twelfth Night party devoted to the sight-reading of a play. Clearly, we were not leading hermits' lives.

With our changes of jobs, new friends came into our orbit, even as some old ones drifted away. Into the mid-1980s we lived a fairly busy urban middle-class social life. And after we built our out-of-town retreat in the early 1970s, we often had visitors there, both family and friends. (Now, we average one overnight visitor a year.)

Whatever the reasons, in the past decade, our social life has thinned down to a weak broth. And there is no gay component whatsoever. Deaths, in our age range, are certainly a factor. Last fall, our last New York friend, one of nearly forty years, succumbed to cancer. His wife had died a number of years before that. And so many people have moved away. We do keep in touch by letter and the occasional visit— always ours. Almost no one we know comes to New York any more.

The fallings-apart have different causes. In the case of one couple with whom we were very close for years, contact ceased for reasons no one can recall—the only one who might have known has died. Our closest gay-couple friendship came to a bizarre conclusion:

We had done so much together, spent so much time with them—

Ron reviews all this chillingly well: the attrition has been alarming. Aside from the deaths and departures, part of the cause may be that we strike others as being sufficient unto ourselves, since we do everything together.

And, frankly, we do so much *more* than anyone we know—and maybe *that's* off-putting. We're also the youngest—in spirit. I'm sure our heavy cultural schedule and our passion for travel intimidate people—though neither of us pushes these pursuits into anyone's face.

. . . Astonishingly true! Like I've said, we're the youngest, most venturesome folks we know.

In my defense (glancing ahead at Ron's account, I see a defense is called for) I'll say that *since* our retirement, I've made more effort to replace lost friends than Ron has. He prefers to cling (sometimes desperately) to old relationships and never seeks new and fresher ones. One might point out that I benefit from this tendency of his!

dinners, theaters, trips, holidays—
and then, suddenly . . . well, perhaps not so suddenly. After retiring and moving out of the city,
one of the pair became increasingly
caught up in a return to the fundamentalist Christianity of his childhood. Mutual visits had become
unpredictable—sometimes pleasant, sometimes edgy. I wrote them
to arrange a visit to our retreat on
the occasion of our anniversary, a
celebration we had shared with
them for many, many years. When
there was no response, I phoned to
inquire and was stunned by the ex-
planation: the fundamentalist had
taken profound exception to comments Al had made, in a letter,
about the infamous Republican
convention of 1992. "I'm a lifelong
Republican and it's pretty fundam-
ental to me," he said. So a relationship of thirty-five years came to a
bitter and silly end.

But we're both responsible for
some of these separations. My
acts are those of omission; as in
other aspects of life, I let things
drift—the phone call not made,
the letter not written or written too
late. Al's are those of commission,
not in person, but by letter. Never
one to withhold an opinion, he ex-
presses himself forcefully in type-
script. In certain instances when
friends have done something an-
noying, Al has lectured them by
letter about their failings, a couple

This old friend went weird.
His current home in upstate
New York—shared with his
longtime companion—is stuffed
with literature from the old
Moral Majority, much of it rail-
ing against the perverted homosexual "lifestyle." He wor-
ships Jerry Falwell, who would
happily slap the two of them
into a concentration camp for
"queers." Go figure.

I've had to reconcile myself
to Ron's looser notion of "lover
loyalty." Over the years, he's
maintained friendships with
people who've proved unacceptable to me (migawd—one
of his professional cronies
turned out to be a cofounder of
NAMBLA!) or who have been
guilty of major social breaches.
One woman—a close mutual
friend—behaved so badly (and
proved so incapable of apolo-
gy) I felt a break was inevitable;
but Ron continues to lunch with
(and exchange birthday and
Yule gifts with) her to this day.
In contrast, I can think of at
least two occasions where
friends (one male, one female)
proposed a relationship on specific terms of exclusion of Ron
—whether they were personally uncomfortable with him or
jealous of my devotion to him
was never clear. In each case,
I abandoned the friendship,
feeling strongly that any relationship that barred Ron was
invalid.

But then, I recognize that
I'm an obsessive and tend to
be exclusive about core relationships. "Love me, love my
lover" has been my operative
motto, and it's been limiting.

of times in such sharp terms that they felt they had no recourse but to withdraw. (In one case, I've remained on friendly terms with the "offender," but it's somewhat awkward.)

And lastly, I reluctantly wonder whether people find us unengaging or off-putting. No one wants to be considered boring. I think we do interesting things and can be good company. But evidently others may not agree. If this sounds like a whine, I don't mean it that way. It's just one of those things that happens with time. I'm sure we'll continue with our epistolary contacts and the odd visit here and there, and recall with affection the friendships of the past.

> And we can always re-screen those two movies!

PROBLEMS? WELL, AL'S HAD ONLY ONE (BUT IT'S BEEN A PIP!)

by Al

In-laws are rarely a major bonus in any marriage, but I've been saddled with a mother-in-law from hell. I had no clue, going into our relationship. Ron's parents seemed friendly enough when I kept appearing on their doorstep as the college buddy, even after the groves of academe had long been left. His father was much older than his mother and beloved by all, including me. This couple was the nucleus of an extended family on both sides in their Tacoma-Seattle community. Ron's father had been well on his way to presidency of his bank when he was struck down in his prime with a heart condition that rendered him a semi-invalid for the rest of his life. His wife (let's call her Sis as

> **AL (BESIDE HIMSELF) RESPONDS:**
>
> When Ron and I outlined this eight-part account, we fully intended to hold to our formula of alternating authorship of main texts and side commentaries. This section, however, resists that format. I wrote the main text well over a year ago, but stuck it in a drawer, since our editor preferred receiving the sections in numerical order. In the interim, we were contacted by a campus archivist who flew east to interview us about organized gay life at Stanford in the late 1940s. We told him that (as we've stated in "The Stanford Start") there *wasn't* any, and our interviewer went on to press us for details of our long life together. When

many in her double family do), though young, inexperienced, and with no education beyond high school, promptly became the bread-winner, working up to a responsible position with the Red Cross. I greatly admired her for that—and for her part in raising so splendid a son.

It was only after she became a widow that I had to face the fact that there was little *else* to admire about her. Having lost her husband, she seemed determined to regain her son, and her resentment of me became palpable. She obviously blamed me for dragging him off across the country, to settle in New York City; in truth, Ron had always hoped to live here—he had just never told her. At any rate, Ron proved inadequate to the situation that developed; blame it on the only-child syndrome.

The fact that it's a classic plot-line (from *Hamlet* to *The Silver Cord*) doesn't make it easier to live with—this realization that one has wed a mama's boy. But there's a possibly helpful lesson in our long experience with ad-justments to family. Though I never pushed Ron in my family's face as my lover (this just wasn't done back in the 1950s), I took pains from the start to make it clear that he was my chosen life mate and my first responsibility ("forsaking all others"). So Ron was from the start accepted by my parents and two older sisters (indeed, the middle sister—who's made a career of obsessive attachments to notably unavailable

> he asked if we had had any problems, I thought of this sec-tion (already written but un-seen by Ron) and—striving for an honest answer—I told him: "Only mother-in-law stress."
>
> Ron's reaction was electric, cutting off further discussion: "Don't make what I'm going through any harder," he snapped. At that moment, I realized I could not present Ron with this section and ex-pect him to make the usual marginal response. The wound of his mother's long decline is too fresh, and his resentment of the truths I've revealed here would be too intense.

> Yet to omit this section as if *my* past pain (and whatever the reader can learn from its causes) had no importance, seemed equally unaccept-able. The only solution, then, is the one I'm implementing here. By the time this all ap-pears in public print, the situa-tion will be less emotionally charged, and my words to the left should be accepted in their original context. At any rate, my "beside-myself" com-ments absolve Ron of any re-sponsibility for this section.

men—promptly fell in love with Ron, agog that they share a No-vember birthdate).

Ron, on the other hand, was never able to bring himself to pres-ent me to *his* (much broader) family as anything but college pal and roommate. A San Francisco aunt (one of his more sophisticated relatives) did realize we had become inseparable and took Ron aside to caution him about the fragility of homosexual relationships. But once he had assured her of our permanent commitment, she became wholly accepting. That was pretty much *it*, though. Neither she nor Ron ever discussed our relationship with other family mem-bers. In fact, Ron took great pains to render me as invisible as possible, rarely including me in gatherings of the clan, and virtually never mentioning my name—especially to Mama.

It has been excruciatingly painful, over the years, to hear Ron on long distance, describing our life together in the singular, as if I didn't exist.

"Oh, I've been building some closets for my loft, and on week-ends I drive my car up to my country place to work on my projects there," he would report. (Accurate translation: Ron's been helping me construct closets I designed, specced, and ordered lumber and paint for . . . and then we've driven our co-owned van upcountry to work on projects I've initiated there.) So outraged have I been by his subterfuge, I've had to leave the room to avoid hearing his side of the conversation during these all-too-frequent long-distance calls.

His unwillingness to be honest served to encourage his mother in her battle with me for "possession." An early example:

I innocently proposed to Ron that a summer visit to Spokane's World's Fair might permit him to see his mother (the costly 3,000-mile distance between them was, back then, a consideration, and he had not visited Tacoma for several years) while at the same time I could see if my Seattle sister could join us. We both proposed my idea (Ron, of course, avoided identifying its source) and both women accepted. I immediately made a reservation for Ron and myself through the Expo '74 accommodations office, and asked them to send campground data to my sister (this is the sister who had earlier declared her love for Ron); she was then driving a minicamper with a single bed. Ron sent data to his mother so she could arrange her own lodging, advising her I had already applied for a twin-bedded room for us.

Several months later, as the date for our convergence on Spokane drew near, Ron checked with his mother as to where she would be staying. "Oh," she airily informed him, "I never applied; I've decided to stay with you, in your room." So I was to move into the gutter.

Wait: it gets better. My life mate actually had the temerity to propose this arrangement to me! "Mother's decided you can stay in your sister's camper."

Expletives deleted here. Needless to say, I told "Mother" to stuff it, and Ron scrambled to find her lodging.

All four of us managed to get together once, during the fair, for lunch. Ron's mother was insufferable to my sister, arching a lip as she inquired about the campground. I couldn't believe this creature! On what conceivable grounds was she feeling superior to my sister—this woman of humble ranch origins and no education? Once Ron (properly embarrassed) had squired her away, my sister sighed: "She infantilizes Ron." And I nodded sadly. "Trust me," I said, "Ron's never like this except with her."

This encounter did yield one positive result: my sister fell out of love with my lover. So how did I deal with such a mother-in-law in all the years since? As little as possible. Ron made pilgrimages to Tacoma. Inevitably, she made a couple of visits to New York City, and endeavored to ignore me in

I guess my refusal to be imposed upon is much the same as what Ron referred to in the previous section on friends. I take pains never to hold friends or relatives to a higher standard than I offer in return. But, alas, today's social world is one of lazy compromise and lowered expectation. I've always felt that anyone I dealt with deserved to know where they stood with me; they all come to realize they can't stand *on* me.

Our main difference (as Ron persists in telling me) is that I'm *meaner.* I grew up with two older sisters taking advantage of me (psychologically *and* physically) to further their territorial ends. Ron's an only child, never having to assert himself against siblings. I'm in no position to knock this—hey, it helped mold him into a person remarkably easy to live with. But there are times when his bend-over-backward agreeableness drives me up the wall.

The result of this basic difference in our personalities is that, once we're gone, survivors will think of Ron with greater affection. They may not *respect* him as much, but they'll be able to come up with luscious eulogies.

my own home. But I simply ignored back, shaking my head in wonderment at how someone I love more than life could, in turn, be so devoted to someone who wished I did not exist. Again, put it down to biology—especially where an only son of a widow is concerned.

The lesson to be found in our experience? My way of introducing my life mate to my family lays a far better foundation for a couple's future than Ron's attempt to ignore the need. Over the years, Ron has been included in my family Christmases and major birthday celebrations; we've traveled with my elder sister both here and abroad, renting a houseboat with her to explore Lake Powell, and even flying her to Bali, where she took my favorite portrait of us, posed in a temple gateway like suppliants, wrapped in the requisite sarongs. I seem to be entreating, "We're together, please. Admit us both."

The whole disparity of our approach to family came crashing in on me while I marched alone in New York's recent massive Stonewall 25 parade past the UN, behind the mile-long rainbow flag. *'Twas risky of you, Ronald,* I thought, *to desert me on the eve of this momentous occasion.* I never felt so undervalued in our forty-three years together, surrounded here by young same-sex couples from all over the world, openly embracing and kissing in celebration of their devotion to one another. And where was *my* lover? Off yet again to Tacoma, because Mama (a frail creature, now, in her mid-eighties, who had resisted all family efforts to get her supervised care) had fallen and—of course!—fractured a hip. Hardly life-threatening, and something her many nearby relatives could have taken care of until he could conveniently get out there again. But no, Ronny must drop everything to jump on the next plane, leaving me with a fistful of tickets to Gay Pride Events we had chosen—and a lonely Stonewall march.

But as I stepped up First Avenue, I realized it was well past time for me to "declare myself." No more (I assured myself) would I accept Ron's keeping me invisible. Any future flights to Tacoma would have to be discussed as to what, precisely, they might accomplish. And if I *ever* again heard him on the phone to family members erasing me from a report on our mutual activities, I would just pick up the extension and say, "Hi, this is Al. Just wanted to clarify that I *do* exist in this partnership . . . and it's not *Ron's* country place; it's *ours.* "

Heady moment! Of course, this firm resolve dissipated somewhat during a series of subsequent calls from Ron (in Tacoma/Seattle) to me (laboring alone on yet another country project). His continued frequent trips there are now essential, since the trauma of his mother's accident accelerated her mental decline. Ron has been needed to get her properly settled into the care situation she so long resisted. And I'm left telling myself (over and over, during his absences) that one of the reasons I love Ron is that he's such a responsible person. Even though his taking upon himself all her affairs has cut deeply into Ron's time and energies, his mother has inevitably diminished as an intruding factor in our life together.

But how unfortunate that the problem has been resolved only by accident; I remain convinced that Ron's reluctance to clarify our relationship to his family has caused me years of avoidable distress.

So, after forty-seven years that's the *only* problem I can name? Well, if I work at it I can come up with one more: Ron does often squeeze the tube of toothpaste (or K-Y) from the middle instead of the end.

As I've indicated above, the major portion of my text was written over a year ago. Several months later, I revised these last paragraphs to update the account re Sis's deteriorating condition. She's never left her nursing home since her fall, just before Gay Pride Day '94 (except for several hospital stays) and Ron's recent trips west have been essential. They're now depressing, since her mind has gone and communication with her is over.

Still, Ron won't be ready to deal with my presentation, here, of the "problem mother-in-law" for months to come. There's a strong tradition in western culture that one must not speak ill of the dead or dying—as if this sad condition automatically bestowed beneficence. I may someday have to remind Ron of his own impatience at the instant statesmanship Nixon achieved by dying (he was even honored with his likeness on a stamp). Death doesn't expunge the record of a person's misdeeds, and I'll always find it very sad that Sis denied herself a full relationship with a loving son by her stubborn refusal to acknowledge his marriage.

THE RETIREMENT PROJECT

by Al

The most startling thing anyone says to us (and we get it a lot—from younger friends, family, and strangers we meet on trips) is, "You both took *early* retirement? Why on earth? I can't imagine what I'd *do* with myself! I intend to hang on 'til they *make* me retire."

Our response to such declarations is to shake our heads in wonder. It strikes us both as pathetic that people let their profession dominate their life. For us, though we both held responsible, long-term executive jobs we were good at, work was simply what paid the bills—it made possible a rewarding lifestyle with a comfortable home, good dining (in or out), and a rich cultural life. We took pains to assure adequate pensions so that the life we had made for ourselves would not end, once no salaries were coming in; thus our lives since retirement have involved only minor scaling-down, financially—an adjustment more than compensated for by all the extra time we have to do things together.

> RON RESPONDS:
>
> There's certainly a shock when your monthly income drops to a half or a third of what you've been used to, and half-price subways and movies don't compensate. Still, the dry-cleaning bills are less. It just becomes a matter of managing resources.

It strikes me that gay couples have an advantage here. Same-sex pairs are likely to have more similar interests in the first place, so are less likely to wonder how they'll "stand one another when we're both home all day." We've had straight couples voice such concerns about retirement—especially those who've maintained conventional roles: he the breadwinner away at the office; she the homemaker and child-rearer. "The thought of him underfoot, barging into my kitchen at all hours—!" one wife confided to me about the husband who was contemplating retirement.

Well, if any such concerns are entertained by any young gay readers of this book, let's hope we can assuage them with our own experience. Except for those financial constraints, the joys of retirement cannot be overpraised. Being at last in full charge of one's

own schedule—every day in the week from getting up to going to
bed again—is a reward that makes all those years of indentured
servitude truly worth their toll in compromise.

Have I ever missed the perks of
being a magazine editor? Being
wooed at lavish lunches or cocktail parties by PR types? Paid to
travel to distant cities to cover

> I never got wooed. I was
> the one with the expense ac-
> count. But those trips sure built
> up frequent-flyer miles.

stories or conventions? Lord, no: I now choose my own restaurants
and destinations. And my home city is twice as rewarding when I
can choose to attend weekday rehearsals, previews, and receptions
denied to the nine-to-fiver. When people ask, "But doesn't time
hang heavy?" we're incredulous. The thing that continues to amaze
us is how we ever found time for all that office stuff. Our daily
schedules continue to be so packed with commitments (ranging
from mundane chores to lofty cultural pursuits and travel) we can't
imagine how we accomplished all this while *also* working long
hours for somebody else.

Yes, though we had challenging jobs, it never occurred to either
of us to confuse our careers with our lives. So—especially when
things got professionally less-comfortable or pleasure in the work-
place deteriorated—we both welcomed the chance for early retirement. In the case of both of our corporations, it wasn't financially
feasible to retire before sixty-two. I reached that blessed plateau
first, being two-and-a-half years Ron's elder, but had to hang on,
chafing, for an interminable extra half year to clean up editorial
projects I knew would go to pot if I walked away from them. This
still gave me a two-year head start on Ron when I finally gave
myself total freedom as a Christmas present in 1988—and found it
as heady as I expected. Ron envied me my independence and
I—unfettered and fulfilled—encouraged him to join me in it as
quickly as he could. Since the final years of my career had been rife
with stress and conflict, I embraced control of my own time and
energies with immense relief; the only thing missing was Ron to
share it all with. So things got even better two years later.

The secret of a successful retirement together? In our case: having been an active, busy couple, sharing a rich mix of experiences.

Any such couple will find that the extra time retirement provides simply enriches what they've enjoyed all along.

In different ways, Ron and I have always been "project people." I'm so goal-oriented I can't conceive of progressing through life without specific set intentions to

> I don't think of myself as a project person at all. I've never been goal-oriented. I drift. And since Al is so goal-oriented, I drift in his wake.

work toward. Ron, though less goal-driven, was always oriented toward a retirement target. Finding role models in his San Francisco aunt—a career woman who invested in a canyon hideaway—and mutual Manhattan friends—a couple who bought an estate in Vermont to which they would flee when city pressures became too great (often inviting us along)—it was Ron who early on pressured us to shop for a country retreat.

We began our search while still employed, first looking within a hundred-mile radius of Manhattan (which we both knew would always remain our nucleus) and, when properties this close in proved beyond our means, expanding our horizons. One thing our friends' experience had taught us· choose a retreat within a two-and-a-half hour drive from the city. Wrestling a car five hours or more into the Vermont mountains after a grueling week at work never seemed that appealing.

Our search gradually narrowed and focused on the Upper Delaware Valley. The Delaware is the last free-flowing major river in the Northeast and as soon as realtors began to display its charms to us, we were hooked. That's another advantage of being closely attuned

> We agreed on certain basic criteria (after price and distance): rural, trees, stream.

in attitude and aspiration: we avoided contention ("I'd prefer ocean frontage." "No, the privacy and remoteness of the mountains!" "Well, at least property on a *lake*!") and the moment we set foot on the eighteen acres that was to become Shadowglen, we both knew our search was over.

We had both been willing to consider a "handyman's special" and indeed inspected a number of abandoned do-it-yourself cabins that simply needed a fresh infusion of determination. But in the end, we decided on the purchase of raw land, the development of which would be entirely to our design.

I go into all this here because of our shared conviction that any for-the-long-haul couple (gay or straight) should have a long-term project that extends well into retirement. We perhaps overdid it with our mountain acres through which a stream cascades, but the principle is sound. Find something you both believe in fully, and make it the anchor of your retirement relationship.

It needn't, of course, be country property. It might be the creation of an ideal love nest in the heart of town. Or it could be an agreed-upon program of travel, domestic or foreign. But couples shouldn't assume that the accommodations they've made to one another during the period they've pursued separate careers are necessarily going to translate into an ideal retirement relationship. In analyzing other couples' fear of retirement, we've concluded that it's a mistake to quit work "cold turkey"—without mutual plans for *investing* that great boon of additional time together.

If the project you choose is a house you build from scratch, be prepared for some strain on the relationship. This is a demanding commitment, since it's a project that's never completed, and the oft-frustrating labor involved has challenged many a marriage—gay or straight. On the other hand, when you're literally building your future working side-by-side, the sense of shared commitment is probably greater than any you could expect to achieve from another mutual endeavor.

Coming off a profession of do-it-yourself, I've been a bit obsessive in pushing project after project at Shadowglen. I've now promised that the ambitious dome theater we're finishing up will be the last construction I involve us in (Al's last erection?); Ron would prefer to turn more attention to maintaining what we've already built—and to our vegetable garden.

One alteration that Shadowglen has made in our scheduling is our reluctance to travel during the summer. Our mountain country is

> I've made many dumb decisions in my life—socially, sexually, financially, occupationally—but the prize for lack of foresight was to agree when Al was offered the (nearly) complete panels for a dome; they would otherwise have been sent to a dump. "What a waste," I foolishly said.
>
> This project has come close at times to ruining retirement and has cast a shadow on my enjoyment of Shadowglen. I don't have all that many hours left in my life and far too many of them have been spent on this folly. But I agreed to it, so on we go.

at its best then and it seems perverse to leave it for long periods. Winter in northern Pennsylvania, on the other hand, is more of a challenge than we wish to face, now, except for brief check visits. Trudging through thigh-deep snow quickly loses appeal at our ages, as do frozen water lines and car chains. So we now plan our major travel—southward!—for January through March; and during summer and fall our Manhattan loft becomes our *city* retreat, to which we flee to recharge our cultural batteries.

It truly seems we've found the best of both worlds and have fine-tuned the balance between urban stimulation and rural relaxation.

Shadowglen is not, of course, our only shared project. Maintaining the city loft also takes an investment of time and energy, as does our photographic record of our travels and projects.

One major annual project is *not* shared, though it's an endeavor we both pursue—separately. You should see our loft in early December when each of us is privately at work on the hand assembly of his own Yule card. We've

> Al's cards focus on photographic remembrances of the year, plotted out well in advance. He fails to mention that his are elaborate too, in the year-end written summary that accompanies the card.

been making personal cards for over forty years and wouldn't dare stop now; once you establish this tradition, scattered friends around the globe expect it of you. Our "project approach" here is identical: we each formulate the idea and keep it from one another. Screens are erected around separate work areas during the assembly process—which in Ron's case can get fairly elaborate. (To commemorate our recent Russian trip, he painstakingly simulated a black lacquer box for each name on his long list; for one of our Olympics years, he hand-assembled seventy tree ornaments consisting of Santa Claus hanging by his knees from the five properly colored Olympic rings.) When prototype cards are finally completed in each enterprise, they are formally exchanged. I confess I find this moment a highlight of each year.

How do couples manage without mutual projects and traditions?

CODA

The writing and editing of our joint account has stretched over three years and, as we conclude it, we're celebrating our forty-seventh anniversary. In closing, let us respond to the family values rhetoric so popular with the radical right. We've had many years to evaluate those highly touted, exclusively heterosexual values within our own family structures, and what we've personally witnessed adds up to a chilling list:

Shotgun weddings
Induced miscarriages (no known abortions, oddly)
Casual divorces (many)
Costly mistresses
Matricide
Child abandonment
Murder by a greedy wife (my own father's misbegotten
     second marriage)
Suicide
Fratricide
Surgical sex switch (wife held hubby's hand as he went under
     the knife)
Widowhood as relief (a sister "prayed" for her cheatin'
     husband's early death—even while he was flying bombing
     missions in the Air Corps)

All this mess and catastrophe within the confines of our two "average middle-class" families— and all created by certifiable heteros. I've often had to realize that

> And if we started cataloging friends and acquaintances, we would have to add their frequent disappointment and discontent with their offspring . . .

the relationship Ron and I have built and maintained is one of the few stable love matches in either of our families. Where my two sisters are concerned, I'm the sole sibling who found Mr. Right— the sole sibling whose own marriage reflects the stability of the parental example.

You can appreciate, then, why we'll be rolling on the floor, gagging with hysterics, when telecasts from the next Republican convention feature the Two Pats somberly assuring us that heterosexuals have the corner on marital stability, and that same-sex marriage is a threat and affront to family values.

Once we recover our compo-
sure, we may just start planning a
wedding trip to Hawaii.

> Can we order the flowers
> for our leis?

UPDATE

Since this was the first collaborative essay commissioned for this book, it was completed several years ago. To make it as current as its companions in this anthology, the authors offer the following update, section-by-section (main texts by Al, kibitzing by Ron).

Life Doesn't Begin at Forty

For the sake of emphasis and consistency (and from personal pride) I have updated all references to our number of years together: we've just celebrated our forty-seventh anniversary. . . . In light of the several accounts of "open marriages" we've accepted for this anthology since ours was written, my concluding statement now sounds harshly judgmental. Monogamy still seems to me an essential basis for any true *marriage*, but there's obviously a diversity of gay unions where it's *not* mutually invoked, without lessening the sense of commitment.

> **RON RESPONDS:**
>
> The necessity of legal protection of rights relating to property, finances, and medical matters becomes more apparent with age. We *think* our wills and property arrangements and medical directives forestall potential hazards. But as Arch Brown's account in this book ("Dance to the Music") demonstrates, the omission of a single small phrase can create costly, time-consuming, and wearing problems. . . . Re the monogamy issue, I question Al's subtitle for this book: possibly "Commitment" would be more accurate than "Fidelity"—but that's a subjective call.

The Stanford Start

Happily, there's much to update where Stanford is concerned. That imposing chapel I mention still dominates the Inner Quad, decorated with pictorial mosaics outside and in. But this nondenominational campus church became the first in the nation to give formal permission for gay commitment ceremonies (Harvard's Memorial Church followed suit, led by its famously gay pastor, Reverend

Peter Gomes). . . . Re Ron's marginal memory of my Village room: although I don't recall the incident, I would have been titillated to have an attractive friend catch an after-shower glimpse of my penis and find it of interest. I remain flattered that (fifty years later) he still does. Frankly, these days—at seventy-two—my genitals are the least-changed, most-functional (and therefore my favorite) part of my body.

Despite Stanford's importance in our lives, we didn't maintain much connection with it. We lost touch with nearly all of our friends, and individually we visited the campus only rarely. After the early 1950s we weren't there together until my sixtieth birthday.

But we have become enthusiasts of the Alumni Association's travel program—the association has us in its files as life partners. And we've both included the university in our wills.

Careers and Finances

The major update of this section: Since writing it we've established an upcountry joint account to take care of shared costs of expenses there. It's working out smoothly, and proved a boon to organizing royalty payments on this book: since our publisher has a policy against payments to more than two co-authors, we're able to deposit royalties into this account and write personal checks to the other contributors. And, as so many financial transactions are shared, we've come (after all these years) to see the value of maintaining one joint account.

For reasons touched on in this section, Ron retired with superior resources (he certainly spent the bulk of his career with a superior company!)—so, bless him, he's been most generous in "tiding me

Hooray for the 401K. Proceeds from that, plus income from a modest unexpected inheritance, have relaxed the pinch we felt in the first years of joint retirement.

over" lean periods when my liquid assets haven't quite matched expenditures—especially for accelerated travel plans. Example: Since it was *his* choice to celebrate his upcoming seventieth in Japan, he's covering most of the cost. I hope to be able to afford the cake.

Cultural Pursuits in Tandem

Nothing's changed here: the cultural pursuits, though we're both now in our seventies, have grown even more intense, and we've nearly filled those stacking cubicles for theater/concert programs we had just built and installed when we first wrote this section. Our pursuits these days (since we're both retired and no longer have occasion to travel separately) are *all* in tandem. They include summer performance festivals such as Charleston's Spoleto, Glimmerglass Opera, Caramoor; we're frankly surprised we don't spot more gay couples at these events. . . . In light of the new television miniseries *More Tales of the City,* let me expand on my lack of enthusiasm for Armistead Maupin, gay chronicler of 1970s San Francisco. I guess I'm one of the few "gay spokespersons" who defended PBS for its decision not to sign up the sequel to the original series (produced in San Francisco by British television) which PBS ran in early 1994. I didn't think the original shows did our gay cause any favors, and I'm just as happy the new batch aired on limited-access Showtime, instead. Oh, sure: Marcus D'Amico was personally appealing as Mouse (he's replaced in the new series) and his goodnight kiss in the convertible on an SF street remains one of the memorable "breakthrough" TV images. But author Maupin is a moral lightweight who blithely celebrates the pot-and-bathhouse culture of pre-Plague San Francisco; I never felt his denizens of Barbary Lane did a thing for gay rights.

> The first episodes had a quirky charm, but the show got tackier and tackier until it became unbelievable, off-the-cable-car-tracks soap opera.

> A word should be said about the increase in the number of engaging gay-themed works in theater *(Party, When Pigs Fly, Last Session, R&J)* and film *(Kiss Me, Guido, Beautiful Thing, I Think I Do, Gods and Monsters).* It's also heartening to find appealing gay characters— not psychotic or doomed or suicidal—in mainstream films *(My Best Friend's Wedding, In and Out, As Good as It Gets).*

In a recent issue of *OUT Magazine,* this era is eulogized as the Gay Golden Age! But what's to be expected of a magazine that prints a guide to current circuit parties and tabulates this season's drugs of choice? It's as if those male bimbos of Sex Panic! are accepting the welcome miracle of protease inhibitors as license to return to the mindless promiscuity and doping of the 1970s. This will, pressed to extremes, come to a similarly bad end.

Stick around, Larry Kramer; looks as though "the community" may be needing your acerbic scolding yet again! Meanwhile, one element of the gay scene seems eternally determined to pursue an ugly, self-destructive lifestyle; there remain among us too many emotional cripples whose only concept of "fun" is to degrade themselves; and their *least* concern is that they unfairly give the vast majority of us a tarnished reputation as a result. We're tarred with the brush of your highly publicized irresponsibility, guys—and getting tired of it.

> For the arts in general in our society, the picture remains bleak. After the admirable Jane Alexander retired from the National Endowment for the Arts, she revealed that in an endeavor to show congressmen what it was all about, she often invited them to events at the Kennedy Center—and found that they usually went to sleep. Their opposition was not about Mapplethorpe pix of dicks.

How Many Corners on a Globe?

Since we both have a deepening sense of mortality, our travel planning has accelerated and intensified. Obviously, only a finite number of trips is still possible, so it's become more critical to plan them fully ("We will not pass this way again") and more frequently. Our fullest travel years to date were 1996 and 1997; we dubbed them both *Wanderjahr*. On New Year's Day, 1996, we flew to Nairobi for a camera safari and hot-air balloon trip over the Serengeti, then flew on to the Seychelles to cruise that archipelago in the Indian Ocean; in June, Ron gave me a surprise seventieth birthday trip to Venice; in July we drove to the Olympics—in both Atlanta and Savannah; in September we flew to Puget Sound for a spectacular whale watch (three pods of orcas converged at the prow of our ship); the month of October was spent on a sailing yacht cruising the Turquoise Coast of Turkey. January 1997 was devoted to an exploration of Southeast Asia, climaxing in a long-denied visit to Cambodia's Angkor Wat; both March and June saw trips to southern states (Florida and South Carolina respectively); after an October jaunt up the Pacific Coast, we were off to Morocco. Most of these trips were "packaged," with groups of strangers; the era of youthful independence—of striking out on our own, clutching $5-a-day travel guides—is long past. On all but one such group tour, we were the only male couple, yet there was never an awkward moment.

The principal update here is that we've softened our rejection of specialized gay travel. In Key West we signed onto a day's all-male snorkel cruise and found the group not only congenial but (once the sailboat anchored at the reef and all clothes were shed—even those of the gay captain and crew) pleasant to ogle, as well. On a recent trip to Napa Valley we overnighted at a gay resort along the Russian River and enjoyed swimming in their pool beneath towering redwoods, then dining in their upper-deck restaurant overlooking it. Our Morocco trip was booked through Family Abroad, a gay-owned agency we learned about through our subscription to *Out and About* (a lively international travel newsletter, edited by a long-term gay couple, Billy Kolber-Stuart and David Alport). Though our tour hadn't been billed as all-male, it turned out that way. I wouldn't characterize any of our companions in Morocco as dedicated travelers—not even the two singles (from Chicago and Atlanta) who were travel professionals. Most of the group dutifully followed our assigned Moroccan guide through the labyrinths of medina streets in each royal capital, but the level of commitment seemed less high than with mixed groups of our past travels. (Several of our Morocco guys were dedicated *shoppers*—certainly another legitimate reason to seek out exotic destinations.) But what advantage, really, was there to traveling with an all-gay group? The "freedom" to remark on an attractive native waiter or ask our decidedly nongay guide about local gay life (in Morocco: nil) didn't strike us as significant.

So, while we're glad we've broadened our options and would not hesitate to sign on for another all-gay tour headed someplace we wanted to go, we still don't feel *compelled* to "travel gay." Two months ago, we were exploring remote Mayan sites in the jungles of Belize, Honduras, and Guatemala

> The incipient infirmities of old age make us realize that we had better undertake these more-demanding trips while we can. I was using a cane (post-ankle fracture) in Morocco, and Al resorted to it in Central America. True, one of the most vigorous temple-climbers on the Mayan trip was seventy-nine—but you never know.

with a Smithsonian study group, no less—back to being the only same-sex couple—and our next two trips abroad will be with Stanford Alumni.

A final travel update: we were in Belize when the tourism minister of the Cayman Islands denied landing rights to an all-gay cruise ship chartered by Atlantis Events. *Out and About* (and other gay publications) characterized the Caymans as homophobic and called for a boycott. Some lauded Belize (where the banned ship—the *Leeward* of Norwegian Cruise Line—docked instead) as enlightened by comparison. Not so! I picked up a local newspaper—a dreadful little tabloid called *Amandala* which proclaims itself "The newspaper with the greatest circulation in Belize"—and was jolted to find it virulently homophobic throughout. Virtually the entire issue (dated Sunday, January 18, 1998) is devoted to antigay diatribes. Let me quote from the page-two editorial, headlined "The Malignant Mulatto," which is a racist attack on Belize Minister of Tourism Henry Young (who had had the audacity to approve the alternate docking):

> We are seeking to explain why, although most of you Creoles are puzzled by Henry Young's immediate and stubborn stance on the matter of the toxic homosexual cargo of February 1, why we at AMANDALA see the decision as merely the predictable product of the confused mulatto mentality . . . which rules Belize. . . . It was into this world of the white God that Henry Young was born. . . . It did not matter to the traditionally malignant mulatto that the European had enslaved the black man and murdered the red man. . . . And now this Belizean multimillionaire has told Belizeans that we should welcome what Cayman and the Turks and Caicos refused—a shipload of toxic homosexual cargo.[1]

This editorial stance—rife with outrage and condemnation of everything not pure-blood black (and assuming no *black* could ever be gay—strictly a "European depravity"!) is reflected in variously by-

> The local Belizean Smithsonian guide dismissed the whole thing as ridiculous, saying that the paper represented a minority view (size of minority unspecified).

lined reports and columns throughout this issue. Yet I hasten to point out that this is an *opposition* rag; it does not reflect official Belizean policy. We found the country gracious and friendly as we traveled its back roads. But—oh! the educating we all must do!

Friends and Social Life

This bleak report of nearly three years ago has altered for the better. When we took on the editing of this anthology, we adopted

> Our warmest relationship is with a heterosexual couple, but they live in another city.

and expanded a "new circle." Though we've not met most of the writers in this book (most of whom have proved to be disappointing correspondents), we consider them all potential friends and have enjoyed the back-and-forth required to get their accounts into print. And recently we were privileged to attend an astonishing party a few miles from our country home. New friends our age (who had been neighbors-up-the-road for several years—oft-mentioned by mutual country friends but unmet until a chamber music benefit a few months earlier) host this affair annually around Halloween, with an ever-expanding guest list limited to established male couples in the area. The area is rural, so we were amazed at the number (fifteen) and variety of such couples. We've had our retreat up there for nearly thirty years and simply never guessed we had a legion of gay neighbors. This potluck dinner party filled the hosts' house with lively conversations in every corner; not one flounce, screech, or cruise the whole evening; attire featured neither studded leather nor chiffon; topics discussed ranged from books and movies to dependable local roofers. It was confirmation that real-people male couples are in abundance everywhere—exactly the message this book was meant to promulgate.

One thing about this category, alas, has not changed: as Ron confessed three years ago, though he bemoans the situation, he does nothing to rectify it. Any attempts to meet new people or follow up on nascent bonds made with travel

> I must admit I'm becoming increasingly antisocial. Encounters are wearing and casual ones with strangers are particularly difficult. I have nothing to say. But Al does keep trying.

companions must always stem from me. I've come to realize that most people who complain of too few friends aren't willing to expend the effort to cultivate new ones. In all this rumination on friendship, I've had to conclude that I have unrealistically high standards where it's concerned. Relationships that other people blithely call friendships often seem to me to be merely acquaint-anceships. I detect no great bond there; these people will often belittle their so-called friends to other so-called friends. While I probably miss a broader social life as much as Ron does, I've never hungered for a plethora of acquaintances: too often they just com-plicate and clutter one's life without enriching it.

As for Ron's private woman friend, she's become a tolerated nuisance to me. He still has muffled phone chats with her and creeps out to join her for lunch every few weeks. I keep hoping he'll come to realize by himself that she's unworthy of even this minor strain on our relationship, but he clings to her desperately. "My one remaining New York friend!" he cries. She, of course,

> I don't actually creep—it's more like walking. And it's her habit not to leave her seat at intermission. Al really should be able to understand her attitude. When he dismisses people from his life, he considers them dead. I'm sure that's the way she feels about him. (Her un-forgivable sin was not to come to a party she had committed to and canceling at the last minute.)

relishes her secret role and the fantasy she's formed that I would attack her if we chanced to meet. At one chamber music concert all three of us happened to attend, she remained quivering in her seat during intermission rather than face a lobby encounter. A rather absurd neurotic, is she? Or am *I* neurotically possessive?

Problems? Al's Had Only One

The problem outlined here has long since been resolved—but in the saddest possible way: through the decline and death of "Sis." My first impulse was to omit this section, but since the problem had been very real, very painful, I now feel it would be dishonest to do so. (Another update: since the original writing I've lost both my elder sisters, so am as sibling-less as Ron.) It was painful not even being able to share Ron's grief as he attended his mother's final descent into dementia and death. As a dutiful only child, he had the whole burden of seeing her cared for and then buried, and he faced all the decisions about the disposition of her effects. I could offer only cold comfort and the assurance that things would be taken care of on this end during his continued trips to the Northwest. How different all would have been had I been integrated into his family from early on! But something truly significant has happened in the last couple of years. No longer conflicted with his mother's enmity for me, Ron has opened his remaining family (a heady network of aunts, uncles, and cousins) to me. Since I've now lost much of my own clan, I've much appreciated acceptance into his. For the past two years we've visited the Northwest *together*, and Ron's relatives have welcomed us with group lunches and dinner parties. Departing from one of the latter, I gratefully received the closest thing to a blessing anyone in Ron's clans has bestowed: Ron's cousin's very R C. husband stood at his door with a host's farewell; clapping a hand on my shoulder he said: "Take care of each other." (We will, we will—for all the time that's left us.) Meanwhile, the "only problem—but a pip!" in our marriage is no more.

I had not read the account until asked to provide comment for the update. There's nothing I didn't know or sense about Al's resentment of my mother. He had good reason to feel resentful. I often didn't handle things well. But there's not much to be gained in commenting at length. Al's capacity for resentment and need to get even have always amazed me. Maybe it's genetic: his parents spent much of their time battling enemies. Just as he is puzzled by only-child behavior, I am mystified by sibling relationships—not only his with his sisters (whom he has lost in the sense of severed contact with) but also those in my own extended family.

He seems to forget that he was integrated into my relationships with those relatives to whom I was closest—a paternal aunt, who is very fond of him and whom he has visited a number of times; a maternal uncle and aunt, who were always very hospitable to him; and most especially a maternal cousin (the only relative who ever lived nearby)— we visited her and her children quite often: they stayed with us at Shadowglen, and the girls grew up thinking of Al as much of a relative as I am.

The Retirement Project

Looking back, our "retirement project" had another advantage—it got us out of Manhattan during the Sleazy Seventies! We acquired the country property in 1970, and our attention for the next decade was strictly fresh-air (Ron got into vegetable gardening while also helping me build against the monthly deadlines of my Leisure Home series in *Popular Science*). Thus oriented, we had little time for more than a flicker of distaste at reports of the dank bars, abandoned piers, flashy clubs, and orgy parties where "ever-wilder things went on." Every weekend and many vacation days we were speeding upstate. Not that the wild things would have presented any temptation; neither of us had ever

> Of course, this book became Retirement Project #2. As usual, Al has been the driving force, and I've followed along, with about the same energy and enthusiasm I brought to the dome.

been into the bar scene or gave a damn about being "with it" where the escalating drug scene was concerned. Still, our decade's focus on Shadowglen spared us all contact with Studio 54, the Anvil, or Mineshaft—or the childish exhortations of Gay Talese. I recently plowed through the Seventies section of Charles Kaiser's decade-organized history titled *The Gay Metropolis* and truly felt that Dante was conducting me on a tour of the inner circles of Hades. Somehow, having it all so succinctly summed up brought home its true horror. This was not hedonism; it was grotesque obsession. It should be noted that not only gays were "making this scene." Heteros flocked to Studio 54 and other dives, so eager to get at the drugs and sex inside they happily stood in block-long lines, desperate to have the Steve Rubells of that insane world admit them to hell. Several of Kaiser's informants were still ecstatic in recall. Talese was espousing constant anything-goes sex, while his loony wife intellectualized his excesses. "It was the Weimar Republic reborn!" one of Kaiser's voices gushes. Exactly: and just as the then-unprecedented decadence of the last years of Weimar opened the gates to the greater depravity and death-obsession of the Nazi era, so the lunatic license of the sex-and-drugs 1970s paved the way for the ghastly Plague years. I'll be eternally grateful to have been spared both.

As for the Plague itself, to even *begin* to deal with the early mainstream view of it, one must force oneself to remember one's own first encounter with what was to become the epidemic. At the start of the Fourth of July weekend in 1981 a medical writer for *The New York Times* headlined his report "Rare Cancer Seen in 41 Homosexuals" and went on to say most of the cases "involved homosexual men who have had multiple and frequent sexual encounters with different partners, as many as ten sexual encounters each night up to four times a week."[2] Unquote! *Ten* different sexual partners per *night*? In heterosexual terms, this was perverse behavior any mainstream citizen (myself included) could only associate with a desperate street-corner hooker. No one *I* knew could conceive of such a lifestyle. Although I never quite sank to thinking "they're getting their just desserts," or even "they've brought it on themselves," I had little choice but to buy into the "us-and-*them*" attitude that prevailed throughout society during the 1980s. "How *could* anyone live like that and expect the rest of us to accept it?"

In my case, it was only with Paul Monette's fine AIDS memoir *Borrowed Time* and Craig Lucas's script for the 1990 film *Longtime Companion* (no "s") that reeducation began. These meditations on the Plague forcefully demonstrated that the horror could happen to *real* people—not just to mindless sybarites bent on their own destruction. And the ultimate response of the gay community was remarkable: compassionate and angry, determinedly protective and outraged. Our behavior in the late 1980s and 1990s has been, largely, as commendable as our excesses in the 1970s were repellent.

Unlike several other writers in this book, I had the AIDS shadow touch my life so lightly I hesitate to relate the incident at all. You don't, somehow, expect the Angel of Death to visit you in the guise of a vertically challenged periodontist, but that's what happened to me in June of 1989. In the course of a series of dental appointments to have a crown fitted and installed, my mouth became inflamed and my dentist prescribed an antibiotic. On my next visit, two weeks later, the condition had not improved. "Can't be gingivitis," my dentist decided. "The tetracycline would have cleared it up. So no point in renewing the prescription. I'm referring you to a periodontist." So casually can a nightmare begin. The little, youngish periodontist's plush office was in Rockefeller Center, and after a perfunctory rubber-gloved inspection of my sore mouth, he declared—almost impishly, "I've never *seen* such a condition, mind you, but I'd guess it's an early sign of AIDS!" This viciously careless diagnosis sent me, of course, for an immediate HIV test. Though I couldn't conceive how I could ever have been infected, my first concern was for Ron. (No, I realize, looking back, it never occurred to me that he might have been the source of infection—

such is the absolute trust of monogamous love.) But if the result came back positive, could I (in my ignorance) have infected *him*? (It also never occurred to me *not* to be tested; I had never understood for a moment gays-at-risk who "preferred not to know.") At the clinic, I was much impressed with the professionalism—and absolute anonymity; you weren't asked your name but were assigned a code number—of the testing program set up by NYC's Department of Health. I had an unexpected sense of release as the vial of blood was drawn: the decision was now irrevocable. Now I only had to reconcile myself to the two-week wait for the verdict. I never mentioned the test to Ron in the interim. Sweating out the results was hell for me; there was no reason to put him through it, as well. Happily, I was decisively negative.

One thing surprised me during the tortured wait. At the end of the 1980s, testing positive was still taken as a death sentence. Much as this possibility obsessed my waking hours for these two weeks, it never penetrated my dreams. My subconscious continued to entertain itself with its usual surrealism as I slept; no shadow of AIDS darkened these colors. Yet the night after I told Ron of the ordeal, the *release* of concern did manifest itself: in my dream I methodically and efficiently garroted a pygmy periodontist.

Regarding that startling (absolutely factual) list that concludes our original joint account: I'm glad to report no further fuckups by heterosexual kin. But I must clarify one item we included: that sex-change operation was eagerly sought by my married nephew— a successful politician who headed the city council of a midwestern capital. I recall with gratitude that this young man absented himself from a critical reelection campaign to join a family gathering in Los Angeles for the funeral of my mother in the mid-1970s. Following that, no contact. He had never been a correspondent, so I had been startled to learn from the newspapers—in April 1984—that my illustrious nephew had become a niece. I had never met this transformation until the fall of 1996, when his/her side of the family converged on Seattle to celebrate the seventy-fifth birthday of my five-years-older sister (it was to be my last reunion with this full clan). At that time, nephew-become-niece had driven all the way from the Midwest—the first leg of a transcontinental circle which was to continue down the Pacific Coast, across the southern states (to take in a transgender conference) before turning back up the East Coast to New York City. In an avuncular mood, out in Seattle, I urged niece/nephew to look me up, back East; once she/he did, I treated her/him to lunch at my club. Each Tuesday this group gathers at the glorious National Arts Club on Gramercy Park for cabaret entertainment and a speaker, and my niece-nephew fit right in (though I would venture to guess this was the first transsexual guest ever to lunch with the group; I simply introduced her/him as my niece). After lunch, the two of us strolled down lower Fifth Avenue, chatting easily before we had to split for separate destinations (back to the Midwest for her/him; off to Turkey for me). As we lingered a moment beneath the Washington Square arch, my niece/nephew suddenly announced: "I've always been so grateful to you, Uncle Al. It must have been tough growing up gay in the 1940s and 1950s, but I always knew you'd got through it, and once you got together with Ron, it always gave me confidence that a good life was possible."

I was thunderstruck. At base, this was a poignant moment—a distant nephew whom I had never known well enough to discuss such things with (I had never thought about his being gay; I had not been invited to his wedding, never met the bride) was now telling me I had been a role model. But he was addressing me here, beneath Washington's arch, as a woman—and *this* is an uncle who winces at tattooed forearms and is slightly sickened when confronted with a pierced nipple or septum. *This* uncle celebrates nearly seventy years of pride in being a gay male. And now this uncle's being told he was the inspiration for this nephew's having his genitals "surgically inverted?" *This* uncle could only smile wanly and wave farewell.

We still correspond (this is, despite appearances, an intelligent, productive person), but I can never pretend to understand the compulsion toward self-mutilation. Do I think people with such a compulsion should be free to go through with a sex-change operation? Since there are surgeons willing to perform it, of course. It harms no one but themselves and is therefore more easily justified than most abortions. But can I ever embrace the practice? No. In fact, those gay-rights activists who try so desperately to be politically correct and all-inclusive, who end up claiming to speak for GaysLesbiansBisexualsTranssexualsTransgendersS&MleathermenDykesonBikesCrossdressersTransvestites, remind me of a car dealer that sponsors the weather reports on my upcountry radio station: by the time his commercial has identified him once or twice as "your JeepEagleChryslerDodgePlymouthPontiacChevroletCherokeeVolvoHonda dealer" there's scarcely time for the weather.

Sure, all these fringe minorities-of-a-minority have civil rights, but loopy superliberals who hop about proclaiming "nobody's free until *all* are free" make no pragmatic sense. They need to be reminded that nobody *is* entirely free—nor should we be. We all have obligations to our fellow creatures, including the obligation not to thrust perverse peculiarities in their faces out of an adolescent intent to shock and discomfort. I live in hope that more and more gays will grow up to acknowledge that "conform" is not a dirty word in every context. If there's a party I really want to attend and the invitation dictates "black tie," I dig out my tux. It's really that simple: let's *earn* that place at the table. Bruce Bawer reports that one gay-press reviewer of his fine book wrote along the lines of: "If that's what's involved to sit at the table, I'll settle for take-out." Fine. If your taste runs to junk food and plastic forks, you've every right to make that choice. Just don't whine about exclusion.

The same mail that brought the contract for this book from our publisher also brought me a summons for jury duty at State Supreme Court. The juxtaposition seemed appropriate, since the main message of this book is that we American gays are basically like everyone else, with the same civil responsibilities. We pay our taxes, we try to vote intelligently, we serve on juries. It remains galling that we are still denied perhaps the most basic of all human rights—the right to have the state recognize and sanction our most stable, committed, and nurturing relationship. DoMA must go. It is counter to everything we respect in American democracy. We are not second-class citizens; DoMA is second-class legislation, conceived, written, and signed into law by second-class minds.

New York City

NOTES

1. The malignant mulatto (editorial). 1998. *Amandala* (Belize), January 18, p. 2.
2. Lawrence K. Altman, 1981. Rare cancer seen in 41 homosexuals. *The New York Times*, July 3.

Fraternity Brothers

Carle Elkins with Patrick Ellis

Patrick Ellis and I celebrated our thirtieth year as life partners on July 4, 1997. Although we are collaborating on this narrative, I (Carle Elkins), will be the scribe while Patrick peruses his favorite magazine, *Gourmet*. He has promised me a proper feast when this is finished.

Before we start on the somewhat rocky road to nirvana, let's go back ten years prior to that commitment day in 1967.

It was a clear and starry night on the campus of a small central Florida college in 1957. Patrick was knocking on doors in search of prospective fraternity pledges. I had just returned to college after three years in the Army and was decked out in my best U.S. issue T-shirt, pecking away at a vintage Royal.

Little did either of us know the knock on that door was the first note in a melody we would continue composing for the rest of our lives. Now, find a K (for knock) on your keyboard, and you can start your own symphony!

To this day, Patrick claims he had a revelation when he opened my dormitory door—an aura struck him. Must have been blinded by that bright white T-shirt! He was persuasive and we became fraternity brothers—straight fraternity brothers I might add, for it would be many years before we realized and admitted our true orientation.

We feel those years of close friendship have been a major factor in the success of our lives together. During the next two years we shared all those memorable college experiences: going home to meet each other's families, rooming together off and on and, yes, fighting and arguing as friends are wont to do.

We graduated about the same time, Patrick going into teaching and I changing my biology major to photography. This decision eventually took me to California for a degree program and of course separated us seriously. We were still straight, mind you, but we might have been the only people who thought so!

We kept in close touch and when I flew back to Florida for a family visit, Patrick was the first person I saw. We still laugh about that reunion. My plane was very late, Patrick had held the bar down with martini olive pits, I had gained twenty pounds, and he walked right by me in a daze. How he ever drove us from Miami to Key Largo, where he was teaching, is still a mystery. But friends do what friends have to do!

Patrick always accused me of being the world's oldest student but I did finally return to Florida, degree in hand.

Patrick was teaching in Miami by this time, and just where do you think I found a job? That's right, with a well-known Miami Beach photographer.

Although Patrick lived in South Miami and I on the beach we still saw a lot of each other.

It was another of those clear, starry Florida nights and we were riding around Key Biscayne talking about our lives, problems, and aspirations when we stopped in a vacant lot overlooking the bay. Now, why would two straight friends choose such a romantic setting for a chat? Well, we comforted each other . . . held each other . . . kissed each other. Did I say the "K" word, and I don't mean "knock?" Add another note to our developing melody!

Odd to think back on that time and those days in Miami and realize we still didn't get the hint that we were really more than just friends.

Patrick had a good job with the school system, but I had to get on with a career—and soon. Looking to start or buy a photography studio on the coast, I found a small place for sale in Daytona Beach.

Here we go, separated again—but at least not by the entire country. Patrick would drive up to see me and I down to visit him. However, we were each beginning to explore a totally new life experience that we weren't ready to share.

I was still dating and, while driving around Daytona Beach, my girlfriend pointed to a bar, indicating it was a gay bar. Well, that was a Tuesday night; Wednesday I was in there—and the rest is history. I will never forget that first moment I held the man I met there—the first time I had ever really touched another man in this way. I knew at that instant who I was and the true sexual orientation with which I was born.

I was in my late twenties but I have never regretted not coming out sooner. The values gained from family and society served me well in adjusting to my newfound identity.

Patrick had a less easy time of it. He met someone while at a convention and felt very uncomfortable with the whole concept. Although he continued to have occasional liaisons with men, it would be several years before he would accept his sexual identity.

Shortly after we both had "come out," as they say, I was visiting Patrick in Key Largo. Over probably too many drinks at a local bar, Patrick confessed his experience, hoping but not knowing that I would approve or at least understand. Boy, was that evening a mutual eye-opener! I launched right into my infatuation with the cute blond I was seeing and the happiness I felt that Patrick and I shared another bond in our friendship.

We continued to visit between Daytona Beach and Key Largo except now we went to gay bars, at least in Daytona. Patrick almost got asked to leave the Hollywood bar when he laughed uproariously at the first drag show he had ever seen. You knew those girls were serious, but that night a few of them should have kept their pants on.

Although he had returned to Miami, Patrick continued to lead a quiet gay life, but I let no grass grow under my feet as I embraced my new lifestyle.

Meanwhile, my photography business was not doing well. A friend sent me a job application for an aerospace company in West Palm Beach. I was hired in the photography department, sold my business and house, and moved to Palm Beach County.

The shock of going from being your own boss to working for a very strait-laced national corporation cannot be overstated. I had to endure occasional overt remarks by co-workers, but I ignored them and generally got along very well.

It was about this time that Patrick and I, fed up with lousy relationships and loneliness, began to think about a life together. It had been a wonderful ten-year friendship, and on the July 4th weekend in 1967 we made the commitment as life partners. I remember the moment as yesterday, as we lay down together for the first time. I knew this was the man with whom I would spend the rest of my life.

Although I tried diligently, I was unable to find employment in the photographic field in Miami. Ultimately, Patrick moved to join the Palm Beach County school system and I continued to work at "the rocket factory," as it was affectionately called.

Some of those early years were a test of our stamina. I wasn't happy with my job; Patrick followed the lead of many good teachers, fed up with shifts in educational reform, and left teaching to open his own shop specializing in silk flowers and accessories.

It was also the beginning of the wild 1970s and the chant of love in the air caused more than a little friction in many circles. We had our moments there, we experimented, lived the life, and expanded our senses to the point of seeing the value of our relationship.

Our lives began to stabilize as my job improved and Patrick joined the world of retail. We owned our first home together and began to develop mutual interests that would bring much happiness in their pursuit.

Travel and collecting became passions we embraced fervently. The combination of those two hobbies bonded us even closer—particularly trying to bring back half the Orient in carry-on luggage. We ultimately have covered much of the earth from the Pacific Rim to Africa and most exotic cultures between. Also, through antique shows and craft fairs, our house is filled with wonderful memories: tribal masks to cocktail shakers, stoneware to bronze dragons— with a few tributes to Adonis thrown in.

We lived in Jupiter, Florida for the next twenty-five years. Patrick would go on to join the world's most prestigious jeweler and I would stay with the rocket factory, producing film and video programs for our corporate giant.

Probably one of our most trying times came as we had just sold our house and were making plans to build. I embarked on an extended assignment, taking me to South America for long periods of time. Patrick was left to pack up, deal with his father's death, move in with a friend, supervise the new home construction and, oh yes, work.

The stress of separation, living in limbo, problems with the new house, and not being able to really share any of this was a real test of our tenacity.

We survived that ordeal, but it wasn't until we retired and put that house on the market that we actually realized how successful our lives together had become. We lived in a small community, and families from every walk of life came to us expressing their regret at our leaving. It is wonderfully rewarding to know you have lived your life to the best of your ability, becoming a contributing member of society—and that people actually noticed.

Although we both took early retirement and moved to Key West in December 1992, then north to the other end of the state—St. Augustine—in September 1998, some of those same neighbors keep in touch and stop by. In these resort cities of diverse lifestyles, we've lived and loved as always, respecting and trusting each other. Jealousy has no place in our lives. No matter how great the disagreement, we never retire at night in anger. We try to be grateful for all we have, not regretting what we don't, ever working together.

Does anyone ever reach nirvana? Life is too great and challenging to settle on any plateau. That's the knowledge we've acquired — our final K. At age sixty-three (me) and fifty-nine (Patrick), we happily advise younger couples: "Keep on adding notes to your melody and don't look back."

St. Augustine, Florida

A Long Road for Soul Mates

Walter van Nus with David Cassidy

Some long-term relationships not only endure, but also *begin*, because of spiritual affinity rather than sexual excitement. One might even argue that if high erotic expectations are absent from the outset, one later avoids the difficult transition, often a failure, to an open relationship and platonic affection. Such, in any case, is my tentative conclusion after twenty-three years of life with David. At its outset, of course, this understanding lay far in the future.

David's life began in Orillia, Ontario, but he spent much of his childhood in the port city of Kingston, in the same province. Here, where Lake Ontario narrows into the St. Lawrence River, a Royal Navy base helped defend Upper Canada against American invasion during the War of 1812. Kingston's first member of parliament, after the Dominion of Canada was established in 1867, was the country's first prime minister, Sir John A. Macdonald, who is buried there. These associations helped provoke David's interest in Canadian history, which in the early 1970s he would study at the University of Toronto.

I was born in Holland, only six months after David's debut. Postwar Holland seemed to offer few opportunities for my father, who—like many Dutch people—had formed an attachment to Canada when Canadian troops liberated the Netherlands from Nazi rule in 1945. And so, when I was a four-year-old blond moppet, the family emigrated to Canada. Settling in the small town of Arnprior (just north of Ottawa), we found few Dutch-speaking friends, and the pressure to assimilate was intense. Since my first language—both spoken and read—was Dutch (my mother, a teacher, saw to that), I felt isolated in my kindergarten class, and I suspect that my shyness and preference for books and music to people stem partly from that experience. But so does my interest in Canadian history.

My parents could not explain Canadian traditions; very well, *I* would master the history of Canada and understand the place better than most with long pedigrees. Thus, in the early 1970s, I too would be studying Canadian history at the University of Toronto.

Coming out in the mid-1970s was easier for David than for me, but it was easier for both of us than for the preceding generation of gay Canadians, because of crucial amendments made in 1969 to the Criminal Code of Canada. In the United States, where criminal law falls under state jurisdiction, the campaign against "sodomy laws" has been localized and lengthy. Indeed, in some states, it has still not succeeded. In Canada, the federal parliament has this power. In the United States, the president and the state governors do not dictate to the legislative branch, whereas in Canada, the prime minister and his cabinet are the leading members of the majority party in the House of Commons, and caucus discipline is much stronger. And so, in 1969, when the prime minister determined to remove the state from the bedrooms of the nation, as he put it, it was done quickly, and on a nationwide basis. Pierre Trudeau's government amended the Criminal Code to permit gay sex between two consenting adults in private. This reform encouraged gay organizations to become more visible, and to publicize more openly such services as counseling by telephone and drop-in centers. The Community Homophile Association of Toronto (C.H.A.T.) was formed in 1973 to do both sorts of good works, and advertised them by such practical means as posters on downtown utility poles. It was C.H.A.T. that allowed me to meet David.

David is a born organizer. At the age of twelve, he set up a Community Puppet and Kids Show in Kingston. During his high school days, he got so involved in extracurricular activities that he had to repeat his senior year (which, in Ontario, was grade thirteen), whereupon he organized other such students into a "Grade Fourteen Club!" At the university, the scope of his activities was widened to include the student newspaper and the college rowing team. He joined C.H.A.T. in 1974, and quickly became its treasurer. In particular, the job meant managing the funds collected at C.H.A.T.'s Saturday-night dances.

Whether born or made so, I'm a recluse. While David danced up a storm at C.H.A.T. on Saturday nights, I would be alone in my rooms at Massey College, a graduate (and not yet coed) residence at the University of Toronto, only a few blocks west of the gayest streets in town. Massey College fostered a cloistered life deliberately, even through its architecture: the Resident Junior Fellows' rooms all faced an interior courtyard. Underneath our genteel corporate appearance (complete with academic gowns worn to dinner), there operated several homoerotic cliques to whose true nature I remained oblivious, recognizing assorted advances only in hindsight. Instead of responding to these chances, I became increasingly depressed, without knowing why. Still, I had splendid friends there, who shared my passion for classical records and for croquet. My fellowship expired in the summer of 1974, and I had to move to my own apartment off campus. Lonelier now, I had to face facts. I remember the day the light dawned: I was walking along St. Mary Street, which runs east from the University to Yonge Street and its record stores. The same poster kept appearing on one utility pole after another alongside me. I don't remember the exact words. "Gay and Afraid? You Are Not Alone!" or something similar. Below the slogan appeared the C.H.A.T. distress-line number; I surreptitiously copied it down. That evening, I finally dialed the number, and was lucky to speak to George Hislop, the founder of C.H.A.T., who calmed me down, and suggested that instead of facing the sexual pressures of a gay bar, I attend the next drop-in at the C.H.A.T. premises on Church Street. This I did, and was taken home by an attractive musician named Robert. Rob (still a good friend) soon gathered that I was too frightened for sex, and patiently tucked me in. He decided I needed to learn to relax with openly gay men, and on Sunday morning invited some friends to join us for brunch. Among the crew was an effervescent imp, with big expressive eyes and a melting smile, named David Cassidy. But a stout and catty queen dominated the conversation, and I learned nothing about David. I returned to C.H.A.T. the next Saturday. David was there, dutifully supervising the cash flow in between bouts of dancing on the second floor. Recognizing me as I sat shyly by myself, he took me by the hand and led me downstairs, where we sat on the stoop (in full view of St. Michael's Cathedral!) and talked for the first time. Our common interest in history at once came to the fore.

I marveled at his capacity for reaching out to people, from which I've benefited ever since.

After the dance ended, we went to his tiny apartment on Maitland Avenue, and spent the night in a bed just big enough for David alone (provided he didn't turn around much). For this and other reasons, we slept little. So began a lifelong relationship, but at the time, neither of us thought so. David, being more experienced, assumed I was another neophyte who badly needed an understanding friend now, but who would soon be experimenting with one man after another. I liked David enormously but didn't appreciate his "faggier" friends (still don't, I confess). More important, the cuddling couldn't substitute for the sexual joy I longed for, and had never found.

About two months later, David took me to Metropolitan Community Church, and at the social following the service, I met the third corner of the triangle, Michael. Like David, Michael excelled at taking the initiative socially and sexually, but the resemblance ended there. David was dark-haired, short, and slender; Michael had sandy-colored hair, and stood a husky six feet tall. David liked oral sex; Michael focused exclusively on the anal approach. That night, I learned in Michael's bed that I did, too.

In the autumn of 1974 and the winter of 1975, my passionate liaison with Michael continued. Meanwhile, David had found someone who shared his sexual tastes: Raymond. During these months, I thought the uncertainties had ended. I still saw David socially, but had a hot lover of my own. My morale in the clouds, I was completing my PhD thesis quickly. Michael, who hailed from Edmonton and wanted to return there, suggested that I apply for a sessional lectureship at the University of Alberta. The university surprised me by accepting. So there we were: I would move to Edmonton in August, where Michael and I would soon live together, while David and Ray settled down in Toronto. Then, one winter's evening, I met David only to find him as he had never seemed before: solemn and tense. As we parted, he handed me a sealed envelope, and asked me to read it carefully after his departure. I read his profession of love, and was torn apart. I cared for him as I'd never done for a friend before, but I cared about Michael, too, and Michael fulfilled me erotically in a way that left David cold. I told

David that we were sexually incompatible and could only be friends. Besides, I would soon be leaving for Edmonton. I still saw him after that, but felt a cold sadness as my departure approached.

Meanwhile, my fantasy of a home life in Edmonton with Michael was fading. He ran his own successful business in Toronto, and as August neared he became vaguer about his commitment to move west. I discovered that he slept around, and had a fondness for underage adolescents. And what—besides sex—had we in common? We both loved 1930s musicals and late Romantic orchestral works. But he knew little of history or politics. And then there was the difference in height. With David, I felt comfortable walking side by-side; with Michael, I felt like a kid brother. More seriously, the kid brother role was one Michael wanted his lovers to play. He would bring one out of the closet, introduce one to gay literature and organizations, and expect to be idolized for it. Since I was two years older than he, and had achieved far more educationally, this scenario was doomed to failure. As I flew to Edmonton in mid-August, I believed that both Michael and David would soon be only memories.

At the University of Alberta that September, I busied myself having my thesis professionally typed, and writing a set of lectures. Late that month, David called to announce that he would take the train west to visit relatives in Saskatchewan, and proceed from there to Edmonton in time for my birthday on October 5. Neither of us knew that Michael had decided to surprise me by arriving unannounced for the same event. (Lacking self-confidence, I underestimated Michael's genuine affection.) Two days before my birthday, I welcomed David to my apartment. When we slept together, I felt contented and complete. On October 5, Michael arrived, and the atmosphere soured. That night, Michael shared my bed, and David was demoted to a sleeping bag in the living room, where he cried and finally drugged himself to sleep. I had to take action: another night like the last one and David might drug himself to oblivion. Yes, David and I were sexually mismatched, but he had traveled all this way to reaffirm his love. As for me, I now knew that I would never find peace without him. I chose to live with my soul mate.

The decision in principle was made, but much remained to be decided. Having given up high school teaching in disgust, David had become night manager of a photo-finishing firm. He quickly came to hate that, too, and now relied on unemployment insurance benefits. But to keep those checks coming, he had to return to Toronto. My appointment at the University of Alberta would expire in May. Both of us disliked Edmonton as gay-unfriendly, but no university posts were available in Toronto. In November, the answer came from the chairman of the History Department at Concordia University in Montreal, who invited me to apply for a tenure-line position there. (The senior member of my thesis defense committee had just evaluated the department and had extolled my merits.) Think of it: cosmopolitan Montreal!

My day-long interview took place on December 5, and that evening I flew to Toronto to spend the Christmas break with David. I left David's number with Concordia so that the verdict would come quickly. In the meantime, however, the national director of the Progressive-Conservative Party had offered David a job at the party's Ottawa headquarters, a post that could have led, in time, to a senior position and considerable influence. David was prepared to sacrifice this chance, and instead move to Montreal, where no job awaited him. In mid-December, as we watched *Another World* (of which David and his sister were rabid partisans), the good news came from Montreal. We danced around the room.

On May Day, 1976, David and I flew to Montreal, and have lived here together since. Despite the unease created by Quebec separatists, we've flourished in one of the world's most multicultural and tolerant cities. But in doing so, we both left behind families who lived in the Toronto region. David had come out to his parents before we left. As traditional Catholics, they found the topic distasteful. Yet they love David very much; he had always been such a sunny, helpful child. They acquiesced to his demand that we share the same bedroom while visiting, yet still call me "David's friend." Both of his parents share an impish sense of humor, which helps lighten our occasional visits to their apartment. David's brother and sister are more relaxed about the subject of sex, and his grown nieces and nephew exhibit the far more gay-positive approach of many their age. As for my parents, my father had left my mother before I came out, and my relationship with him withered thereafter. My late mother, always a freethinker, had little difficulty in accepting us, and her beautiful tapestries on our walls attest to her eventual warm support. My four siblings also came through for us, except one brother who became a fundamentalist Christian preacher. Oh, well, there's one in every family tree, I suppose.

Since 1976, both our careers have been Montreal-oriented. David soon found his true calling through another outburst of volunteer work, this time for Ville Marie Social Service Centre. As usual, he made himself indispensable and in 1977 was hired full-time. Later, he would add a Master of Social Work to his history and education degrees and become a social worker in pay scale as well as in practice. In 1985, he organized the first Canadian National AIDS Conference, held in Montreal, and then co-edited Canada's first anthology on the subject. He has since organized local HIV-positive and PWA support groups and published many articles in professional social-work journals on such topics as the impact of clients' deaths on AIDS support workers. He also encouraged gay social life in Montreal through a gay fraternity and a gay couples club. As for me, I was already expert in the history of Canadian urban planning before moving to Montreal. I soon fell in love with the history of Montreal and its older suburbs, developed lecture and seminar courses on the subject, and published papers in that field. We are both deeply rooted now in our adopted city.

But most of our friends aren't interested in our professional lives. They want to know how, in a subculture noted for brief relationships, we're still happy together after almost a quarter century. At first glance, we indeed do not seem suited. Most startling to outsiders is our sexual incompatibility. As well, David is an activist, whereas I'm an observer of life. He networks like crazy and, even when home alone, keeps busy counseling by phone. While something of a dynamo in the classroom, I really prefer solitude much of the time. And I couldn't network if my life depended on it. (I'm tenured, so it doesn't.) I cultivate a few friends with whom I share interests; David spends time with all sorts. Moreover, while I am (some would say, *icily*) calm, David is moody, even mercurial. His duties as a social worker now consist mainly of arranging for the care of elderly people who can't manage anymore. Like other provinces and states scrambling to balance budgets, Quebec has cut social service spending, and the frustrations of his job often leave

David (who is also an antipoverty activist) grumpily impatient by the time he gets home. As a university professor, I have more autonomy and choose the timing and sort of work I do to an extent rare among the salaried. The historian's role reinforces my cool detachment, and I dislike emotional outbursts. Our friends observe these differences and ask how we can live together at all.

In the first place, while our professional lives rarely coincide, we enjoy many common interests. Among other things, we both follow politics keenly, read about history, study the varieties of religious belief, and love live theater, PBS, summer evening walks, and trips to New York. In addition, we share friends. David has introduced me to some wonderful people suffering from AIDS. Thus, while I've not known most of the 300 PWAs whose deaths David has had to endure, we have both known some of them. In particular, we adored Dan Rice, an ebullient Native man with one of the sharpest wits and most selfless souls we've met. When I remember Dan, I can more easily identify with David as he recovers from the death of yet another friend. And, of course, we also have in common close friendships with quite healthy gay men and women, not to mention some terrific gay-positive straight people, who make both of us part of a familiar cluster.

In the second place, differences can be complementary as much as divisive. Yes, I dislike his grumpiness after a day's work, but my calm patience helps cool him down. Yes, I do think his penchant for taking initiatives has nearly led to burnout, but his initiative also spurred us to buy a home before house prices took off in the 1980s, and to improve it in all sorts of ways. If he's apt to launch household projects, I'm good at the detail work that brings successful completion. As for sex, we recognized the fact of our different tastes at the outset, and made our relationship open from the beginning. We have seen many relationships end when the initial passion fades. Our initial entente obviated the need for a later and painful transition to a more platonic union.

As well, neither tries to remake the other in his own image. David finds it hard to understand how I can remain aloof from the world's immediately pressing problems, and I don't think it makes sense to commit oneself to so many projects that nothing is done as *well* as possible. But I wave him off cheerfully to his next meeting, and he leaves me curled up with my book. Even our house was chosen to allow each of us (literally) enough space. It's a two-story Arts and Crafts "cottage" (as Montrealers still call them) dating from 1928. The finished basement serves as David's headquarters, and my den occupies the largest bedroom on the second floor. This way, the ground floor separates our activities. He can play his disco music while I listen to Shostakovitch; he can counsel a client while I prepare a lecture. Much autonomy alternating with shared pursuits: that's what works for us.

But one cannot dissect and analyze all the ways a relationship becomes a lifelong solace for both partners. Why is hugging David so wonderful? Why do I like to watch him sleep? How does he make me double up with laughter? When two souls interlock, an island of contentment forms which lies beyond the realm of reason.

Montreal, Quebec, Canada

The Rise from Rascals

Al and Lew Griffen-O'Connell

LIFE IN THE HOLLYWOOD HILLS

by Lew O'Connell

I, Lewison Burns O'Connell, was born May 25, 1937, the only child of Joyce Ivy Burns O'Connell and Lewis William O'Connell, in a Christian Science Birthing Center in Pasadena, California. Joyce was a Busby Berkeley dancing girl and a direct descendant of the poet Robert Burns. Lewis (known as Connie) was a cinematographer in the movie industry, working with directors Howard Hawks and Cecil B. DeMille. The old saying about being born with a silver spoon in my mouth doesn't apply. I was born with a silver service for *eight* in my mouth. During my first few years of life, I lived in the luxury of Beverly Hills, California, with nurses caring for me and many internationally known entertainment personalities fawning over me and showering me with lavish gifts. As I struggled through school years, it was difficult for anyone to control what one teacher termed "this frisky young man." I was transferred through all of the best schools on the West Coast until finally I managed to graduate from high school. I then tried college and, when that didn't work out, I joined the naval reserves. During this period, I was experimenting sexually with male friends in college and the Navy. Ultimately, societal pressures forced me to marry. It was certainly a marriage of convenience—and to satisfy "Mother." From this marriage there were two abortions and finally the birth of a daughter (with whom I continue to have a comfortable relationship, though she has her own family in California).

It was no surprise that during this ill-fated marriage, I was continuing my escapades with many male sexual partners. Eventually, my wife and I divorced, freeing me to find a male lover and settle down in the bedroom community of Studio City in the San Fernando Valley. My first love interest (which lasted for eleven years) was with the film librarian for Metro-Goldwyn-Mayer studios—a fellow named Tom. As that relationship ended in 1974, I flitted about West Hollywood, into one affair after another—none of which lasted more than a few months. During this time I was employed at Disney and Universal Studios as a sound editor, working on numerous successful TV series such as *The Bionic Man* (starring Lee Majors) and *Baa Baa Black Sheep* (starring Robert Conrad). My lifestyle during this period included regular Hollywood Hills gay gatherings of many famous and less-than-famous legends of screen, stage, and television. During the Mother's Day weekend of May 8, 1977, I spent the first part with a male flight attendant in Long Beach and then did the obligatory Mother's Day brunch with my parents at the Beverly Hills Hilton. After dropping them off at their home, I ventured over the hill to West Hollywood to the popular Santa Monica Boulevard gay bar Rascals. It was there that I met Al Griffen.

LIFE AS A CHARLESTON HUSTLER

by Al Griffen

I, Alton Dannie Griffen, was born on November 2, 1947 in Charleston, South Carolina, the first son and third child to Mary Cherry Griffen and Dannie Elmo Griffen. Mary was the typical school lunchroom worker and Dannie was a boilermaker laborer at the naval shipyard. My childhood, growing up in the low-country farm region called Ferndale—a rough-and-tumble area—was not an easy one. Working before and after school each day, I did find happiness each weekend with my father—either in the surrounding woods, hunting, or in the swamps and streams, fishing. My times spent with my father were my happiest as we shared many hours and my father taught me all the *manly* things. My school years were remarkable: I was an excellent learner and constantly brought home high marks and honors. My high school years were spent at a special preparatory school in downtown Charleston (this was provided through an expense-paid tutorial program by the school board) and it was there, at the early age of thirteen, I first experienced hustling. My male classmates taught me how to cruise the Battery, the waterfront park at the tip of Historic Charleston, getting picked up by wealthy older gentlemen and being paid for sexual favors. The old saying "today's trade, tomorrow's competition," must have been written with me in mind. My experiences in high school led me to an opportunity as a bellhop at one of the exclusive downtown hotels. It was there that I plied my trade as a hustler and— due to the restrictive liquor laws of the area—also bootlegging liquor for the local Mafia. This led to the opportunity to become a young bartender at Charleston's only transvestite-hooker bar, in the historic Slave Market area. There I oversaw the comings and goings of many a drunk sailor paying to get his rocks off before heading back to the base. It was also while there that I first experienced man-to-man sex as a willing participant, instead of as a bought commodity. Still, saving my earnings from all these escapades, I had enough to go off to college at the University of Houston. There I met my first true love, a giant of a man, thirty years my senior. That rocky relationship continued for almost four years until I finished college and returned to South Carolina (with the elder lover heading off to Saudi Arabia on a two-year work contract). During my years as Director for Special Education for a small-town school district in South Carolina, I received a grant to study at the University of Lund in Sweden. There I continued my studies, attaining my doctorate in behavioral psychology—appropriately enough. Here was this young kid from a small backwoods upbringing, studying and traveling through Europe at the tender age of nineteen.

When I returned to the States, I set out for California, a big step for such a young man. Upon arriving in Los Angeles, I first went to a gay bar on Santa Monica Boulevard. The first night there, I met a beautiful blue-eyed, blond-haired Mexican named Gordon. Gordon befriended me and took me home to his apartment in the Hollywood Hills. Gordon and I had a stormy three years together as I tried to mature in an abusive relationship—and also tried to kick-start my professional career. My job at the Los Angeles Area Chamber of Commerce exposed me to many international business and government leaders, some of whom offered me many favors. In January

1977, I finally had enough courage to leave Gordon and strike out on my own. By this time, I had become a senior consultant with one of the leading management and financial firms in Los Angeles. I found an apartment on top of a tall building above Santa Monica Boulevard, with a 180-degree view of the Los Angeles Basin and downtown. This apartment was only three blocks from the popular gay bar Rascals, so I became a regular.

On Mother's Day—May 8, 1977—I drove my best friend in my first-ever new car to the downtown MCC church. On our way back to West Hollywood, my brand-new car was broadsided by a non-English-speaking, nine-months-pregnant illegal alien from Mexico. Heartsick and depressed, I went to Rascals to drown my sorrow, and while there saw Lew O'Connell for the first time. I made it a point to place myself beside Lew wherever he went in the bar. Gay bars still intimidated me at that time; I usually hid in dark corners and was always shy about striking up a conversation. My cruise method was to always let the other guy speak first. And so for two and a half hours, I followed Lew around the bar until Lew finally spoke to me. We talked for a while and I invited him to dinner. Lew accepted and that was the start of our twenty-year relationship!

LIFE EVER SINCE

by Al and Lew Griffen-O'Connell

Al was standing in the corner of Rascals, a popular neighborhood West Hollywood cruise bar, when he saw Lew walk through the door. Al noticed Lew because he was drop-dead gorgeous, wearing a red-and-black-plaid lumberjack shirt, worn jeans, and boots. His long, flowing blond hair and dark beard made him a striking and imposing figure. Al told his best friend, Beattie: "That is going to be mine." Beattie laughed and warned Al that Lew looked like trouble. Al couldn't bring himself to strike up a conversation with Lew, but the first time he saw Lew smile, he glimpsed a tender and affectionate side that made Al want him even more. Al's style when in situations like this was to place himself next to the person he was admiring, hoping the other man would be the first to strike up a conversation. In this case, Al followed Lew around the bar for more than two and a half hours. Finally, as they were standing by one of the exit doors, Al turned toward Lew and looked out the window of the door. Lew looked at Al and said, "Is it still raining?" Al replied that it was and on such stunning repartee are lifetime relationships founded. They began conversing, exchanging information about themselves. After half an hour more, Al asked Lew if he would like to join him for dinner. Lew told Al that he had had a rough weekend and wasn't interested in sex. Al countered: "I didn't say, 'Do you want to fuck?'; I just asked you if you would like to have dinner with me." This candor intrigued Lew, so he accepted Al's invitation.

They left the bar and walked down Santa Monica Boulevard to a little restaurant named Theodore's. They sat for two hours eating and talking. After dinner they walked back to Al's apartment where they had wine and continued their conversation. Lew made a sexual advance and Al just melted. They wound up in bed that evening. The next morning as Al was preparing to leave for work, he placed a house key and a five-dollar bill on his desk. He went into the bedroom, woke Lew gently, and told him he was leaving for work and would like Lew to be there when he returned that afternoon. When Al returned home, Lew was there cooking dinner. They went to the gym where Al worked out, and afterward returned to Al's apartment. This arrangement went on for two weeks and finally one evening at dinner, Lew pulled a cloth pouch from his pocket and took out two gold bands exactly alike. He placed one ring on Al's finger and the other on his own.

That evening, Al became extremely stoned and unloaded on Lew his beliefs about what would make a happy union. He told Lew that he would never be a one-man man. He had to have his freedom to be with other men. Lew, cautious, agreed that theirs need not be a monogamous relationship. During the next three months, Al and Lew lived together in Al's apartment, and Lew slowly educated Al to *his* lifestyle. Lew owned his own home in the San Fernando Valley and worked at Universal Studios. Lew convinced Al to give up his apartment and move into Lew's house in the Valley. Al bought Lew's mortgage and became half-owner in the house.

Lew's occupation allowed him the freedom of not being in the closet at work; on the other hand, Al's profession demanded that their relationship remain secret. Eventually, Al went to work for Howard Hughes's Summa Corporation as director of industrial engineering. During his years at Hughes, Al had to live a double life, never letting anyone at work know about his home situation. During this time Al and Lew remodeled the Valley home and created a hedonistic paradise behind the four walls of their love nest. Eventually, Al changed jobs and worked for a medical-products manufacturing giant, Puritan Bennett. But here, too, Al had to keep his private life a secret.

During these years Al and Lew struggled with their choice not to be monogamous. At times there were some close calls as they accepted each other having sexual encounters with other men. They also played around with other couples and an occasional three-way. In 1979, one day while at work, Al suffered a heart attack and was rushed to the hospital. Lew was listed on Al's personnel records as the person to contact in case of an emergency, so he was notified of Al's condition. Lew rushed to the hospital and for the next few weeks stayed by Al's side as he recovered. During this time they made several momentous decisions to alter the course of their lives: not only would their future relationship become monogamous, they would also both leave their West Coast jobs, sell their Valley love nest, and move to the property they had purchased on a lake in South Carolina.

To backtrack for a moment: During these two years, Al and Lew and Lew's parents had traveled to South Carolina several times to visit Al's family, which included two married sisters. Al's family and Lew's parents hit it off and they all became one big happy family. In this respect, Al and Lew were lucky to have such loving support from both sides. It was during one of these visits that Al and Lew had purchased the lakefront property with the thought that it would be a good vacation getaway and potential retirement spot.

Now, back to where we left off: Lew convinced Al that they should move back to South Carolina. Lounging in their Jacuzzi, after work, Al tried to explain to Lew the hazards of living in such a conservative area, and that being near an extended family could prove tedious. Lew would have none of Al's warnings. So they sold their home in Los Angeles and moved to Pinopolis, South Carolina, a small pine-land village with a population of about 400. Charleston was over thirty miles away. When they moved, they also took Lew's aging parents with them. During the next six years, Al and Lew remodeled their lakefront home while Lew's parents lived in a double-width mobile home next door. Al's family took care of Lew's parents when Lew and Al traveled. The two families grew very close.

Following these good years, Al's parents died, and in 1983 and 1985 Lew's father and mother also passed away. Lew's only family at this point was his daughter, whose San Francisco wedding provided a unique note: Lew's ex-wife chose to stay in the background, relinquishing her mother of the bride role to Al, who was thus seated in that traditional chair and appears (in her stead) in the wedding photos. Life in South Carolina did indeed prove to be very tedious. The neighbors refused to accept them; the only redeeming value that Lew and Al had was that "they are such good boys to take care of their aging parents like they do." It was frustrating to Al to try and be a part of the community only to be shunned by everyone. It also was humorous, in that the men who shunned them in public often sidled around in private trying to have sex with Lew and Al. But that was the way most of the men were there: publicly straight, but privately longing for sex with other men. Al was also beginning to feel smothered by his family. There were very few days that he wasn't faced with some sibling crisis no matter how little or how big. Although Lew had looked forward eagerly to sharing Al's siblings and nieces and nephews, having them underfoot, unannounced, and laden with problems ultimately palled.

It was in 1985 that they heard about Key West, Florida. They took a two-week trip to Key West and fell in love with the area. They made the decision to move there, and to further commit to a new life together, they decided to merge surnames. They found a lovely open-water lot with a sunset view on an island called Lower Sugarloaf, where the community of Sugarloaf Shores had become established. They bought the lot and signed a contract with a builder to have the home of their design built. Over the next year, Lew worked at the Casa Marina Hotel as a gardener, while also overseeing the construction of the house. Al stayed in South Carolina trying to sell their home there. They saw each other for one week a month during that year; Al would go down to Key West to take care of matters regarding the construction. Problems with the contractor led Al and Lew to fire him with only the shell of the house constructed. At this time, part of their five acres on the lake in South Carolina was sold, so Al closed up their house and moved to Sugarloaf. There Al and Lew finished the house by themselves. During the period from 1986 through 1989, they did nothing but work on the house, landscaping the yard, putting in a swimming pool, dock, and boat ramp. Also during this time, they became active members of the Sugarloaf Shores Property Owners Association (SSPOA). They were accepted in the community without reservation.

It was here that Al became politically active, first being elected to the board of the SSPOA and eventually serving two years as president. During this time, all elected officials in Monroe County knew that to win the Sugarloaf precinct, they would have to win Al Griffen first. Al and Lew held fund-raisers in their home for political hopefuls that they supported. The first year, two county commissioners, the sheriff, the superintendent of schools, and other political officeholders sought the public support of Al and Lew.

At one point in 1989, the little contract station post office in Sugarloaf was going to be shut down. Al and Lew launched an effort to keep it open and their efforts paid off—but *they* had to operate the station. So they worked six days a week at the little post office. It was there that everyone came to really know Al and Lew and likewise Lew and Al came to know everything about everyone who lived on the island. During this period, Al and Lew became active in many civic, social, and charitable organizations. Al kept operating the post office until March of 1997, hiring local islanders to work there for him.

In 1993, Al was hired by the Monroe County Sheriff's Office to develop a video production unit. It was Al's years producing his own political talk show on the local cable channel that led the sheriff to offer him this position. The sheriff had one caveat, though: if Al was to take on the position, he would have to give up his TV program and cut back on being so politically visible. Al, excited at the prospect of the new opportunity, agreed to the sheriff's request. So Al, an openly gay prominent political person, became a special deputy with the Monroe County Sheriff's Office.

During the years since Al started that job, other deputies, male and female, have felt comfortable enough to come out of the closet. The sheriff relied on Al as the liaison with the gay community, even to the extent of having Al organize his campaign in 1996—a campaign that saw the sheriff overwhelmingly reelected by a 70-to-30 percent margin. The sheriff also won every precinct that was predominantly gay. This was some feat, since the local Gay Lambda Democrat Club supported the opposition to the sheriff.

Lew and Al have since sold their open-water property and have purchased a house that was built in 1968; they are currently remodeling it. Al continues his work with the sheriff's department and has been assigned to the prestigious HIDTA (High Intensity Drug Trafficking Area) Task Force, which is a program under Attorney General Janet Reno's supervision. Al works successfully with the agents from the FBI, DEA, Customs, and ATF—all as an openly gay male. Al's current project is convincing the Monroe County Commission to adopt a domestic partnership ordinance and a human rights ordinance. At present it looks as if these will be accomplished with the unanimous support of the county commission, and Al expects both to be in place by the time this account sees print. Lew is now landscaper at the prestigious Little Palm Island resort.

Al and Lew have forged a life together from broadly different backgrounds—a life that has encompassed successful accomplishments, socially, politically, and professionally. They continue to work and play together in Monroe County and considered themselves extremely fortunate to have opportunities to make a difference. All this from that meeting at Rascals.

Sugarloaf Shores, Florida

A Bond Strengthened by Grief

David Withers with Ron Dinkins

I've often thought of putting our story down on paper and wish that I had kept a diary over the years because I think our tale is one worth telling. My partner, Ron, and I have been together for sixteen years. We live in Cayce, South Carolina, which is a suburb of the capital city, Columbia.

Like most gay couples, we have had a lot to overcome and deal with in our relationship. At the time we met, I was just coming to grips with admitting I was a gay man trapped within an eight-year marriage. Ron was also trying to come to terms with *his* sexuality. We met on Senate Street—a place here in town where homosexuals cruise late at night. It was that longing for something that neither one of us had experienced at that point in our lives that brought us together. We both wanted more than sex, we wanted a relationship.

We moved in together within a month of meeting—probably for all the wrong reasons. I was very hesitant at first. I had only been out of the relationship with my wife for one short month, so I was still dealing with that. As much as I wanted a man in my life, I didn't know if I was ready yet to commit to anyone else so soon. Then there was the age difference: Ron is nine years younger than I. And then there was the big issue (in my mind) that I was the first man he had ever been with. I didn't think that we had a chance to make it together long-term, but I knew that I would enjoy it while it lasted and decided it was worth the gamble.

Since that chance meeting on Senate Street sixteen years ago, something wonderful has happened. We have fallen in love and remained together, growing deeper in love as time has gone by. It might have been lust that brought us together, but it is love that keeps us together.

As with any other relationship, we have had our troubles and heartaches. It has not always been easy, but it has always been something that we both wanted and were willing to work at and fight to keep alive.

Over these past sixteen years together, we have had to deal with such issues as maturing together. We have had to step in and help raise Ron's much younger brother while his family was going through difficult times. That meant adding a child to our relationship within the first two years. Then there were the growing pains when my earliest fears were met and Ron felt the need to experience the company of another man. We lived apart for only a month but it took time to rebuild the relationship. It was a difficult time for both of us.

Later in our relationship, our first home was destroyed by Hurricane Hugo—while we were in it! That was an emotional time that has left us changed forever. Though our home was torn apart by the forces of nature, our relationship grew stronger through it all. Shortly after rebuilding our home, my father passed away suddenly. Ron was right there by my side through it all. My parents loved Ron like their own, and my mother was comforted by his presence as much as I was. Because my mother was handicapped, we purchased a house across the street from her and moved to be near her so we could help her. We had only been there about a year when she became ill with cancer and died. It was the most difficult time of my life. I don't think I could have made it through without Ron. He was there every day at the hospital with me, right by her side. During this two-year period, I also lost all but one of my biological aunts and uncles and my one remaining dearly beloved grandmother. Without my relationship with Ron, I would have felt I truly had nothing left in life.

If fate had not given us enough trials to endure, it gave us AIDS to deal with as well—*both* of us. Ironically, I feared telling my family because I didn't want them to worry and have to deal with my illness. Little did I know then that I would outlive them all and have to bury each one of them. This illness has once again done something I thought impossible. It has brought Ron and me even closer. Through it all we have been there for each other and we know that we always will be no matter what the future holds.

I've told you about the hard times. We've experienced much joy and happiness as well. We have wonderful friends who love and support us as does Ron's family. I too have a cousin who has been like a sister to me. She and her family now live in my parents' house across the street with their three-year-old and nine-year-old. Both children call us Uncle Dave and Uncle Ron. We are blessed to have them in our lives. While we are both "retired" at this point (I as local postmaster), we stay involved in our community, both the gay and straight. It is important to both of us to give something back.

I would like for the world to know how happy I am to be in this wonderful loving relationship; we both feel God had a part in bringing us together and helping us stay together.

Cayce, South Carolina

*   *   *

Editors' note: A phone check just before this account went to our publisher was answered by the family member the author speaks of so fondly above. She revealed that both David and Ron had been hospitalized, and that Ron remained in critical condition. Courageously, they again authorized publication of this account, and we include it as a tribute to a union that endured exceptional adversity.

As this book goes to press, a note from Withers confirms the tragic story: Ron Dinkins suffered an aneurysm while he and David were vacationing in DC in September 1997 and died of complications following surgery. "My life has been turned upside-down," David writes, "and I've had a hard time getting anything done."

Opposites Attract:
Enduring Clashes in Personality, Generation, and Culture

Cheh Cho with Jack La Wren

If asked, twenty-some-odd years ago, if I'd ever thought I would live through a long-term relationship, I probably would have adamantly denied that possibility. I still haven't fully realized that I have, in fact, been in just such a relationship for a little more than seventeen years now. Our relationship had several strikes against it, even before it ever started. There are not only language difference, a major age difference, and religious differences—all of these are compounded with cultural differences and a pronounced difference in social backgrounds. If we believe the old adage that "opposites attract," then an example of just what this means can readily be seen in the relationship that has developed between Jack and myself. We did, of course, have a few similarities between us: we were both males, we both prefer to sleep with men, we are both considered relatively intelligent, we are both native-born Quebecois, and we are both bilingual. Between the two of us, our travel miles could probably circle the globe a few times around. There is relatively little in the way of compatibility between us, yet somehow our relationship has survived some tumultuous clashes.

Although we were in very different careers when our relationship started, they have by now become very similar. Example: we have both (at different times and in different places) been teachers. I started teaching high school and progressed through private college up to graduate university level. I still teach at that level and am presently completing the requirements for my PhD to gain access to a tenure-track teaching position at the university. Jack taught at the undergraduate university level, but no longer teaches because he didn't really enjoy that environment. From a different angle, both of us are working within the social services sector but where I am a clinical social worker and educator, Jack is involved, almost exclusively, in social service administration and social policymaking.

As with most couples (gay or straight), we had to go through the process of discovering and comparing each other's abilities, capacities, and limitations in relation to the various tasks that each of us would adopt within this relationship. We both cook pretty well, so that daily decision is based more on who's available to do it on any given night. Although Jack is bigger physically and, in my opinion, is more intimidating than myself, I'm the one who defends our property and confronts the neighbors when necessary. Jack gives in much too easily, whereas I cannot be swayed no matter what excuse may be presented. Coming from an "off-the-streets" background, and being one of thirteen children, I am, without a doubt, much more aggressive than Jack could ever be. We take advantage of what each of us has or does best toward making our relationship work. For the most part, our division of labor is based on not only physical attributes but ability, experience, and/or availability—never on traditionally assigned male/female roles.

I was born in the dead of winter, February 1959, as the last of thirteen children: six girls, six boys, and me. It's as if my parents equally distributed genders then finished off with a mix so as not to upset the balance. When I was three years old, my biological father died, leaving my mother and grandmother to fend for a tribe of children. We were placed in foster care shortly thereafter. As a result, I spent most of my early childhood and adolescence going through a series of thirty-something different foster homes. Being in thirty different homes averages out to a new home every two and a half months or so. At the age of nine, I moved into a home where several of my biological siblings were already living. I ended up spending most of my adolescent life there or in close proximity. These foster parents played a critical role in our family since they actually scoured the countryside looking for all of our natural brothers and sisters. The mother was an American Jew and the father was a Welsh Anglican. The five of us children were born to Chinese parents although none of us claimed any affiliation to that cultural community except through appearance. We were brought up in an environment that was based on cultural differences and were each given the choice of which culture and religious upbringing we wanted to follow. Only one of my sisters and myself did *both* a First Communion and a Jewish rite of passage—in my case a Bar Mitzvah. As a result, my natural brothers and sisters are about evenly split between Jews and Anglicans.

Being a ward of the foster care system, I was made aware of the fact that by the time I hit age eighteen I would have to be totally self-sufficient. Instead of going through the academic stream in high school, I was inadvertently pressured into going through the *vocational* stream to ensure that I could get a job upon completion of high school. I received my initial training in professional cooking and spent many years in the restaurant and club business, sometimes working several jobs simultaneously. Somewhere in the back of my mind I always had the notion that I would work for a while – enough to get somewhat secure—and then return to school. From the time I was six years old, I wanted to become a social worker and show those people how to do their jobs properly—obviously a result of having lived through the foster care system.

My personal interests and hobbies are as varied as my work-related experience. I collect stamps, rather informally; I also collect anything "strawberry" (e.g., dishes, refrigerator magnets, candles, whatever); I design and make clothes, on occasion; I enjoy reading fantasy novels (in the same genre as J.R.R. Tolkien's trilogy), though since returning to school I haven't really had the opportunity to do much recreational reading; I like cooking for special occasions (i.e., for a lot of people); I spend a lot of time outdoors puttering in the garden; and I thoroughly enjoy just vegging out and sun-worshipping.

By the time I was twenty years old, I had already had several serious relationships with men, but none lasting for more than a couple of years. The last relationship ended with the discovery of my partner in bed with one of my best friends. Needless to say, a huge fight ensued and that relationship came to an abrupt end. I only mention this because of the profound effect that it would have within our present relationship.

Jack was born during the height of summer (July) in 1933, third of four children in a very French-Canadian family; in my opinion, at least, they are all very Parti Quebecois-oriented. Because I am predominantly Anglophone, only one of his sisters will have anything to do with me. There is some communication with the other members of his family because I am fluent in French and have degrees from two of the French universities here in Quebec. For the most part, though except for Jack's sister Micheline, the only interaction with his family are births, weddings, and funerals (the usual family obligations). Jack and his family being Roman Catholics, our gay relationship is never discussed—or even acknowledged, for that matter. His work environment is the same. They don't need to know and Jack insists that his private life remains exactly that, private.

Jack's career as a social service administrator has allowed him the opportunity to travel to the Orient on a regular basis. In many ways, this satisfies his penchant for Oriental culture—and Oriental men. Like an inordinate number of French-Canadian men, Jack has this "thing" for Asian boys, and I guess I fit the bill. Jack, for a man of sixty-four, is incredibly well preserved. He visits the gym three times a week and is probably in better shape now than when I met him eighteen years ago. Jack's family, from a predominantly upper-middle-class background, encouraged the pursuit of higher education. Jack holds several master's degrees in political science (Université de Montréal), sociology, and economics (University of Chicago). He also began a PhD at the Sorbonne in Paris but never completed it. He began his career teaching sociology at the Université de Montréal but didn't like it and subsequently changed to social service administration, where he is still active.

Jack's favorite pastimes and hobbies include photography, unusually copious pictures taken on each of his Oriental vacation trips; I guess the travel itself counts as a hobby, as well. He's been a faithful visitor to every antique dealership he's ever come across, for as long as I can remember; he likes to do little manual projects within the house and garden, to the point where half of the basement space in our house is devoted solely to his workshop, tool storage, and general materials supplies. He also likes to cook, on occasion. But the one thing that he enjoys doing the most (which drives me around the bend, so to speak) is collecting dishes. Although many of them are nice, unique, and original pieces, most of them we do not need. The problem stems more from the fact that we have long since run out of places to put them. He has bought dishes that I have had to find space to store. I doubt very much if he even remembers what they look like, but he continues to buy more and more.

In late summer of 1979, I was twenty years old when I met Jack, who was, at that time, forty-seven. He was (and still is) quite a good-looking man. Although only slightly taller than my 5' 8", he was sturdily built and definitely had all his lumps in the right places. Although he appeared to be older than myself, when we first met I really had no idea of just how much older. He was quiet and somewhat shy, bordering on timid except when it came to pursuing me.

We dated somewhat noncommittally from August until December of that year before anything serious started to come of it. We officially became a couple when I moved into our house on January 20, 1980. When we decided to make a formal relationship agreement, I made the condition that if he were going to screw around and play the field, that he was to tell me first! He could not wait for me to find out by walking in on him in the middle of something with someone else, or worse, find out from the neighbors or our friends. Since I had just gotten out of a relationship that ended for that very reason, I didn't want to risk a repeat. Effectively, I felt that if I took the fun and the challenge out of it, it wouldn't appear to be so enticing. I must admit though, that the first time he did take advantage of the agreement, it was not easy for either of us to deal with. And when *I* then took advantage of it, it seemed to be just as difficult for both of us. Needless to say, our relationship has survived it and may even be more solid because of it.

The honeymoon lasted for a little more than two years before beginning to wane. I was very much in love with him and he with me. We had adjusted to our new living arrangement with considerable success. The house was not completely finished when I moved in so we had the good fortune to have something to concentrate our efforts and our frustrations on. We were both kept so busy with our individual careers and the remodeling of our home that we really didn't have time to get into any serious trouble, relationship-wise.

Our relationship is built on things much more important and self-perpetuating than sex. Even though some of Jack's extracurricular activity has been long-term, relatively speaking, I know that no matter how long he sees a particular guy, I'm the one who wears his ring (quite literally) and I know that he will always come home to me when it's over. And, I think that he knows that I will be there to pick up the pieces, after the end comes. I feel secure enough knowing that whoever might pose a threat to our relationship wouldn't stand up to any outright confrontation with me. They would have to be better looking or more suited to Jack's tastes, be more intelligent and better educated (compared to my nine degrees, this would be highly unlikely), or incredibly wealthy for Jack to choose them over me. They would also have to prove to him that they could run this house and interact with him (faults and idiosyncrasies included) better than I can. I have the advantage of seventeen years of experience in doing just that.

It is not my intent to imply that sexual relations between Jack and myself are nonexistent, not fulfilling or satisfying, or that sex is no longer pleasurable for either of us. For me, whenever we have sex, it is pure "fireworks" every time, even after so many years. My only regret is that it happens with less and less frequency. I guess we're just getting older. The infrequent occurrences makes us really appreciate it all the more when it does happen.

It is truly incredible that our relationship has survived at all, considering some of the obstacles that we had to overcome. Our languages were the first experience with conflict, particularly in relation to which radio stations the house sets were tuned to—not to mention which television programs we would watch. This led to us not wanting to watch television together at all. The problem was solved when we purchased an additional TV set. The radio has been allotted to a first-come-first-served basis. But Jack still adamantly refuses to buy an English language newspaper, even if I give him the money to pay for it. Then again, he won't ever buy cigarettes for me, either. Jack has never smoked, but he tolerates my doing so.

Another adjustment that we had to make was in relation to holidays and family events. With the varied religious background of my family and the staunch Roman Catholic faith of his, this is no easy task. We decided that every other year, we would have a menorah and my Jewish traditions at Hanukkah, followed the next year with the Christmas tree and traditional holiday observances of his French-

Canadian upbringing. So far, this arrangement seems to be an amiable solution. He still is very reluctant to wear a kippah at occasions where they are required, but then again, sometimes, so am I. More and more now, I am working within the Jewish community, and Jack is still somewhat apprehensive about accompanying me to some of the functions I am supposed to attend. I'm not certain if this is because of an uneasy unfamiliarity or discomfort with the Jewish religion and/or culture—or is it simply that the conversation at such functions is usually in English?

Another big obstacle that we had to work our way through was that of the very large age difference (more precisely, the generation gap). In my opinion, this problem was much more pronounced at the beginning of our relationship. I suppose that, at the age of twenty-one, forty-something seems a long way off. The difference was also much more noticeable by being compounded with the different generations of our respective friends. My friends were much younger than Jack's and would not mingle comfortably, no matter what we tried. Aside from that, our attitudes toward things were, quite literally, generations apart. For all intents and purposes, I probably had an easier time adjusting to this than did Jack. Since all of my brothers and sisters are older than I am (my oldest brother is the same age as Jack), their friends were a lot older than me and my friends. Although adjusting to this was somewhat difficult as I was growing up, I would imagine that having had that experience has better prepared me to deal with Jack's friends.

But the hardest difference to deal with was the *pace* of our lives. My lifestyle is (in Jack's eyes) spontaneous, erratic, and unpredictable, whereas my opinion of Jack's comportment is that it's too systematic, too calculated, and too rigid. His emphasis on the importance of politics is exactly opposed to what I think politics is good for. I will admit that although some things have come closer together as time elapsed, *that* one still holds us apart. By now, the age of my friends is not all that distant from that of Jack's friends and there is more potential for intermingling of the two groups.

Both Jack and I are actively involved in our neighborhood association and have been members on the association's board of directors, in different capacities and not always at the same time. Ordinarily, I avoid politics in my life, but Jack has a certain propensity for it. He has even been involved in the politics of the Municipal Council of Montreal and, to a lesser extent, in the broader provincial political arena. We both joined the neighborhood association for very different reasons. For him the allure was the political forum and the impact that he could make in relation to the administration of the association itself and on the municipal level. For me, the attraction was more a means with which to create a formal sense of connection with my neighbors, my neighborhood, and how things were done that would have a direct impact on our home, our property, and our ability to ensure access to whatever we needed that would improve our living environment. There was, of course, the added social context created by the association, in which getting to know our neighbors and our neighborhood could provide additional help, support, or resources, if ever we happened to need them (e.g., the added security of the neighborhood watch program and having friends to count on in case of emergency). We have had our confrontations in our discussion of these matters but generally don't discuss issues that are strictly political because of the unnecessary tensions and/or frustrations they can cause.

Ultimately, Jack and I have adopted an unspoken rule about not discussing language, religion, and politics. Aside from the occasional snide remark concerning the language or mentality of the other, we have found that this unspoken rule has managed to avert much more serious disputes.

There were times when Jack planned to entertain people from his office in our home, so I cooked and cleaned with him, but when it came time for his guests to arrive, I had to go somewhere else so that he wouldn't have to explain our relationship to any of them. My friends think that I should never accept that kind of situation, but I don't think that it is worth making a fuss over. He is very much committed to me and our relationship, but his belief is that this type of intimacy needs to be expressed to me alone and that the outside world does not need to be either made aware of it or forced to acknowledge it. In the same vein as sharing the right to have "extra-marital" affairs, I think that this type of situation depends on the two of us having a very strong sense of security in who we are as individuals, who we are as a couple, and how each needs these identities to be recognized and/or acknowledged.

I think that one of the most difficult adjustments—or at least the one that has taken most of our energy (it's also the one we have been dealing with for the longest period of time)—is the pursuit of higher education and all that comes along with it. Aside from the obvious points of contention such as the expenses, the student loans, and the sudden lack of earned income, our biggest battles were over the choice of field I decided to pursue.

Teaching and social work seemed to have hit a vulnerable spot in both of us. My dedication to those fields was matched only by Jack's apprehension. It was as if that choice was just too close for his comfort. It laid us wide open for potential conflicts as to who knew more about what, who was right and who was wrong. Part of the apprehension in the two of us came from my feeling the need to prove myself to Jack and Jack's need to protect his territory (after all, he was there first). Ironically, it wasn't until I reached the second graduate degree that Jack showed any interest whatsoever in my academic achievements.

In a discussion that we've had concerning this issue, Jack stated that since I had received awards of recognition and, by that time, had already had several formal publications in various academic journals, he could acknowledge I must be "good at it." When I was first accepted to do a Doctorate in Social Work (DSW) in Boston, and was awarded a prestigious fellowship grant from the Quebec government, Jack became much more interested in what I was doing. For a very long time, I had sensed Jack's regret at not having finished his PhD and thought that he was living out his unfulfilled dreams by seeing me finish what he had started. When I made the decision to quit Boston, I think I put a lot of undue stress on our relationship. But the commute back and forth from Montreal to Boston had really cost us a lot. Obviously, the physical wear and tear on my body and on Jack's nerves had really begun to take its toll.

I would leave home at about 2:30 to 3:00 a.m. on Thursday, arrive in Boston in time for my first class, do the second class after an hour and a half break, then start the trip home, arriving at midnight on the same day. Making this trip also depended on the weather and the road conditions, which could prolong a regular six-hour trip into as much as eighteen hours. Some of the winter storms in the White Mountains of New Hampshire can be inconceivable. That year of commuting cost three cars and a lot of anxiety and/or aggravation and seriously shortened both of our life expectancy rates.

Still, I was very concerned that Jack would have a difficult time dealing with the fact that I wanted to quit, considering that I was taking away his "second chance" for getting a doctorate. That fear, I now see after the fact, was mostly in my own mind. Yes, he was disappointed, but he was more concerned with my health and state of mind than with the doctorate. He was really supportive and encouraging when I made that decision and through my severe depression that followed. We maneuvered our way through that situation together, as we had so many others before.

All of that seems so far away now since I got accepted into a joint program of the Université de Montréal and McGill University for a PhD in social work. Not only does this new situation combine the two cultures and languages, it also puts me back onto my own home turf. It gives Jack more of an opportunity to interact in the process. And, to make it even better, I was awarded another fellowship grant from the Quebec government.

*   *   *

It can be reasoned that tragedy is a true test of a relationship. If this is true, then our surviving seventeen years together can be documentation. During our relationship, we have endured several traumatic situations. First my adoptive father died, followed eleven months later by my mother. Although their deaths were attributed to old age, the turmoil that these situations caused within my family had a significant influence on our relationship, not in any really adverse reaction but more in bringing us closer together. In spite of Jack's discomfort in dealing with my family, he did not hesitate to accompany me through all the family obligations and their aftermath. When we are really caught up in the height of crisis and invaluable support comes from an unexpected source, it has a very significant influence on our ability to function appropriately. Jack's unconditional support was invaluable in helping me deal with my rather large and distraught family. Even though I had not counted on his being so involved and supportive, I truly appreciated the fact that he was there.

A few years later, the husband of Jack's sister Micheline was killed in a devastating and horrific truck accident. The effect this accident had on Jack's entire family (including me) was amplified by the sudden shock and the fact that, of all the members of Jack's family, Micheline's husband was the most liked. Micheline had met him in high school and married him directly upon finishing school. She had never known any other man. She was inconsolable. With her situation, Jack was almost as devastated as she was. Micheline needed special attention that she could not have gotten on her own in her apartment, so I moved her into our house and took care of her. Jack's emotional state did not permit him to make any kind of decision (either for himself or for her), so I had to take control of the situation. After the fact, I think that initiative was a turning point in how Jack's family perceived me, and how the relationship that Jack and I shared became somewhat more intense. For the very first time, he allowed me to take care of him. Without having much choice in the matter, he seemed to realize that I was capable and that even though his family and I usually hadn't gotten along very well, I still stepped in and took care of them all as though I had every right to do so. I think that his family also began to see that if someone needed help, I would do what I could, regardless of how distant and cool our interactions had been up to that point. I guess that Jack and Micheline saw a facet of my personality they had not expected to see. We have become much closer since then. Even the rest of their family is more respectful of my right to be included as a peripheral member of that family. I would imagine that, much as in any heterosexual couples' relationships, dealing with the in-laws is just as difficult and tension-causing for each member of that couple.

More recently, one of my brothers fell ill and refused to be put on medication or a treatment regime that would control his illness. He wanted the illness to run its course and get it over with as soon as possible. If he had agreed to take the medications that would have been prescribed, I'm fairly certain that he would still be alive today. He chose not to do anything that might prolong his life. As he got gradually more and more incapacitated, he decided that he wanted to die at home. His wife is a head nurse in a coronary care unit at the Jewish General Hospital and, he declared, would be qualified to take care of him in his own house. But, as he needed more and more care, the daunting task of providing it overwhelmed his wife. My brother didn't want anyone in the family to know of his illness so he forbade her to call on any of us to help. In the last few weeks of his life, his wife defied him and called me because I was the closest of all of our siblings, both emotionally and geographically. She was really desperate for help.

Needless to say, when I found out the true situation, I was incredibly angry at him for his refusal to treat his illness. To my way of thinking, this decision constituted suicide on my brother's part. After the initial shock and anger, I arranged to help in providing his care. I ended up going to sit with him all night, every night, so that his wife could get some rest, and at other times as well, when she just needed a break. Even during the day when his wife and I were there together, we got no rest from the task of taking care of him. We couldn't ask any of my other brothers or sisters to help because he wouldn't allow it. His wife's family is spread out across the United States and in the Philippines. Although they could not be counted upon for physical, concrete assistance, they were all forthcoming with moral support and encouragement. Upon notification of his death, they all made arrangements to arrive in time to attend his funeral. In the meantime, we felt that we should at least try not to aggravate his situation and to take care of him by ourselves for as long as we possibly could. With my brother's nontreatment, and his "willing" himself to die, at least he didn't suffer much longer after that. On the day that he died, all hell broke loose in the family.

Jack was very instrumental in refereeing and trying to keep the peace. He was very supportive and understanding, not only to me but to all the rest of my family as well. For quite some time I had been in such a state that I could not think clearly without reenergizing the incredible anger that I was feeling toward my brother and his situation. For me, as with most Jews, to give up trying to treat or cure an illness is like giving up on life—which is bordering on sacrilegious. I had a very difficult time coming to terms with his decision, but what made me all the more angry was the secrecy surrounding it and our inability to call upon other members of the family to help in taking care of him. Even several years after the fact, Jack and I are still dealing with fallout from that traumatic event within my family.

One of the long-lasting effects of experiencing the illness and death of my brother was manifest in our making plans for what each of us wishes when we each get to that point, and what happens after our deaths (e.g., living wills, powers-of-attorney, last wills and testaments, etc.). For both of us, it became apparent that we needed to ensure that the other would be protected through formal "succession" arrangements. We felt that this had to be strictly legal—incontestable in a court of law because, as of yet, gay relationships are not legally acknowledged, nor formally sanctioned, either in Canada or anywhere else in the world. We have even gone so far as to have made arrangements for our funerals. This has given us both a certain level of comfort and has reduced some anxiety—each knowing the other won't have to deal with the same type of experiences we've had in my brother's case.

Another hurdle that Jack and I have had to leap on a consistent basis is that he does not express any emotions whatsoever. He doesn't get loud and angry when things don't do well. There's no sign when he's happy or sad or when he's frustrated or hurt. He just doesn't exhibit any type of emotion, as a general rule. It has taken a very long time for me to learn to pick up on some of his subtle means of communication. I, on the other hand, am the exact opposite. I will let anger, frustration, anxiety, or whatever be put right out front for all to see. I get loud and angry and then it's over. Once the emotional outburst is past, I can get on with finding the most appropriate or effective way of dealing with the situation. Jack doesn't understand this pattern any more than I understand his. Although we cannot change each other's natural behavior patterns, at least we are more concerned with figuring them out and learning to recognize what any given behavior signifies—and what to do about it, if anything. After seventeen years of trying, I can't whole-heartedly say that we have mastered it yet, but I do think that we have become better at it. Although it can be rather difficult at times to live with what I teasingly refer to as "an emotional cripple," I would imagine that it is just as difficult for Jack to deal with someone as up-front and volatile as I am. I'm not really certain whether this is a cultural thing, a generational thing, simply unmatched character traits, or profound differences in our personalities. I think that it could be all of these at once.

At this point, I have a difficult time remembering what life was like before I met Jack and got into this relationship. I don't believe for an instant that I would even be able to envision life without him. On second thought, not only would I not be *able*—I wouldn't *want* to think about life without him. Not only have we shared a relationship for a very long time, but we are still truly friends, lovers, and inextricable soul mates. If I had to sum up where it is that we want this relationship to go, I would be hard pressed to come up with a good response. Jack could not answer that question either. What we did agree upon though is the fact that it doesn't really matter where it goes, but how it gets there. It is mutually imperative that we get there together. We are both prepared to use our own and each other's strengths and abilities to get wherever it is that we are going—even if this means that we each have to "countercompensate" for any inabilities or insufficiencies in the other. It seems that our relationship, long ago, became a sort of self-perpetuating one. We have created and nurtured a healthy interdependence. We have both learned a great deal from sharing our lives, but I'm fairly certain that we also had to unlearn a lot. It is well known to the two of us that the only way that this relationship could have any chance of surviving would be for us both to aim toward respecting and/or maintaining his own individuality; all the while interweaving each other's personal habits and characteristics, our combined strengths and weaknesses, our individual personalities, and our individual and combined preferences, hopes, and dreams into one cohesive unit. Ironically enough, I think that this is exactly how we got to this point. And with God's help (no matter which one's), we will continue to live and grow, together. Yes, we have had to deal with a lot of differences between the two of us—had to deal with a lot of challenges to make our relationship work; but we have met most of them. Those that we have yet to deal with, we've at least learned to adapt to, or manipulate into something that we could find a way to live with.

Neither of us got into this relationship believing it would last forever. I think that we both feel it could end, at any time. It just might be this noncomplacency that is keeping it alive. I think if I were to feel that this relationship is indestructible, I wouldn't be so willing to give in or make compromises when necessary. If this relationship is worth anything, then it must be worth fighting for, protecting, and perpetuating.

We don't, for a moment, believe that what I've described here is really all that different from what happens in any other intimate relationship between two people. Nothing can be said to be unique to either a gay relationship or a straight one. In both types of relationships, these things need to be worked out and adapted to. Even it if seems to take an awfully long time, believing that the relationship will be worth all the effort in the end will be the only way that this can be achieved.

Montreal, Quebec, Canada

Together at the Bars

Morgan Whittaker with Ed Guillory

We met the night of February 11, 1981, in a bar called Chaps on the Upper East Side of New York City. Ed was avoiding going home to his apartment mate (also his ex)—an Anglican priest. I (Morgan) was avoiding going home to my parents in New Jersey, with whom I was living due to my (own fault) financial difficulties. We were both sitting there, minding our own business, when a man came in and propositioned me with himself, coke, and/or grass. I declined all three. Ed noticed this and, laughing, started talking—as the would-be trick left for other territories. The talking and many more drinks followed, as did dancing. Information was exchanged: we were both thirty-three, both comfortably out—although my parents (aware deep-down) drew an Irish Catholic veil over the situation. I had never directly told them I was gay; at the time, knowing their Catholic attitude toward life in general, it was just easier not to discuss the matter.

As we danced and drank, we marveled (appropriately) at the fact we had both grown up in northeast New Jersey, just a few miles from each other. All too soon it was last call—4:00 a.m.—much too late for me to get a bus back to New Jersey. So, Ed invited me home, in spite of prohibitions on such by his ex. We were so drunk anyway, it really didn't matter—nothing could have happened.

When 7:00 a.m. came around, the alarm went off. We staggered up—after less than three hours' sleep—cleaned up, and left the apartment, Ed walking the dogs, and me on my way to the Port Authority terminal to catch a bus back to New Jersey. Ed had to go to his job at Bloomingdale's flagship department store on Fifty-Ninth Street; I had the day (Lincoln's Birthday) off from my job as a paralegal at the Chelsea office of the Legal Aid Society. I gave Ed my telephone number and headed back to New Jersey. I had good feelings about the previous night, but figured it had been just another drunken night, another trick missed. Ed obviously had the same kind of feelings, because a week later, he phoned me with an invitation to come in to New York for a long weekend. He had the place to himself for a week and was having a dinner party that Saturday night.

I went into the city, met Ed again, and things started. Ed had his party, mainly with people from Bloomie's, but it was a good time for me to meet his friends, both straight and gay. It was a fun party, went on and on, and the next day, I was a hungover mess. However, later on, things improved. We had our first sex together, and it was wonderful. A couple more days together and a real relationship began.

But after those few days, we had to part. Still, there was something there. We wanted to see each other again—and we did so. Ed talked to his ex, who agreed to let me come on visits. Soon, it became more than a quick wham-bam, thank-you-man thing. We were developing a real relationship.

Things progressed, and as Ed's situation with his ex deteriorated even further, the relationship between us ripened. Finally, after a big fight between Ed and the ex, it was time to cut loose. We ended up in a hotel on West Ninety-Third Street: one room, twin beds (which we tied together, to make a double), on Broadway. That lasted for a couple of years. All this time, the total relationship continued to develop—sex, yes, but more important, the love and caring. On weekends, we drank a lot but, at the same time, had fun, and more loving. But we couldn't feel we were truly making a home—not in an Upper West Side hotel.

By now, Ed had terminated his career in retail in favor of a job at what was then the Bowery Savings Bank.

Then, on a snowy day in February 1983, an ad appeared in *The New York Times* for new apartments opening up at the South Street Seaport in Manhattan—a spot in New York that was being redeveloped. We went downtown and immediately signed for a studio with a sleeping loft. We loved it; it was perfect for us. Moving was not easy in any way, but we did it and thanked whomever for being able to. We had a great time there—wonderful location and great local straight bars (the best of which was an Irish place) that accepted us as we were. Also, we were at the connection of all the subway lines, so we could go to Greenwich Village whenever we wanted.

Ed worked with a lady at the bank who had friends in Key West. They invited her down for a visit, and she loved it; so she told Ed all about the place. She also warned him about how gay the town was. (She didn't know about us?) This was, of course, long before Key West's hyper-advertising in gay publications. Intrigued, we decided to take a one-week vacation in Key West; it was wonderful! We enjoyed the town and the people we met; some as friends, and one or two in after-the-bar relationships.

We went down again the next year for two weeks and had *such* a great time, we decided we wanted to move there. Living in New York, with its constant expenses, there was no way to put enough cash aside, but then something happened. Ed's dad passed away, which gave us some money. And the decision was made: we were going to do it.

So, in January 1987, we did it all: got our stuff packed up by professional movers in New York and took off with our dog and cat and headed south. We knew what we were getting into: New York City prices and rents—at low wages. But we figured it was worth it—decent weather most of the time (we quickly adapted to the attitude that anything below sixty-five degrees was *cold*). And since we already knew some people from our visits, we easily became assimilated. I soon got a job at a major hotel and had become its food and beverage office manager until the staff was downsized last year; I then went to work in a gift shop and lasted a year before the tourists wore me down. Happily, I've part of my parents' estate to tide me over while I seek a tolerable nine-to-five. Ed has kept *his* hotel job—in the accounting department.

We've been here in Key West/Cayo Hueso since then and have loved the life we've had in our eleven years here. By that, I mean our life together, and sometimes with new friends, before and after the bars.

We live at the upper end of Key West's main drag—Duval Street—just two blocks from the Atlantic surf. It's a relatively quiet section of downtown and usually, right after work, we meet at a neighborhood straight (but gay-friendly, like most things in Key

West) bar. Most often, a good night out is a fine dinner (no problem getting *that* here) and after-dinner drinks somewhere.

Some nights (generally when we both have the next day off) we'll head to midtown, where the gay bars are. On occasion, depending on our proclivities and the quality of the clientele, we may invite someone home for more fun (safe, needless to say).

We're still proud parents of two adoptees: Wookie, an eight-and-a-half-year-old sheep dog/collie/God-knows-what female—and Fulton, a mostly Russian Blue male cat of fourteen, named for the street we lived on near the Seaport—because Fulton was "fixed" there.

The most important thing is that we not only love each other, but we really care about each other. We recently both turned fifty and are determined to enjoy the rest of our lives together. After this many years, sex, while still fun, is not the most important thing. It's all the other parts of a relationship that really do the thing. Hey, seventeen years—*something* has worked!

Key West, Florida

Dance to the Music

Arch Brown

PRELUDE

Whenever my mother would ask why I wasn't getting serious with a girlfriend, I would always answer that she shouldn't worry, "I would be married by the time I turned thirty." I knew this was a lie. I would never marry. I had been actively gay since the age of twelve and I certainly wasn't going to magically change at twenty-nine. But it seemed to keep her quiet. At least for a while.

But now I *was* twenty-nine. And indeed I was ready to settle down, although I was sure my definition of marriage was very different from hers. I had left for New York shortly after graduating from college. For seven years I had been romping through the big-city gay world. I had had many men, and a few short affairs. A few longer ones. Nothing had worked out. But in the past few months I had gone through a major transition; I had my first executive job as a merchandise coordinator for a new department store *and* I had just signed the lease on a spacious seven-room apartment, with a bit of a view of Central Park. I felt almost like an adult. Was I ready for a real relationship? I had always felt that any kind of a pairing was best if both parties came together when they were self-assured and had something real to offer one another.

THE HESITATION WALTZ

It was Labor Day weekend, 1965. There weren't many places to meet other men, as New York City had managed to close down most gay bars because of the World's Fair. After all, they didn't want visitors to think there might be "queers" around the city. One of the places that had survived was Stauch's Baths at Coney Island, directly behind Nathan's Famous, where there were private dressing rooms, steam rooms, and segregated nude sunbathing on the roof. Most of my friends were away for the holiday weekend and so off I went on the subway to Brooklyn.

The day was only partly sunny and there weren't too many people slinking around the dank hallways. On the old tarpaper roof were the usual gangs of older local men who seemed unaware of the gay population that surrounded them, and a couple of large gay groups with bleached hair and long fingernails. There was this one guy lying on his stomach, but every time I caught his eye he would turn his head away. I couldn't tell if he was shy, or uninterested. But I kept staring. He had a body that was simultaneously lean and voluptuous. His face reminded me of an elegant Renaissance painting: large pale eyes and a strong Roman nose.

Suddenly it was pouring rain and everyone scrambled downstairs. The steam rooms filled quickly. I followed. And there he was again, standing now against the slimy wall and once again averting his eyes. I even tried to get him into conversation, but he only nodded back. I gave up and went back to my locker. But the Fates intervened. It turned out he had the locker directly across from mine. He found the coincidence funny, and it seemed to open him up more. We began to talk. His name was Bruce, and he too lived in Manhattan. Conversation flowed freely. He was going to leave and asked if I was ready to go. But now it was my turn to pull back. For some reason I decided that since I had just arrived a little while ago, I would stay, hoping the weather would clear. He invited me to dinner that night and gave me his number. I said I would call later that afternoon, but I wasn't sure I would. Maybe I would get my rocks off in the steam room.

He left and I hung around for another hour. The rains cleared, but the clouds didn't. It was getting cooler. Most people were gone, and I finally gave up. As I was headed up the street to the subway, there he was again. Some force was at work! He said he had stopped for a hot dog and had been walking on the boardwalk. We took the subway together. He was funny and bright. And he had opinions— on politics and art and economics and gay rights.

By the time we got back to his beige-and-tweed apartment, I was charmed. We had drinks: vodka and sesame crackers with blue cheese and sour cream. We made love. We went out to dinner: cannelloni and Chianti. We made love again. I spent the night.

When I got home the next day I told my roommate (I had just taken in a friend named Michael, who had been kicked out by a boyfriend) that I had met "the man I was going to spend the rest of my life with." Michael made some crack about my wash-and-wear wedding dress, but I knew I was right. Not only was I attracted to Bruce sexually, but he seemed right in every other way. We were almost the same age. He was also from the Midwest. His parents, like mine, had a stable marriage and he had a strong moral background. We both liked art and opera and politics and swimming and architecture and Chinese food and ballet. At the same time we were very different. He had a doctorate in pharmaceutical chemistry, worked in research, and had the focused mind of a scientist. Compared to me, he had come out much later in life, and he'd had much more trouble with being gay. He led a much more closeted life. He was a much more *serious* person. He had so little confidence in his artistic side that his apartment had been done by a decorator from Macy's. He was taking a course in French just for the hell of it.

All of these differences made him very attractive to me. Being a scientist made him almost an exotic. All my friends were ribbon clerks and bartenders. I liked his seriousness, his intelligence, his not being the typical arty fag. I was in love.

We made a date for the next weekend. He came over to my crazy pad with the awning-striped wallpaper and street furniture. He loved it, but my cat figured things out immediately and growled at him all night. She was losing her primary position and knew it.

We started to date casually. Maybe once a week. I didn't know it at the time, but he was also seeing someone else. I had met a few other men and kept all my options open. But within a few months we were talking on the phone every evening and seeing each other several times a week. We really *liked* each other. There was a comfort level that neither of us had felt before. There was nothing we couldn't say to one another. If there are such beings as soul mates, he was mine.

When it came out that we had both been seeing other people, we hesitated to impose rules on each other. Still, the one serious relationship I'd had in New York, with a young NYU student named Jack, had fallen apart because of infidelity. I saw no reason to lose Bruce over some one-night stand. He was mine. And I was going to keep him.

GRAND PAS DE DEUX

The following summer we rented a small cabin together in Connecticut. It was only a shack with no electricity or plumbing (gas lamps and appliances, a very odoriferous outhouse). But it was on a small island that sat in the middle of a forty-acre lake. There was total privacy. We could run around nude all day long. Paradise. The ultimate honeymoon.

We invited a few friends out for weekends, who mostly thought we were crazy to put up with all the inconveniences. But we loved it; having to row the luggage and groceries and cat over in a boat was great fun; eating by candlelight in our tiny screened-in dining area was magical. Bruce's parents came east from Michigan, and we took them out to the cabin for a day. They were delighted with the place and seemed to like me. And I was charmed by them. They were funny and intelligent, and immediately accepted me as a part of their family. It never seemed to matter that it was a man who had married their son.

And married we were. The commitment was secure. The following winter we decided we wanted a more permanent summer place. Almost immediately we found a small cottage overlooking the Housatonic River. After much discussion, we decided Bruce would buy the cottage and I would buy a new car. (Bruce was sure about us, but less sure about entangling our finances.) In order for us to afford all this, it meant he would have to give up his apartment and move in with me and Michael, who was still ensconced in the tiny maid's room.

The three of us got along fine. The biggest problem was deciding who was going to carry the garbage down four flights. Bruce was terminally fastidious. If the trash was anywhere near the top of the can it *had* to be taken away. Michael and I would let it pile up till it was falling onto the floor. So, I made up a new rule. If something bothered one of us and not the other two, then the nose that was out of joint had to handle it; if Bruce was upset by the garbage, then he should get rid of it. And it worked. It became a lifelong pattern for us. If something bothered either one of us, we took care of it. Don't make a scene. Screaming or throwing dishes never helped anything.

Of course not everything can be solved so easily. But we soon learned a technique that would get us through the next twenty-seven years. When one of us was really angry or upset and losing control, the other would call a time-out. We would set up a meeting within the next forty-eight hours, usually at cocktail hour, to discuss whatever problems there were. This gave each of us time to cool off and try to find out what was really at the root of a situation, so when the discussion *did* happen, things got worked out. We both desperately wanted a life together. A relationship is always made up of tiny compromises, and we worked hard at making it happen.

Life was good. Our jobs progressed and were satisfying. We bought subscriptions to the opera and ballet. We began to have dinner parties and an annual New Year's Eve cocktail party. All my friends were delighted by Bruce. He seemed quiet and shy and would seemingly remain in the background for most of the evening. But then, and always at the perfect moment, he would throw out a zinger of a one-liner that had everyone on the floor. A circle of friends began to form. We discovered that we even had a couple of old friends in common, most importantly Lester, whom we each had known for several years, and who had been instrumental in my getting the apartment where we both now lived. He became Bruce's closest lifelong friend, and he and I are still in close contact after all these years and miles of separation.

And Bruce and I discovered we had been at the same Halloween party a couple of years before. We remembered cruising each other, and he remembered my caveman costume. But we hadn't spoken. Neither of us could remember why. Maybe we weren't ready.

Almost every weekend we would drive up to our cottage. We added a deck and built a pier down on the river. In winter we would sit in front of the fire and watch the sunsets. In summer we would swim and garden and go to flea markets. Friends would come up for a weekend, but they were usually too bored by our quiet country life. Michael would come up with us occasionally, until he moved to California with his new lover—the same man that Bruce had been dating when we first met!

I had been told about Bob but had never met him. He had moved to Los Angeles soon after Bruce and I had gotten serious. When he came back for a visit, Bruce asked if we could have him over for dinner. I was curious and said yes. He turned out to be this delightfully goofy and very gentle man with a deep sexy voice and a shiny bald head. Michael fell instantly in love, and two months later had moved to L.A. So, for the first time, Bruce and I were alone.

But not completely. There were occasional tricks we met for threesomes. And we would each go out occasionally for an evening on our own. The extracurricular activities never were a problem. They were an accepted part of gay life in late-1960s New York. And we were proud of our openness. When, several years later, Nigel Nicolson published his successful book, *Portrait of a Marriage*, a study of his father's open relationship with his wife, Vita Sackville-West, and her "ladyfriends," Virginia Woolf and Violet Trefusis, Bruce felt it affirmed our easy lifestyle.

FLESHDANCE

Being together seemed to give each of us new strengths, to feel more aggressive and adventurous. Jess, a young man working under me at the department store, was being fired for having been discovered reading *Playboy* in the display office. He had been told by the display director to find some contemporary typefaces. Jess was gay and certainly wasn't perusing a girlie mag for fun. But the store would not accept this story and wanted to fire him. The director and I stood by him, and we eventually lost our jobs as well. I was proud. I was right. I was unemployed.

But Bruce felt I was doing the right thing. We believed we could survive on one salary while I looked for a job. We didn't count on my coming down with hepatitis two months after I had lost my health insurance. The doctor wanted me in the hospital, but we couldn't afford it. Bruce took care of me at home, and for the first time I saw his true caring personality. His father had been a doctor, and he had studied pharmacy because he truly wanted to help people. This deep need to be of service would eventually be his genius and his pain.

Six weeks later, I was out of bed, but told by the doctor not to look for another job for several months. To occupy my time, I decided to buy a camera and learn photography. I ended up buying a used 16 mm movie camera, which cost the same as a new still camera, and began following Bruce and the cat all over the house. I slowly learned what I was doing and was loving it. I had always been a frustrated writer. Maybe I could make one of those underground movies, which were all the rage at the time. Boy, did I ever!

The first time I took the camera out to Central Park for some outdoor shots, I found "my subject." I climbed up a hill to get a broad skyline shot, and discovered a young man sunbathing in a tiny bikini. I was fascinated by him, and he was fascinated by my camera. So he showed me and my camera his sizable equipment. I gave him my number and told him to call after I had the film developed. He never did.

I quickly discovered the world, or at least Central Park, was filled with exhibitionists. I would take my camera to the cruisy section of the park and usually someone would follow me (actually follow my camera). They would strip in the park or sometimes come back to our apartment and jerk off for my camera. They seldom were interested in seeing the finished product. No one ever asked what I might do with the footage. They just wanted to be filmed.

I had no trouble getting the raw stock developed, and soon I was camera-cruising several days a week. Bruce was fascinated and couldn't wait to see the next reel. He was always eager, at the end of his workday, for the latest "nudie news." Eventually I met someone who wanted to do a scene with another guy. I paired him up with a young blond I had met with the camera and had my first porno. This first star, Big John, made several films for me, became a friend, and eventually lived with us for several months. He too found true love from the bed in the maid's room and moved to Alaska with a humpy redhead. We still write often, now thirty years later.

There were no porn theaters in New York yet, but a new private club showing soft-core porn had opened in the city. I contacted the manager and began making films for them. I slowly pushed the envelope, till I was the first person making hard-core gay films for the public. Bruce would help me with story ideas and editing. I had no trouble finding actors willing to do it for the camera. This nice little Lutheran boy from the Chicago suburbs had become a pornographer. Bruce thought it was a hoot and would refer to me as "my wife, the porn king." But I was scared shitless. To help protect myself, I took Bruce's last name (the second most common name in the country), hoping we could always tell the postal authorities it must be some other Brown. Eventually more theaters opened, and I began making feature-length films. Except for another brief stint in retailing, I never went back to a nine-to-five job.

Corporate cutbacks caused Bruce to lose his research job. He had found research too frustrating, so wasn't that unhappy. And he got a good severance package to boot. He decided he would go back to school to study for his pharmacy license. There were a few months before the classes he wanted would start, so I suggested we go to Europe. "We can't afford to do that! We have to save money. We're both unemployed. You're crazy!" was his expected response. He was always the sane one. But I suggested that maybe crazy was good, maybe this would be the only time in our life we would both be free.

And so we had our first real adventure, six wonderful winter weeks in Spain on a shoestring: two-dollar hotels, fifty-cent dinners, cold showers, hot Spaniards. An incredible horizon opened for both of us. Over the next twenty years our lifestyle would change. There were fewer fancy dinners out. The ballet tickets were cut back. Clothes budgets were reduced. But we did travel: England, Belgium, Italy, Morocco, Holland, Egypt, Mexico, Jamaica, California, Greece, Bonaire, Spain again, Tunisia, Mexico again, England again, Portugal, Puerto Rico.

I continued making films, and Bruce got his license. He got a job in a hospital pharmacy. We had regular income again. The cottage weekends were still a great getaway for both of us. Our only problem was a new uncaring Manhattan landlord. He wanted more money for less service. It was time to get out. Several friends, including Lester, had recently bought row houses in Brooklyn. We decided to go look. We had been together seven years, and maybe it was time to own a house. On our first trip out, we found the dream house: a beautifully restored four-story Italianate brownstone with six fireplaces, parquet floors, and incredible original details. It also had tenants on the top floor, making the mortgage easily affordable. We moved in two months.

Neither one of us had ever felt we were very courageous. The safe and experienced seemed preferable to the unknown. And yet, I had made a major ethical stand and lost a job; we had both changed careers (mine in a still-illegal industry); we had made a major property investment, and we had run off on a European escapade when we should have been counting our pennies. We liked our new selves. These two quiet and conservative men had found life can be fun and exciting and unpredictable. I don't think either of us alone would have turned out as we did. Had we somehow found in each other what I now call the "Adventure Gene"? I think so.

ANNIVERSARY WALTZ

Life in Brooklyn was very comfortable. Bruce found a clinical pharmacist job at a Brooklyn hospital, where he could deal directly with patients, most of whom were mentally ill. He had found his niche. From all reports he was a genius at his work. I continued making films and doing still shots for the gay magazines. When I wasn't busy with the sex industry, I was refinishing woodwork, or planting in the garden. Having a big yard made us realize we were using the cottage less and less, so we quickly sold it, at a considerable profit.

Our circle of friends began to change. Our mostly gay Manhattan friends didn't like trucking out on the subway to see us, and none of our Brooklyn friends had cars to get them around. We had less company and spent more time just being together. Our tenants left, and we replaced them with a delightful young gay couple we found through the local university's gay rights group. We began to socialize with a few of our straight neighbors. Bruce joined the support group for our local library. I edited our neighborhood organization's newsletter. We continued going to concerts, dance recitals, and the baths. And we traveled at least once a year.

If Bruce had to work a night shift, I would go in to the bars in Manhattan. This was the mid-1970s, and Christopher Street was hopping. I easily fell in with a group that would meet on weekends to dance on the tiny floor at Kellers. On Sundays, Bruce and I would often join my new friends, and thousands of other men, for beers on the sidewalks of West Street. New York gay life had changed phenomenally in the last ten years.

For the first time I had a couple of affairs with men I met at the bars. Having evenings free while Bruce was at work allowed me time to carry out more extended fantasies. They would run their course in several months, usually after it became clear I wasn't going to leave Bruce.

We decided to have a big party for our tenth anniversary, and to invite anybody and everybody we liked. When I mentioned the date to a woman who lived a few doors away she responded, "Why, that's our anniversary; we'd love to come." We had never said anything about our relationship to any of the neighbors. But I took a deep breath and answered, "It's our anniversary too. Our tenth. And that's why we're having the party." She smiled and said, "Congratulations. We're only up to number seven."

I found out months later that the neighborhood phone lines were extremely busy the next twenty-four hours as word got around. But no one seemed to mind and everyone came to our party. We didn't want a lot of presents, so we didn't tell most people it was a ten-year celebration, just a party. Closer friends knew, and one gay friend presented us with a ridiculously funny concrete anniversary cake. As he did, all fifty friends, gay and straight, gathered 'round and rousingly sang "Happy Anniversary." We cried. A lot of other folks did too.

In the six years we lived in Brooklyn we never felt prejudice from anyone. Bruce was president of the library group and I ended up running the annual house tours. We had always thought of ourselves as a "gay couple" and presumed we were judged accordingly. But no one gave a damn if we were gay or black or fuschia. You were accepted not for what you were but for who you were. Period. If you were an asshole, it didn't matter what color or sexual persuasion you might be. As we got more involved in the neighborhood we discovered there were other gay and lesbian couples, interracial straight and gay couples, bisexual couples, weirdos, pinkos, and dopers. It wasn't just live and let live, it was "let's all live together." It was an amazing group, and some of these people remain close friends even though we left there twenty years ago. It was a perfect time in a society that we never thought could or would exist, and we were a part of it. It changed forever how we felt about ourselves and those around us.

But after six years in Brooklyn, we both longed for Manhattan. It didn't hurt that property values in our neighborhood were soaring at the time. In fact, we sold the house the day we put it on the market for twice what we paid for it. Making money from the houses we loved was fun!

We bought another, larger brownstone on the northern border of the Village. Again there were several tenants to help with the mortgage. We moved into an empty fourth-floor apartment, which was sunny, but tiny, while I renovated the second-floor space, a former carpet warehouse. With the help of one of my dancing buddies, one of our gay Brooklyn tenants, and one of my recent boyfriends, I spent the next nine months creating a loft apartment for us, including a new kitchen and bathroom from scratch.

THE TEA DANCE FROM HELL

We decided to inaugurate our new place with a Sunday tea dance. We invited about a hundred people, gay and straight, young and old. We opened a large floor area for dancing and moved speakers around it. It was a warm summer day and most of our hetero friends, including all of our recent neighbors, dressed elegantly; the men often in jackets, and their wives in ankle-length summery frocks. But in the gay world, a tea dance meant tight jeans, a sleeveless undershirt, and bulging biceps. The two groups tended to glare at each other the first couple hours. But as the drinks poured and the music was turned up, everyone finally started to dance and get along. Gracefully coiffed matrons boogied with bare-torsoed muscleboys with popper inhalers about their necks. It was quite a vision. Even for New York.

We served a buffet supper, and the two camps again separated. The straights sat poised in the front living area, while the gay boys lounged in the back or out on the terrace. A group of serious Dutch leathermen, in town for a special leather weekend, evidently saw the hunky boys on the balcony over the street, decided this must be a gay bar, and somehow got up to the apartment. So here are all these elegant ladies nibbling at their chocolate-mousse tarts while seven hirsute men in bare-assed leather, chains, and spiked helmets clanged through their midst. The guests were speechless. The Nederlanders were even more surprised. But they stayed. It ended up an incredible party. Nobody wanted to leave. We had become Arch and Bruce Brown, Party People. During each of the next eight years we gave at least one big blowout, always with a very mixed crowd. The largest was a Halloween bash for 400 that stopped traffic all along the block and attracted dozens of people across the street trying to ogle. Everyone knew that anything and everything could happen. Mostly naked people were part of the fun. I guess we had a knack, although I'm not sure I could define it. The parties became famous and total strangers would call trying to get an invite. I once met a guy in a bar, and when he found out what block I lived on, asked me if I knew "those guys that gave the parties."

We loved it. We loved having so many friends from so many worlds who could come together, even if only for a night. Gays have a big advantage over their straight counterparts because they move through a broader social world, meeting lawyers and plumbers and artists. Now our hetero friends were also exposed to "new" people and experiences. And they seemed to love it and many thanked us personally.

We also gave preparade brunches on Gay Pride Day, and held a series of networking parties for gay artists of many different disciplines. And in all those years, we only had one guest's muffler disappear and only one tiny cigarette burn on a chair. No other losses or damage, ever. "If ya give 'em a good time, they'll give good back to you!"

THE COURT BALL

We weren't the only Gay Party Givers in the city. A writer friend was giving himself a costume party for his birthday. His invitation arrived for what was to be called the Court Ball, and either dress clothes or costumes were required. I don't remember how we came up with the idea, but we spent the next several weeks creating costumes. I was to go as King Edward VII, Bruce as Princess

Alexandra, and our friend Lester as Mrs. Keppel, Edward's long-time mistress.

Bruce had never been in drag, had never seemed to have the slightest desire for it. But the night of the party, after Lester had him made up, and he slipped into his velvet gown and pearls, his whole being changed. His posture seemed more elegant. The way he moved his hands and head were perfect. *And* he looked amazingly like the Danish princess.

He was the perfect Royal and he didn't lose it all night long. We brought the house down with our entrance. I had a plaid kilt and a red velvet jacket. My beard was trimmed like the King's and my tummy was padded. Bruce was statuesque, in blue with a train of pale pink flowers. Lester was all black crepe, veils, and jet. I had a relaxed time meeting people, but every time I turned to see Bruce, he was still his regal self, dealing with whomever he was talking to as if he indeed was the King's Consort. It was an amazing performance.

Much later, a bunch of us, still in costume from the party, walked down Seventh Avenue to a local bar. Cars stopped to take pictures. The bar screamed with applause as we all entered. Bruce seemed thrilled with the experience but kept his proper demeanor throughout.

In the following weeks, I tried to get him to talk about how he had felt. He never would. Nor was he ever in drag again. But I always had the feeling he had been as happy that night as any time in his life. It had never occurred to me that he would find pleasure in dress-up. Obviously, after almost twenty years, there were still things I didn't know about him.

THE STAGESTRUCK STRUT

Bruce continued in the Mental Health Center at the hospital, but my film career was dying. Fewer producers were making new films. Theaters were closing. Video was coming in. One of my regular porn stars was also a theater director, and was directing a play to be produced in a gay bar on early weekend nights. We went to see it, and I later told Kevin I thought the idea of a gay ghetto theater was great, but I hadn't thought much of the play. He suggested I try to write one. So what else did I have to do? Bruce and I together came up with the idea of a young gay man coming out just as his conservative father was running for public office.

It seemed to flow out easily, and as soon as it was finished, Kevin had a reading of it in our living room. People seemed to love it and he took it to The Glines, the group that had produced the play in the bar. A few weeks later, Kevin called and asked me to come see a theater space. The Glines would rent it for us if we could get the show up in four weeks. Over the next week we signed contracts, put ads for actors in *Backstage*, held auditions, designed a set, and began rehearsals. Three weeks later *News Boy* opened at the Shandol Theater.

We had the space for four weeks, and the crowds grew nightly. By the end of the run, two independent producers agreed to move it to an Off-Broadway theater, where it had another run.

I was invited to join the Dramatists Guild. I was invited to join The Glines Board. The Billy Rose Theatre Collection of the Library at Lincoln Center wanted copies of the stage manager's handbook and the original script. I was a playwright! I had a brand-new career at forty-three. There were seven additional productions of the play across the country over the next fifteen years.

Bruce was thrilled, or so I thought. But slowly he seemed to be more and more depressed. He eventually went to see a couple of therapists and joined a gay therapy group. He could not ever put his finger on what was bothering him. At least he couldn't express it to me. I felt for the next couple of years that it must have something to do with me and/or my success as a writer. I eventually came to believe the problem was his work. Dealing with the mentally unstable is exhausting work. And he gave it his all, day after day. Seeing young schizophrenics return to the wards, time and time again, wore him down. He simply cared too damned much. And he was not alone. Many of his co-workers became our friends, and the majority suffered emotional complications because of what they had to do day in and day out.

I wrote more plays—*Sex Symbols, Sam's Son*—and had more productions in New York and at other gay theaters across the country. Cities everywhere suddenly had their own gay and lesbian theater. Bruce was always helpful, as he worked on edits and rewrites, painted scenery, and planned opening-night parties. But he just didn't seem very happy anymore. Our life didn't really change much. We still went to the ballet and theater and for our "boys' night out." At about the same time, and the only time in all our years together, we each had an extended outside affair. Bruce was dating a man he had met at the baths, and I had met James, a graduate student at Columbia. Considering the flammability of this situation, there were very few fireworks. Bruce was perhaps more worried than I, but it didn't seem to seriously threaten either one of us and I would happily go out for an evening so he could have his gentleman friend over for dinner. And both affairs were over within a year. Mine ended, once again, because I would not leave Bruce, and Bruce just seemed to eventually get bored with his new friend.

And then came 1982 and the "gay cancer." Billy, who had been my stage manager for *News Boy,* died within the year. One of my dancing buddies went next. One of Bruce's co-workers fell ill. My old roommate Michael was infected. Suddenly, everything was different. We stopped going out. We were terrified to pick up the phone. I couldn't write; how could one write a play for a gay audience now? What could one possibly focus on but sadness? We continued the parties and the dinners. We kept up with our theater-going and travel. I eventually managed to write another play that got produced, *Brut Farce,* a sex comedy set back in 1973. But around us was nothing but hopelessness and hospital visits. Over the next five years, we lost more than sixty friends. All seven of my dancing buddies are gone. Michael died, as did one of our tenants. The friends who helped with the loft renovation are all dead. A couple we had traveled to Italy with died a year apart. Our accountant died. Kevin, the director, died. Many of the actors in my plays *and* in my films are long gone. I remember us sitting together staring into space, too dazed to even talk. Too pained to even cry.

THE TROPICAL TWO-STEP

Although Bruce would never say so, his job was becoming more and more difficult for him. He had received promotions and raises, but the depression was omnipresent. By 1986, his retirement was vested, and he could retire early if he wanted. Every time we traveled, we fantasized about what it would be like to open a gay guest house in the country we were visiting. Maybe this was The Time. Get out of depressing New York and start a new life.

Bruce was reluctant at first. His deep-seated need to be of service to humanity made him stay at the hospital. But he also realized he needed to get out for his own sanity . . . and mine. We very quickly found a property, a former religious retreat, on St. Croix, in the U.S. Virgin Islands. There already were two other small hotels catering to the gay tourist, as well as a few friendly bars and other gay-owned business. It seemed an ideal location. We made a ridiculously low offer, expecting to bargain, but it was accepted immediately. We borrowed money on the New York building, which had steadily risen in value over the past eight years. Bruce gave his notice at the hospital. They gave him a huge send-off party and a memory book filled with glowing tributes I cherish to this day. On my fiftieth birthday, I signed the deed on what was to become Sea Park St. Croix: seven apartments on three acres overlooking a perfect beach and sunset.

For the next six months, life was doing electrical work, painting walls, caulking tile, refinishing cabinets, planting gardens, patching roads, replacing appliances, and buying furnishings. I had always been the sole renovator of our houses, and Bruce quickly got bored with scraping the caulk in seven bathrooms; besides, this was the first time we had ever been together twenty-four hours a day, month after month. We were in a state of constant exhaustion and occasionally would get on each others' nerves. But, cranky or not, we were having a ball, living out another fantasy.

By the following winter, we were open for our first season. We offered very cheap rates to friends, and began to advertise in the national gay press and travel guides. Everyone loved the place, and visitors soon were referring guests. Many weeks that first season we were sold out.

And we loved the business. Most of our guests were young professional gay and lesbian couples. They were often delightful and fun to get to know. There were a few straight guests as well, but that just seemed part of our life's pattern: throw 'em together and have fun. We had weekly sunset cocktail parties to which all our guests and local friends were invited. Soon we were getting references from previous guests, and many repeat customers. We were a hit!

Especially to the local thieves. The local population, called Cruzians, have a belligerent and lawless culture. Descended from the slaves of early sugar plantations, they are one endless family. Everyone has an uncle who is on what passes for a police force. Break-ins and holdups became so bad for our guests we had to hire full-time guards to protect them. We had known there was a crime problem, but hey, we had lived in New York! We could handle this. Wrong!

Anyone in local authority hated us by definition because we had come onto their island. Even the bank tellers I dealt with weekly refused to say "Good morning" in the entire three years we were there. Finding people to help with painting or other minor construction was also difficult. But one learned that there were people from other islands such as Nevis and Grenada who were willing and competent workers. You just never hired a Cruzian. Strangely enough, no one seemed to mind that we were a gay hotel. A few guests got yelled at on the beach, but our sexuality seemed not to be an issue.

Our hotel was a success. We were happy playing full-time hosts. We might be able to weather all of this local aggression. Others had learned how to protect their properties, with fences and plantings and guns. Then Bruce's back started to ache.

It began as sciatic pain in his leg just as our second high season was starting, and slowly got worse till it was unbearable. Doctors. Chiropractors. Physical therapists. It was eventually diagnosed as a disc problem. He had surgery near his family in Michigan. But three months later the pain was back. Another operation. Three more months. More pain. All he could do was lie in bed, maybe take a short walk. Sitting and standing were hell. For five years, Bruce never again was free of pain.

All this time I was trying to run the hotel alone—not an easy task, even though we did have a part-time gardener and one housekeeper after our initial season. I basically couldn't leave the property. I never got a day off. Even if Bruce was there, he was in bed and I couldn't, and wouldn't, leave him alone.

We put the place on the market. Local real-estate brokers thought the place was worth twice what we expected. They were right. We had done what we had come to do and made a bundle as well. Life's music was once again changing and it was time to move on.

THE PHOENIX FANDANGO

The doctors thought a hot and dry climate might help Bruce's back. I had been to Phoenix once for less than a week, but had liked its sprawling suburban feel, even though it was also a big city. We rented a house, sight unseen, and shipped ourselves, our belongings, and the two big dogs we had acquired on the island. They were supposed to serve as guard dogs but turned out to be big pussycats. We called them Eddie and Alex after our famed costume characters.

The rental house was large and had a beautiful yard and pool. But it was 1950s-ugly and we soon began to look for something to buy. We were in a secure-enough financial position by this time that we considered ourselves retired, even though only in our mid-fifties. We wanted a lovely comfortable house for ourselves. It took three months before we found a 1927 storybook-style place with beautiful grounds, a fish pond, and a pool.

As we made minor renovations and started working on the yard, I suddenly realized that I would again be the sole worker. Although Bruce did find a physical therapist who, through exercises, walking, and drugs, managed to lessen his pain, he couldn't really help me rake or plant or paint. He couldn't carry bags of groceries or garbage. It didn't bother me. We had always taken care of each other during illnesses. And if I got too pooped, we had the money to find help, and soon hired someone to mow the lawns and someone else to clean the house. But it *did* bother Bruce. His inability to be active and the constant pain brought the depression back in spades. He seemed lost. There was no enthusiasm for anything. Even our lovely new house didn't excite him. He would try to cheer up for me. But it was phony and we both sensed it.

We tried another trip to Europe but it was incredibly difficult for him. And for me, as I had to carry *all* the luggage. We managed to have a pretty good time anyway, and I have some wonderful memories from that trip—but it was simply more than we could handle. Our days of traveling were probably over.

When we suddenly got a great offer on the Manhattan building, I had to go to New York alone to begin negotiations. A satisfactory price was agreed on and all seemed to be moving forward. It turned out to be a relaxing trip and while there, I had a torrid eight-day affair with a young blond tourist from Berlin named Bernd who was staying at the Y.

Back in Phoenix, we tried to make new local friends. But it wasn't a very sociable town; people live behind huge garages and block fences. Most people were unresponsive. We had many potential guests just not show for a party or a dinner. No one bothered to call and apologize. If they did come they never responded with a thank-you or an invite back. Our only friends were a straight couple we had met many years ago traveling in Greece and a gay couple who had been guests at our hotel.

Life had changed once again. But we still had each other. And that had always been the most important thing. We were partners in the best sense. We would jokingly call each other husband or wife, but we were equals. There never had been any "roles," in or out of the bedroom. We were two men and had equal responsibilities and pleasures. So I cooked more often than he did. He was much better at dusting and wiring. I was better at plumbing and painting. We had long ago given up worrying about who was paying for what. If I had money when he didn't, then we would use my money. This did not mean that we had a joint bank account. Finances were still kept separate although property was either in partnerships or with "right of survival" deeds.

For our twenty-fifth anniversary we spent a weekend in Sedona, in Red Rock Country. We rented a room with a terrace overlooking a spectacular sunset view, and went out to a celebratory dinner at a place the desk clerk said had the best food in town. We shared a bottle of champagne and toasted to our next twenty-five years. When the hostess asked if we were enjoying everything, Bruce responded by saying, much to my surprise, "Everything is perfect, because we're celebrating our being together for twenty-five years." She responded, "Congratulations. And you chose to spend this night with us. How wonderful!" A few minutes later, two fancy desserts arrived "on the house."

When we met in 1965, no two men would have outed themselves in a public place. But now we were comfortable enough to do it in a small resort-town eatery—*and* get a positive response. It had been a remarkable twenty-five years. We had changed and the world had too.

THE DANCE OF DEATH

Bruce was having a lot of trouble sleeping because of the pain; it was not unusual for him to be up just before dawn. Very early one morning, a few months later, I heard a terrible crash in the kitchen. I hollered from the bedroom to ask if he was okay. No response. The dogs began to bark uncontrollably. I dashed to the kitchen to find Bruce sprawled on the Mexican tile floor with blood pouring from his nose. I screamed his name. Again, no response. I called 911.

The operator had me check for his breathing, and then had me try to blow air into his lungs. He coughed up more blood, but was alive. I was still on the phone with her when the medics and cops arrived a few minutes later. I was still bare-assed. The paramedics quickly went about their business. But the cops started asking me questions such as, "Who is this guy? What's been going on here tonight?" I guess I was pretty hysterical and they finally backed off.

They took Bru off in an ambulance to the nearest hospital. I quickly dressed and followed in our car. By the time I got to the emergency room, it had already been decided that they were going to ship him to a larger medical center that handled strokes and neurological disorders. I was told to go back home and get his insurance card to admit him. I stopped by the house and also picked up our address book so I could call his family in Michigan.

When I arrived at the second hospital, I was met by a young resident who had me fill out forms and answer dozens of questions. When I told him I had lived with Bruce for over a quarter century, he asked innocently, "As homosexuals?" Luckily, we had years ago written medical powers of attorney for each other and no one ever questioned my authority.

They had already taken him to surgery. All they could tell me was that he was having a massive brain hemorrhage. I paced around the hospital all day. Late that afternoon I went off to the airport to pick up Bernd, who was coming through for a couple of days to visit me, with Bruce's approval. I went back to the hospital, but Bruce was back in surgery. I couldn't see him.

There were two more surgeries over the next three days. I eventually found out he had suffered not only an aneurysm, but a simultaneous stroke, and a concussion from the fall to the tile floor. The blood flow was so bad they decided they had to remove parts of the frontal lobes, from both sides of the brain. When pressure continued they also removed a portion of his skull from the left front part of his head. When I was finally allowed to see him, I didn't even recognize him, his head was so swollen and disfigured. I almost fainted.

Bernd canceled the rest of his planned tour of the West and stayed with me as long as he could, about three weeks. I never would have made it through that time without him. My love for him and my thanks to him are boundless. At first I was only allowed two brief visits a day with Bruce. But it hardly mattered. He was in a coma and I was never sure if he knew I was there or not. Still, I went. The staff at the hospital was incredible. Even while he was unconscious, there were physical therapists with him several times a day, exercising his limbs and testing his reflexes. It took four weeks for him to begin coming out of it. He seemed to recognize me instantly and smiled broadly, but most everything else was lost to him. When he began to speak weeks later and was asked what happened to him, he said that he "had fallen off a horse."

He was moved to the rehabilitation floor, and a complex daily regimen began. He had to be taught to eat and walk and go to the bathroom. It took five weeks to get him to understand how to feed himself. So I went three times a day and fed him. He was always happy to see me and knew I was some sort of friend, but for many weeks didn't quite understand who I was. When our few other friends came to visit, he was pleased, but somehow confused as to who they were. Slowly, he began to be able to control his motor skills and bodily functions.

Bruce could walk, but with the shuffling gait of the mentally retarded. He could read, but very slowly, and would read the same page of a magazine over and over because he had no short-term memory at all. He could see with effort, but we soon learned he was completely blind in his right eye and could only see the right half of his normal field of vision with the left; he would eat only the food on the right side of his plate. I had been told, because of the lobotomies, he might be aggressive or violent, but his personality was my same old sweet and gentle Bru.

After three months, I suddenly got a call that he was being released from the hospital. The insurance company was telling them it might not pay the rehab bills and although the hospital was fighting the claim, it was taking no further chances. (Two different meetings were set up for me to meet with social workers, therapists, and doctors to help me cope with handling him at home, but neither session ever took place because of staff schedule conflicts.) So two days later I picked him up and brought him home, having no idea what to do with him.

By this time Bruce knew we were lovers and that this was Phoenix, but almost everything else about our home confused him. He thought we were tenants of one of his old fraternity brothers, and a woman friend he had worked with at the Brooklyn Mental Health Clinic was our next-door neighbor. He recognized the dogs, but couldn't remember their names or which one was the female. If I left him alone for a minute, I might find him peeing on the living room carpet or tearing labels off cans in the pantry. If I could manage to get him into the shower, I usually couldn't manage to get him to wash himself or come back out. I tried to get help through the hospital, but the one aide they sent me disappeared after three days.

I couldn't leave his side. I had to keep us locked in the house with the keys hidden. If I had to go to the bank or the market, I had to take him with me and he usually ended up making a scene or wetting his pants. I had a six-foot-tall three-year-old.

I had no idea where to turn. I called health agencies and government agencies but got no immediate help, just vague promises of "Someone will be in contact with you soon." I was desperate! I was crying myself to sleep every night, only to be awakened because he had lost control of his bowels in the bed. We had few local friends, and although many old friends from New York were as attentive and caring as they could be on the phone, I was still terribly alone.

Someone in the home health care department at the hospital finally called after three or four weeks. They began to send out a weekly nurse and a twice-a-week therapist. I bought a chair that confined him so I could leave the room. I learned how to get him to exercise and move more quickly through chores and showers. Then an additional occupational therapist sent to help with his sight and coordination turned out to be our guardian angel.

She quickly got Bruce admitted to a day-care center for the brain damaged. It was a small organization in our neighborhood, set up to help patients relearn simple self-care and occupational skills. Most of the other "students" were stroke or accident victims. *And* she found a state agency to help pay some of the phenomenal costs of such a facility. (The insurance company did make a settlement with the hospital and the state paid for the majority of his time at the day-care center. Had we had to pay all these bills, total costs would have exceeded $700,000.)

For the next fifteen months, I drove Bruce to the Hope Center at 9:00 a.m. five days a week and picked him up at 3:00. He enjoyed going to "school" and made many friends; he may have lost much, but he never lost his charm. And he gained tremendous self confidence. They were an amazing group of therapists and counselors with endless patience and caring. Slowly he began to improve. He began to understand caring for himself and being kind to others. He stopped wetting his pants. He remembered more of the past and began to sort out his mixed-up fantasies from reality. He learned to talk to family and friends on the telephone (and only occasionally make nonsensical statements).

Bruce still could not be left alone, as he would easily wander off. And no one could control his need to eat. He had weighed the same 150 pounds all the years we had been together. He had always been a big, but careful, eater. Now, all he wanted to do was stuff his face. Eventually I had to install locks on the kitchen cabinets and put a chain on the fridge. Nothing I could do kept him from gaining weight. Evidently, his metabolism had changed, and his girth increased.

Through the Hope Center, I learned we could apply for Social Security Disability. This extra money allowed me to hire helpers at home. It wasn't enough to cover hiring licensed home health care workers, but it was enough to hire part-time helpers, whom I usually found by advertising in our local gay papers. Many were HIV positive and couldn't find regular full-time work. Some had backgrounds in the medical field, others did not. But they found it hard work dealing with Bruce, and few lasted more than a couple of months. Others turned out to be irresponsible: one was a chronic liar; one would sneak him forbidden snacks; one let Bruce walk off while they were out and lost him for a while; one ran up huge phone bills by secretly calling gay 900 numbers on our phone; and one simply wouldn't show up many days and finally disappeared.

But several were wonderful, caring men who gave me the freedom to go out for an evening or take in an afternoon movie. I even took off for a couple of weekends to San Diego and Palm Springs, confident that Bruce would be okay. And his only sister, Barbara, and her husband, Hank, came out from Michigan three times to allow me to take longer vacations, all of which were spent with Bernd, my dear German playmate.

After Bruce "graduated" from the Hope Center, he was more able to handle simple household tasks or play games or work in a coloring book. We even had company over for dinner, and went on a few short trips, always with an aide. But he still had to have someone with him all the time and I continued having help several days a week. By now we could have real conversations. The long-term memory was again intact and we would spend long evenings remembering trips and old friends. He could even help dust or sweep, but only what he could see through his half vision. He seemed happy. He would occasionally complain about how growing old had proven so difficult, as if all of this was simply natural. He never worried about his condition, although he was aware that he was some sort of extra burden on me. Strangest of all, the back pain he had suffered for those five years had disappeared!

The sale of the New York building finally happened. But because the supposedly all-knowing lesbian lawyer who had written up our wills and powers of attorney had left out the phrase "real estate transactions," I had to first get a conservatorship. My New York lawyers said I could do this in Arizona and many months, lawyers, court appearances, and thousands of dollars later, I had the papers in hand. (Luckily his family never stood in my way and were exceedingly helpful.) But then the New York title company handling the deal decided I also needed to do it in New York and it started all over again. Only this time it took twice as long and cost twice as much! But the sale finally happened.

We had bought and sold only four properties. We had truly loved them and never expected to really make money from them, just to enjoy them. But each had doubled or tripled in value due to the real estate market and our own improvements.

I decided to spend some of this influx of money on a new car. The old one was quickly giving out on us. I had found one that I liked and had arranged for a test drive when I could bring Bruce along. He was to ride to the dealer with his aide and go with me on the test drive. Then they were to return home while I tried to negotiate a deal. All went according to plan, Bruce was thrilled with the new car, and they left to go back to the house. As I sat dealing with the salesman, his phone rang. The call was for me. It was the aide. Bruce had collapsed in the car and they were now in a parking lot in front of a 7-Eleven a few miles away.

By the time I got there, the emergency fire-crew had already pronounced him dead. He had had another brain hemorrhage. It had been two and a half years since that first terrible morning I found him on the floor. But this time, no one could save him.

His body was sent back to Michigan and he was buried in the family plot, where the Brown family has now included an additional space for me.

CODA

The next six months were simple numbness. I sat. I cried. I stared at blank walls. I ate too little. I drank too much. Sometimes I would remember to take a shower. I would talk to old friends on the phone, but that seemed to hurt more than it helped. I was so goddamned alone! For the first time in over twenty-five years, I spent Christmas with my parents.

It had never occurred to me we wouldn't grow old together. And if one of us was going to go first, it would surely be me—the smoking, drinking, grease-eating pig. Not him—the sane, slim, daily-exercising nonsmoker. Here I was, in a city where I had no close friends, trying to cope with a loss I had never expected.

But slowly I began to realize what I had had. Few people, straight or gay, ever have a love like Bruce. He was kind and caring and joyous and inventive and curious. How many others have known absolute trust? I could be smart-assed or stupid or scheming—he loved me anyway. And I loved him. So did everyone else. *I* can be abrasive and egotistical and condescending; not everyone always thought I was so great. But *nobody* didn't like Bru.

I also began to see that I was free. I had seen myself those last two years as nothing more than a caregiver. This was to be my life and so be it. Now, I could again move forward, wherever that might lead. For months I wrestled with the thought that I was actually feeling a kind of relief. Shouldn't such an idea make me feel guilty?

But grief takes its own course and one does have to move forward, no matter how slowly. One can't mourn forever, and those who do, make the mourning their only life. So I began to go out for dinner or to a bar. I started to write again. I took vacations alone. I learned to be by myself, but that doesn't mean I liked it. To this day, I'll see something in a newspaper or a store window and think, "I have to tell Bruce about this." He'll be with me always.

THE TESTOSTERONE TARANTELLA

Although I would never have believed such a thing possible, I met a man through a personals column. When he first sent me his photo, I thought, well, he'll never be turned on by me. But I called him anyway and we seemed to get along fine on the phone and both commented on the other's voice and humor. We met for a drink. After seeing him in the flesh, I was even more positive he wouldn't want me. But he did and here we are almost four years later.

Buck is a six-foot-three, handsome, very muscular, Italian former Marine (I'm not making this up) who owns his own landscape design and installation company. So, not only does he make me very happy in the sack, he also mows my lawn. He's very knowledgeable about books and history, a cellist, and a fine poet. He took on a major role in a workshop production of one of my plays here in Phoenix and did an incredible job, even though he had never acted before. *And* in 1995 he came in seventh in the worldwide International Mr. Leather contest.

But we are very different people. I'm a morning person. He definitely is not. I'm incorrigibly prompt. He's chronically late. My house always has everything in place, although not necessarily dust-free. He is a compulsive cleaner, but lives amidst endless piles of "future projects." I'm the eternal optimist and work best under pressure. He's much more a Doubting Thomas and deadlines cause him only frustration. I'm a neatly dressed, uptight, Midwestern kind of guy. He hails from torn-jeans, too-cool California. *And* we are from totally different generations. He was only six the year I met Bruce, which makes him twenty-three years my junior. My paternal instincts are brought out by the fact that his real father died very young. We seem to be making it work, though it is often hard for me to keep up with his boundless energy. We aren't living together yet but are talking about it. We've taken several wonderful trips together (Europe, Hawaii, Guatemala) and on a couple of them have managed to hook up again with dear Bernd (the original endless traveler), who was also here for a visit with us this past Thanksgiving. He (like all my other friends) gets along great with Buck.

We do have more obstacles to overcome than Bruce and I, mostly because of the age difference and the fact that we are so incredibly different. It does take a lot more concentrated effort from both of us. But: there is new love in my life. Not bad at sixty-one.

Barbara and Hank still come out from Michigan and dog-sit for us so we can travel. Eddie and Alex have a new regular playmate in Luther, Buck's dog, who looks amazingly like a longer-haired version of my hundred-pound beasts. All three "puppies" turned eleven this winter.

I have started a small foundation in Bruce's memory that gives grants to gay-positive arts projects based on historical subjects (a favorite interest of Bruce's). James, my old boyfriend from Columbia, now a published author, is on the board of directors.

And about two years ago I saw on a publication masthead a very familiar name—Jack, the college-student first-love from the early 1960s that I had left because of screwing around. I dropped him a note, and we're back in contact and enjoying catching up with each other's lives. He's lived in the DC area with a lover for the past twenty years.

I've also had success with my writing. I had a production of my play *Doubletalk* in New York last year, and my latest work, *FREEZE!*, has recently won the Eric Bentley New Play Competition, leading to two more productions. One, once again, will be in association with The Glines organization, which has by now become a Tony Award-winning producer.

So life is still pretty damned good. The music and the dancing continue.

Phoenix, Arizona

Going for the Gold

Geoffrey Charlesworth and Norman Singer

Editors' note:

Only as we were putting the final touches on this anthology did we learn of yet another remarkable pair—who've been together over fifty-three years. They are Norman Singer, retired from a distinguished career in music management, and Geoffrey Charlesworth, well-known gardener (and writer on the subject); they live in the Berkshires (western Massachusetts). Singer is noted for having put Hunter College in the forefront of concert life in New York City, before becoming (in the 1960s) executive director of City Center (home of both Balanchine's NYC Ballet and the NYC Opera). With the opening of Lincoln Center, he managed the Chamber Music Society, proving to be their most effective fund-raiser. As for Charlesworth, the American Horticultural Society, celebrating its seventy-fifth anniversary, has compiled a list of seventy-five classic books on gardening by U.S. authors, which includes Charlesworth's *The Opinionated Gardener*. His second book, *A Gardener Obsessed*, is still in print; the two will soon be reissued as a two-volume set. "Just like Proust," writes Singer. "They contain handsome acknowledgments—even a dedication—to me," he adds. "We don't hide our ties."

Aware we were being unfair by writing this pair for a formal manuscript with such short notice, we were delighted with this response from Charlesworth:

I'm told I must write this letter because Norman would really have liked us to do a joint account for your anthology. But it just isn't possible. The tight deadline is a major factor, but there are a number of others. I don't think I could write anything of value by the end of this month. I know how difficult it is to write biography because I've started my own and only reached age twenty-five with tremendous struggle. Deciding what's possible to write for others to read is one problem; deciding what to omit because other people may be affected in some negative way is a different one. I wouldn't want to write a superficial account (that is, one without a point of view) and at the moment can't spare the time to immerse myself in memories of 1944. We regard our anniversary as the day we met, though we couldn't live together in our own home until 1947.

To which Norman Singer appended:

In our world, what counts for an anniversary? The first encounter? The first "I love you"? The first time we "did it"? I'm enclosing a copy of Geoffrey's "speech" at our fiftieth anniversary party, sumptuously hosted by friends in New York City in October 1994. 'Twas a great affair, attended by my family plus friends from London, California, Florida, and Paris—gay and straight—and with letters to be read from Geoffrey's family in England. But the most memorable sentiments expressed that night came from Geoffrey himself, who read from the prepared remarks enclosed.

As eager editors, we responded at once, asking only for a one-page manuscript of "lead-in" to Geoffrey's anniversary tribute. The following dialogue arrived by return mail:

G: The whole story would take months to write so we will just tell you how we met. It was in October 1944; WWII was still in full swing, but it was to be the last full year. We were both at Bletchley in England. I was working in the "Foreign Office" and Norman was in the U.S. Signal Corps. In fact we were both involved with different aspects of intelligence (code breaking). We were brought together by Scottish country dance (reels and Stathspeys, etc.) and by music (we both like chamber music). A dance group and music in general were part of recreational activities at Bletchley Park. Every autobiography selects a good story out of a mixed bag of exciting events and boring details, so we can't expect "truth" from anybody with enough vanity to write one. Perhaps when I have stopped gardening I shall complete mine. However, after fifty-odd years together, we can both say we have had very good lives so far, with more ups than downs. Old age is not one of the ups, but far better than an early death, since we have had each other to share life with and to love for so long.

N: When a colleague told Geoffrey that at the previous night's session of the Scottish Country Dance Group there was a "cute" (her words) American doing fancy steps in the Eightsome Reel, Geoffrey went to check it out. While we did hold tight hands during the Eightsome Reel, there were no explosions. This happened the next morning when among the thousands entering the gate at Bletchley Park we happened to enter at the same time. That did it. Geoffrey told me he was organizing a record playing session that night, leading to his question: "What's your taste in music?" My prompt answer: "It's very good: late Beethoven quartets" was warning enough of the brash American he was up against. A later disclosure that we both disliked Churchill sealed the union.

G: Yes, he was brash—but very good looking: green eyes and flashing smile.

*   *   *

FIFTY YEARS LATER—THE DINNER PARTY SPEECH

Our Fiftieth Anniversary

Nobody has asked us how we did it, but anyway I would like to tell you about a few of the problems and difficulties of living with the same person for so long a period of time.

First: Don't expect respect because of age. Being old is no great accomplishment. Lots of people do it. Noah was 500 before he started having children. So being seventy-four is no big deal. It also means that Noah was probably married for a good long time so being together fifty years is also no big deal. And since he waited so long to have children he may well have been gay. In any case his middle son Ham was surely the first gay man to be acknowledged in the Bible, and he clearly had an eye for older men. If you think about it, with a total of only four men in the world at the time Ham came out, the percentage of gays in the world was 25 percent. Not even counting Noah. (As usual there is no mention of lesbians. And the four women in the world are just called wives.)

Second: Don't fear age. Old age got poor press when Shakespeare wrote bad things about the sixth and seventh Ages of Man. But what did he know about it? He only lived to be fifty-six. The best part of *my* life started at sixty. The most unbelievable story is that of Faust: he'd have to be crazy to want to go through that whole youth thing again.

Jealousy: Every long-term relationship has this problem. Othello went too far. Whenever Norman or I lose a handkerchief we look for it together until we find it. Little things like this make living in the same house possible.

Living together: If you want to cohabit amicably, give each other space. That means I want my own piece of the kitchen table for mail, my own room for my own computer, my own piece of garden. When we travel together I always take the left-hand side of the towel rail and leave Norman the right-hand side. In the 1950s Menotti wrote a forgettable opera, *The Medium*, with one memorable line we both quote: "I told you not to touch my things!"

How to deal with anger: Next to jealousy, anger is the most difficult emotion to handle. Never go to bed angry. Never waste time and tears on this ugly emotion. Always say you are sorry, always admit you are wrong. Two good white lies are a small price to pay for a good night's sleep.

Shared guilt: The other person is not you. If they do something you don't agree with, either argue, disassociate, or shut up. You don't have to feel guilty for what *they* do. I never let Norman's mother believe I made him leave home.

What was my most difficult accommodation in living with Norman? At Juilliard, Aspen, Hunter, City Center, and Lincoln Center he was always surrounded by musicians, dancers, colleagues of one kind or another who were either sucking up or being sucked up to. I hardly ever knew with whom I could act like a normal human being. So I had to pass up many opportunities to make friends with some perfectly nice people in order to keep his professional life separate from my private life. This means I can never drop names with the same regularity that Norman does.

The second hardest thing to do I never really managed. This was to be uninhibited about telling Norman how much I cared for him and loved him. I can say I love you when I am absolutely forced and sometimes when it isn't actually necessary. But I wasn't brought up to be spontaneously affectionate. So, Norman, you will have to believe that it has always been true and it still is.

Sandisfield, Massachusetts